THE
CHOCOLATE
SPOON

THE

CHOCOLATE

SPOON

ITALIAN SWEETS FROM THE SILVER SPOON

FOREWORD

The Silver Spoon was first published in 1950 and quickly gained popularity, becoming one of the most influential Italian cookbooks of all time. Considered by many as the bible of authentic Italian cuisine, it has sold more than three million copies in Italy, and has been translated into sixteen languages.

Over the years, this iconic brand has constantly evolved to keep abreast of developments in the world of Italian cuisine, strengthening its position as a leading light for those who love good food. And over the past two decades its online and social media platforms have seen steadily increasing volumes of user engagement and a wide audience.

From the authors of the original *The Silver Spoon*, we can now enjoy *The Chocolate Spoon*, an exploration of a food close to everybody's heart: chocolate. The book traces the long journey that brings the "food of the gods" to our table, and provides all the information needed to learn about this very special food before setting to work.

Suitable for novice and experienced home cooks alike, the chapters that follow include classic basic recipes for beginners, through to more challenging recipes and innovative ideas for the more accomplished. Follow the illustrated instructions to master the core techniques required to create the 100 recipes specially designed for this volume, from everyday pleasures to showstopping chocolate cakes for special occasions.

Using different types of chocolate, the recipes within these pages offer inspiration to even the most experienced confectioners, allowing them to try their hand at complex desserts and intensely flavored bonbons.

The Chocolate Spoon aims to be a comprehensive reference guide, which should be kept close at hand for expert instruction and inspiration. It is fully illustrated with photographs that showcase the silky beauty of this star ingredient, which appeals to everyone—because chocolate never ceases to delight.

INTRODUCTION

For centuries a beverage reserved for nobility, chocolate—whether dark or white, milk or ruby, aromatic or spicy—has been transformed into a bar to be enjoyed by all. It has become a raw material of choice in pastry shops and home kitchens around the world, where it is the star ingredient in cakes, mousses, and bonbons.

This book begins with a historical overview that traces the journey of cocoa beans from the lands of the Aztecs to Europe and the world, before going on to describe the process by which these precious brown beans are processed and transformed into refined chocolate, providing all the knowledge you will need to be able to recognize quality products.

Even if you are inexperienced, you will be able to try your hand at working with chocolate right away, thanks to an extensive section dedicated to mastering basic techniques. Each recipe is accompanied by clear instructions, and step-by-step photographs illustrate critical stages of the methods needed to ensure success when making simple or elaborate recipes, creating hollow and solid shapes, and working with decorations and frosting (icing). Starting with the delicate task of tempering chocolate, which is essential to obtain a shiny, malleable material, we go on to show you how to make bonbons and 3-D decorations, while the steps for creating chocolate curls, shards, and bars provide ideas for making even the simplest of cakes look spectacular. Finally, you will find all the directions for making mousses, crèmes, and ganaches—basic preparations that are an essential part of the best-loved desserts.

The 100 recipes contained in these pages range from simple everyday desserts, such as tarts, cookies (biscuits), and pastries, to more elaborate creations. These are as gratifying to make as they are amazing, including Choux Wreaths with Hazelnut Cream and Brittle and irresistible Cinnamon Cannoli with Ganache and Cocoa Beans. You will discover an entire chapter devoted to chocolate candies, an absolute must for chocolate lovers. And there is no shortage of delightful desserts to be served as pudding, or that are perfect for summer—ranging from simple gelato to more complex semifreddi. The book ends with chocolate beverages, such as classic Viennese Hot Chocolate and Chocolate with Port, perfect for warming the spirits on cold winter days.

Everybody can find a recipe suited for any occasion, and experiment with exciting new combinations of flavors and aromas, all showcasing the unmistakable complexity and indulgence of chocolate.

LEGEND

GLUTEN-FREE

DAIRY-FREE

VEGAN

VEGETARIAN

5 INGREDIENTS
OR FEWER

30 MINUTES
OR LESS

PREPARATION
TIME

COOKING TIME
ON STOVE (HOB)

COOKING TIME
IN OVEN

RESTING TIME

STORAGE TIME
IN REFRIGERATOR

STORAGE TIME
IN FREEZER

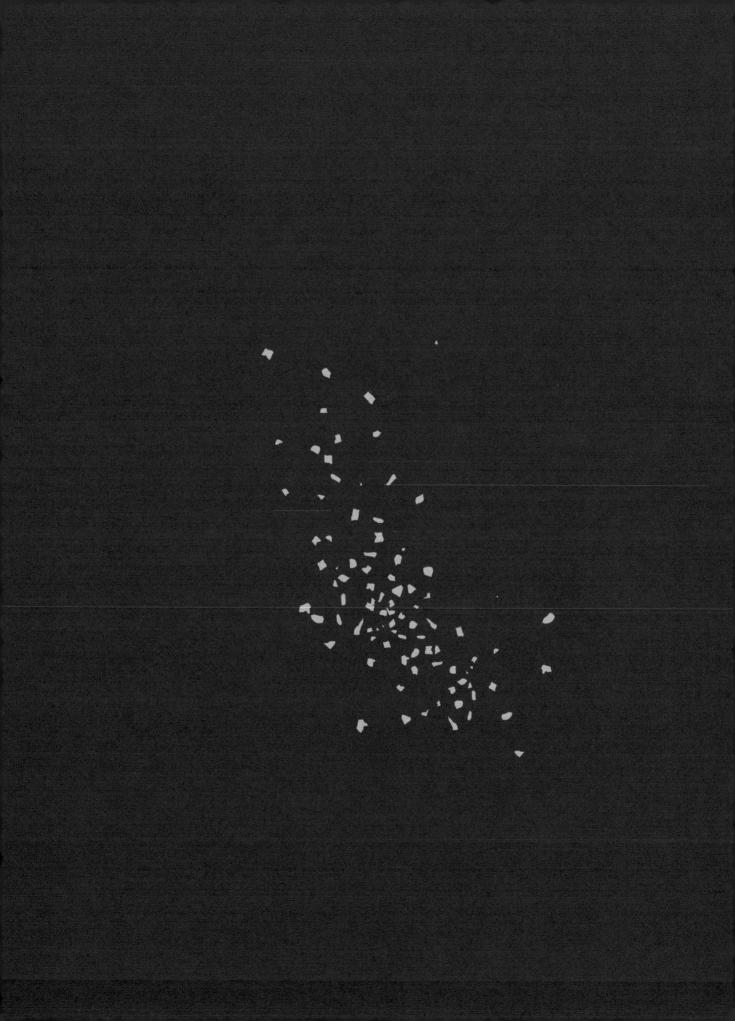

UNDERSTANDING CHOCOLATE

A BRIEF HISTORY OF CHOCOLATE
The long journey of the "food of the gods"

BETWEEN DIVINITY AND SIN

Since the dawn of time, the pre-Columbian civilizations of Central America attributed religious significance to cocoa, to the extent that Quetzalcóatl, one of the most important deities of the Aztecs, was also considered the god of cocoa according to myth. Because it had always been considered an invigorating food with aphrodisiac qualities, it is not surprising that this "brown gold" should also acquire lustful and sinful connotations in later eras, so much so that the Marquis De Sade came to say that it was "as black as the devil's ass."

The "food of the gods" descriptor that is often associated with chocolate comes from the scientific name attributed by Linnaeus in 1737 to the cocoa tree, also known as the cacao tree, *Theobroma cacao*, which is composed of the Greek words *theos* (god) and *broma* (food).

Its discovery, or first cultivation, to be more precise, dates back to the pre-Columbian civilizations of Central America that settled on the coastal plains of the Gulf of Mexico, particularly the Olmec civilization (1550–400 BCE), which was succeeded by the Mayan and later Toltec and Aztec civilizations before being wiped out by the Spanish colonial conquest.

AN ENERGY-GIVING AND VALUABLE FRUIT
Initially, at the time of the Olmec civilization, farmers ground cocoa beans to a powder and then added water to create a high-protein beverage. During the Mayan civilization (250 BCE–AD 900), the cultivation and use of cocoa spread further, resulting in even more complex beverages, for which cornmeal (cornflour) and other ingredients were added to the mixture of cocoa powder and water. However, with the rise of the Aztecs in the thirteenth century, cocoa beans were increasingly cultivated and their use even spread as far as the lowlands on the Pacific coast to the south of the Yucatán Peninsula.

In Aztec times, cocoa beans also became a valuable commodity, a food that served as both currency for trade and a symbol of wealth for the noble class who had large reserves of them. According to legend, Prince Montezuma drank many cups of the cocoa beverage every day because of the supposed aphrodisiac properties attributed to it. Its preparation now involved the addition of pepper, chili, and vanilla. Agave extract or wild honey was sometimes also added, although the drink retained its unmistakable bitter taste, and care was always taken to serve it with its characteristic white foam. It was not until the conquest by the Spanish, who subsequently brought cane sugar to Mexico from the Caribbean, that the cocoa beverage was given the truly sweet and comforting flavor that would guarantee its success far beyond the confines of the Americas.

THE SPREAD OF COCOA
The first cocoa beans were brought back to Spain, to the royal court in Madrid, by Christopher Columbus, although some time would pass before the qualities of cocoa were appreciated. The first admirer was Hernán Cortés, the explorer and conquistador, who disembarked in what is now Mexico in 1519 and succeeded in subduing the indigenous peoples with unscrupulous strategies and great brutality. Trade in the precious raw material intensified in the second half of the sixteenth century, when shipments were regularly sent from Veracruz bound for the port of Seville, and the aromatic beverage began to be consumed and acclaimed at the court of the Spanish kings Charles I (Charles V, Holy Roman Emperor), Philip II, and Philip III. Cocoa spread to France with the marriage of Princess Anne of Austria, daughter of Philip III, to King Louis XIII. The French court soon learned to appreciate the cocoa nectar, and under Louis XIV the drink became extremely popular and beloved at banquets held at the palace of Versailles.

The spread to Italy was slower, which may have been largely due to geopolitical fragmentation. We know that the cocoa beverage came early to Sicily, which was ruled by the Spanish, particularly the regions of Modica and Ragusa. This would give rise to the local artisan production that endures to this day. Early admirers included the Savoy family, which had very close ties with the Spanish court in the sixteenth century, sealed by the marriage in 1585 of Charles Emmanuel I to Catherine of Austria, daughter of Philip II. Little wonder, then, that Turin and Piedmont as a whole should later become the Italian chocolate hub, the place where the first master chocolatiers became established and set up the first artisan workshops to process the raw material arriving from European colonies, while exporting their products to such countries as Germany, Austria, and Switzerland.

It also took longer for the drink to gain popularity in Britain, first reaching the coffee houses of London before the establishment of chocolate houses only in the latter half of the seventeenth century.

AN UNSTOPPABLE PASSION
Cocoa saw an unstoppable surge in popularity throughout the entire Age of Enlightenment and the nineteenth century. Its exquisite flavor was praised by poets and intellectuals, so much so that it was described in the poem *Il Giorno* ("The Day"), written by Giuseppe Parini in 1763, as a part of the morning routine of its protagonist, *il giovin signore* ("the young gentleman"). It was also loved by Carlo Goldoni, in whose plays "cioccolatte," a delightful, steaming beverage that refreshes the soul, often made an appearance. Beyond the borders of Italy, literature repeatedly paid homage to this "brown gold," from Wolfgang von Goethe to Charles Dickens, and from Gustave Flaubert to Guy de Maupassant.

A TECHNICAL AND INDUSTRIAL EVOLUTION
Turin was one of the places that drove the development of the art of chocolate. Paul Caffarel's factory housed a machine for the production of chocolate that was designed to grind cocoa beans in a process much like that of an olive press. The creation of gianduiotto, individually wrapped chocolates mainly containing gianduja, dates back to 1865, when the Risorgimento, the series of wars that brought about the unification of Italy, caused supplies of cocoa to dwindle. Caffarel decided to replace part of the cocoa with hazelnuts, which were grown in great abundance in Piedmont.

It was at Caffarel that a young Swiss man learned the art of making chocolate. His name was François-Louis Callier, and he would go on to open his own chocolate factory on the shores of Lake Geneva at around the time when Dutch chocolatier Conrad Von Houten was perfecting the process of separating cocoa butter from cocoa mass.

Besides Switzerland, the driving force behind developments in the chocolate industry was shifting to the English-speaking world, and in 1849 the Englishman Joseph Storrs Fry, the son of a paper magnate with a passion for chocolate, succeeded in producing the first solid bar.

ARTISAN CHOCOLATE-MAKING EXCELLENCE
An example of artisan chocolate-making that harks back to its very origins can still be found in Sicily today.

In fact, the production of chocolate in the city of Modica still follows a process that dates back to the sixteenth century, when it was under Spanish rule.

Modican chocolatiers grind the cocoa beans by hand on a concave, volcanic stone slab, similar to the Aztec metate, which is heated. Today, however, increasing numbers of chocolatiers are making use of purpose-built machinery.

No refining is involved, resulting in a coarse and crumbly chocolate.

After lengthy experiments, the Swiss Daniel Peter was the first to use the condensed milk invented by Henri Nestlé to create milk chocolate in 1875, while Rudolf Lindt is credited with the invention in 1879 of the conching machine, which perfected the industrial process for refining chocolate, an essential operation.

Across the Atlantic, in Pennsylvania, Milton Hershey founded his first chocolate factory in 1894, laying the foundations of an empire that endures to this day, and whose global success is symbolized by the famous Hershey's Kisses, the unmistakable teardrop-shaped chocolate candies that were invented in 1907. The United States joined the ranks of the largest importers of cocoa and producers of chocolate, to the extent that, in 1925, the New York Cocoa Exchange was established to control the raw materials for chocolate.

Today, together with coffee and sugar, cocoa is one of the most important globally traded commodities, its price set by the main commodity exchanges, such as those in London and New York, and prices are often subject to noteworthy fluctuations. These depend on yearly harvests and speculative activity, but mainly on the quality of the raw material; aromatic, fine cocoa beans can be traded at a significantly higher price than bulk, or ordinary, cocoa.

THE WILLY WONKA CANDY COMPANY

The history of this brand is quite interesting. It was originally founded as Breaker Confections, but its name was changed to honor a character created by Roald Dahl who is the protagonist of the famous children's novel *Charlie and the Chocolate Factory*. The movie version of the book made by director Tim Burton in 2005, starring Johnny Depp as the moody Willy Wonka, is unforgettable. However, the first film adaptation of this story dates back to 1971, and it was actually because of that movie's success, which would raise the profile of its products, that Breaker Confections changed its name in 1980. The Willy Wonka Candy Company was purchased by Nestlé in 1988 and today the Wonka brand is part of the Ferrero group, which acquired it in 2018.

THE COCOA TREE AND ITS FRUITS

In search of superior quality cocoa

As we have seen, *Theobroma cacao* is an ancient plant, with the earliest recorded specimens dating back to about 12,000 BCE. Owing to its characteristics, it only grows in tropical climates, that is, in countries within an area roughly 20 degrees north and south of the equator. In fact, it requires temperatures that do not fall below 59°F/15°C and can withstand very high temperatures, provided there is the necessary humidity. Abundant rainfall throughout the year and humidity rates of 70–100% are characteristic of the tropical countries where it thrives. However, it is a delicate plant that does not like direct exposure to sunlight, and it only grows at low altitudes of up to 2,300 feet/700 meters above sea level. It flourishes in the shade of taller plants that provide it with shelter, including palm trees, such as coconut palms and banana trees.

Today it is grown in more than 50 countries around the world, although bulk production has now shifted to Africa, with the continent supplying more than 70% of the world's cocoa, notably from intensive cultivation in Côte d'Ivoire and Ghana. Brazil, Ecuador, and Peru are the leading Latin American producers, alongside Colombia, Mexico, and Venezuela. In Asia and Oceania, cocoa is widely grown in Indonesia and Papua New Guinea.

COCOA FAMILIES

The cocoa tree is divided into two subspecies, *Theobroma cacao cacao* and *Theobroma cacao spherocarpa*, from which the two main cocoa families, Criollo and Forastero, respectively, are descended. Each subspecies in turn comprises different varieties.

The Criollo cocoa tree, whose name is derived from the Spanish and Portuguese words for "creole," meaning "of local origin," is the type that has changed the least since its origins, and Criollo cocoa is of the highest quality. Its beans, as its seeds are known, have organoleptic properties that produce an aromatic cocoa with subtle nuances, making it highly prized. However, this tree is also a particularly delicate and difficult plant to grow, resulting in very little land being dedicated to its cultivation (it accounts for only about 1% of the world's production). Therefore, its fruits are very expensive, meaning that Criollo cocoa is only used by high-end chocolatiers.

The Forastero cocoa tree, on the other hand, is the most widely grown in the world and accounts for about 90% of total cocoa production. It is easier to grow than Criollo, owing to its good resistance to pests and diseases, although its purple-colored beans produce a bitter, strong-tasting cocoa that is of lower quality and lower cost. Forastero cocoa is used to make most commercial chocolate bars, but also cocoa powder and many industrial pastry products, such as cookies (biscuits).

The hybridization of these two families gave rise to Trinitario, a variety that was first planted in the early eighteenth century on the Caribbean island of Trinidad. Plantations of Trinitario trees yield about 8% of total cocoa production, and its cocoa is considered to be of high quality. Criollo, Trinitario, and the Arriba and

Esmeralda varieties of Forastero grown in Ecuador belong to the category of fine-aroma cocoas, which are of superior quality.

FROM POD TO COCOA

The precious cocoa is obtained from the fruit of the tree, known as a pod, which has an oval shape similar to a small rugby ball and wrinkled skin marked by striations that run the length of the fruit. The pods contain the cocoa beans, which are enveloped in a white pulp, known as mucilage. Freshly harvested cocoa beans are white or pinkish-violet in color and are soft and spongy. They have a bitter taste that does not give an indication of the flavor of the cocoa, which will only develop during fermentation.

As with grapes when making wine, fermentation is also a key stage in the production of chocolate, influencing the quality of the final product, as this is where the cocoa flavors begin to develop. The beans are arranged in special wooden crates with perforated bottoms and covered. The beans must then be stirred at regular intervals to allow them to ferment evenly.

This delicate fermentation process can last from a minimum of 2 days for high-quality beans to a maximum of 8 days for lower-quality beans that need more time to release their aromatic compounds.

During this time, the beans turn their distinctive brown color and develop many of the flavor characteristics later found in chocolate.

The final processing step that is performed on plantations involves drying the cocoa beans. This is usually done by exposing them to the sun for several hours a day on special wooden drying racks or different surfaces. Taking up to 2 weeks, this step stops the fermentation process and removes almost all of the moisture from the bean, which would otherwise rot or turn moldy.

THE JOURNEY AHEAD

After drying, the cocoa beans undergo a quality control process that selects raw beans in good condition and discards beans with flaws that are too pronounced. The beans are then packed into large bags, each weighing between 110 and 154 pounds (50 and 70 kilograms), for shipment worldwide. When you consider that about 25 pods are required to obtain just over 2 pounds (1 kilogram) of dried cocoa beans, you come to realize the huge amount of work that takes place on cocoa plantations.

FROM COCOA TO CHOCOLATE
The transformation from bean to bar

While the growing of cocoa pods and the process of fermenting and drying the beans take place on plantations in tropical countries, as we have seen, the processing that transforms the beans into much-loved chocolate bars typically takes place in Western countries.

Not all chocolatiers make their products from cocoa beans. In fact, the vast majority start with semi-finished products, such as cocoa mass, and even couverture chocolate, which is closer to chocolate than it is to the cocoa beans. This is because chocolate processing is a complex and delicate process that requires expensive, high-precision machinery. As a result, whether a large industry or a small artisan enterprise, companies that process cocoa beans from the pod often only keep a small portion of their production to use in their own lines of chocolate and mainly supply semi-finished products for use by other companies.

The processing of the raw material begins with the cleaning of the beans and roasting in a special machine. There, the beans are brought to a very high temperature, usually 230–302°F/110–150°C, for a period ranging between 15 minutes and an hour. This is a very crucial operation that completes the development of the cocoa aromas and flavors that began with the drying that took place on the plantation. It also has an antibacterial effect on the beans and reduces their moisture content even further, leaving them significantly darker by the end of the process.

COCOA MASS

Crushing and winnowing separates the husk, or shell, from the bean flesh, known as cocoa nibs. Cocoa refining can now begin. The nibs undergo a process of grinding in a special mill, which can be either traditional roller mills or blade mills. This process produces a considerable amount of heat, which melts the fat contained in the beans, known as cocoa butter, and turns them into a thick paste of varying particle size, known as cocoa mass, or cocoa liquor. Often this mixture is cooled, and the solidified mass is turned into cakes that can be stored for a long time or resold as a raw material to other businesses or chocolatiers. Different companies, however, keep this mass in liquid form at a temperature of about 113°F/45°C and then process it into chocolate. Although it seems superfluous to point this out, because no other ingredients have yet been added, cocoa mass is 100% cocoa. More than any other ingredient, cocoa mass is what gives chocolate its characteristics. It is also the sole ingredient in "100% cocoa bars," which have a particularly intense flavor.

Not only is cocoa mass a key component in the production of chocolate, it is also used for the extraction of cocoa butter and cocoa powder, a process that takes place in powerful presses under high pressure. Cocoa butter is separated from the dry solids in the form of a golden liquid. Once properly deodorized, it can be used in the production of chocolate by adding it to the cocoa mass and sugar in order to make it softer and easier to work with.

After pressing, the dry component of the cocoa mass is turned into "press cakes," compact blocks of cocoa with a fat content of 10–15%. This is subsequently turned into the cocoa powder that is found on the shelves of large retail establishments for use in cakes, cookies (biscuits), ice cream, puddings, and hot chocolate.

ON COURSE TO BECOMING A CHOCOLATE BAR

At this point in the process, the other ingredients that will make up the finished product are generally added to the cocoa mass, such as sugar and soy lecithin, which acts as an emulsifier, as well as milk, vanilla, and other flavorings as required.

The different components are then blended and the chocolate undergoes the important refining process that will produce its final consistency and allow it to best express all of its flavors. Several machines are used in order to reduce the particle size of the mixture and give it smoothness, from the roller refiner to the more recent and efficient ball mill refiner. This is followed by another very important process—conching. In addition to further refining the chocolate, conching reduces its acidity and gives it a velvety texture. The chocolate is now ready for the tempering stage, a treatment that involves first cooling the chocolate to about 82°F/28°C, before it is heated up to 90°F/32°C, which allows the chocolate to crystallize evenly and remain stable. As a result, once the chocolate hardens, it will be glossy and smooth, and it will keep for longer.

MODELING

Once chocolate has been tempered, it can be modeled into the desired shape. Polycarbonate molds have made it possible to give chocolate its popular bar shape and to turn it into bonbons and Easter eggs. This is a delicate process that is often still done by hand, with the chocolate left to cool to room temperature before unmolding.

COMPOSITION AND TYPES OF CHOCOLATE

Ingredients and characteristics of a quality product

STORING CHOCOLATE

During the winter months, chocolate should be kept in the pantry, away from light and heat. In warm months, it should be kept in the butter compartment of the refrigerator. Dark chocolate will keep for about 3 years, milk chocolate 1 year, and white chocolate no more than 8 months. If chocolate has a dull color and whitish patina, it means it has been exposed to temperature changes that may have affected its flavor, although it is still edible.

Now that we have followed the cocoa bean's long journey across oceans and through the process that transforms it into chocolate, there are a few more things to know about the ingredients that go into making chocolate, and evaluating its composition. This will allow us to recognize the quality of the product we are about to enjoy or that will be the star ingredient of our favorite desserts.

THE INGREDIENTS

In order to be defined as chocolate, in addition to cocoa mass, the bar must contain at least 1% sugar. Cocoa mass is what gives chocolate its distinctive flavor and intensity. The quality of the cocoa beans that are used to make it and the standard of the manufacturing processes are the basis on which the quality of the finished product is judged.

The role of cocoa butter is to make the chocolate softer and give it a texture that melts in the mouth, allowing us to fully grasp all of its flavors. This flavorless and odorless ingredient is not listed on the label, but its percentage is added to that of cocoa mass, although the cocoa butter content should not exceed 10% in a quality product.

Sugar is an important component of chocolate. It gives it balance and turns it into the sweet treat that we all love. Because cocoa actually has a very bitter taste, the sugar serves to tone down its harshness and enhance its aromatic components, thereby largely contributing to its pleasantness when tasted. Its percentage may vary, but generally a sugar content of 30% gives a good balance of flavor and a properly creamy texture.

Soy lecithin works as an emulsifier, making the mixture more fluid and easier to work with. Moreover, when the chocolate is poured into molds, the lecithin reduces the formation of air bubbles, leading to shapes with fewer flaws.

Vanilla is a common ingredient of chocolate. Its use dates back to its origins, when the Maya and Aztecs used it to flavor their cocoa beverage. The aroma of vanilla is particularly pleasant when combined with chocolate, making it more fragrant. However, it is often used to mask flaws in substandard chocolate. Many master chocolatiers today have stopped using this ingredient in order to focus solely on the rich flavors of the quality raw material they use.

Cocoa powder is sometimes added to chocolate to give strength and intensity to its flavor. However, because it contains practically no fat, its addition can take away from the smooth and pleasant flavor and texture of the finished product.

Since the time of Daniel Peter, as we have seen, milk, generally in powdered form, has been an indispensable ingredient used to make the less strong and sweeter milk chocolate, which is particularly liked by children.

Finally, it is impossible to leave out a product that is a quintessential part of the chocolate made in Italy—hazelnuts. If added whole, the finished product is known as hazelnut chocolate, while if hazelnut paste is used, the result is gianduja.

Liquor, particularly different brandies, is traditionally used as a filling for bonbons. Today, however, it is increasingly common to pair liquor and wine with chocolates. Vintage port, quality Marsala, and Passito di Pantelleria wines are particularly recommended. However, Barolo chinato aromatized wine is probably the best wine to accompany fine chocolate; in fact, the quinine, cardamom, coriander, mint, and cinnamon it contains enhances its most intense aromas.

TYPES OF CHOCOLATE

In a continuously expanding market where many different types of chocolate can be found, it is good to know the main characteristics of the most common ones. Different countries have differing regulations as to how much cocoa should be included in a product for it to fall in to a particular category. The following percentages refer to Italian chocolate.

— Dark chocolate
Dark chocolate must contain at least 43% cocoa mass and 28% cocoa butter. There are dark chocolates to suit all tastes, ranging from the bare minimum to much higher percentages, such as bittersweet, or extra-dark chocolate, which has a cocoa content of at least 70%, and bitter chocolate, with a cocoa content of between 80% and an extreme and very strict limit of 99%.

— Milk chocolate
Milk chocolate, typically light brown in color, contains at least 25% cocoa and 14% milk-derived substances. Many producers and chocolatiers today make types with a much higher proportion of cocoa, about 35–45%.

— Gianduja
Gianduja, also spelled gianduia, is chocolate with at least 32% cocoa mixed with hazelnut meal that originated in Turin in the early 1800s. Chopped almonds and walnuts can also be added to the mixture, provided their weight in combination with the hazelnut meal does not exceed 60% of the total.

— White chocolate
White chocolate contains a maximum of 55% sucrose, a minimum of 20% cocoa butter, and at least 14% milk or dried milk derivatives. In practice, white chocolate contains no cocoa and cannot be considered a true chocolate.

— Ruby chocolate
The latest addition to the market, ruby chocolate was introduced in 2017 as a product made from cocoa beans with a natural ruby color. Created by the Barry Callebaut company, it has at least 47% cocoa, to which a minimum of 26% milk is added. It is also appreciated for the fruity and fresh notes of its aroma.

GETTING STARTED

EQUIPMENT

WEIGHING AND MEASURING

PREPARING AND MIXING

SHAPING AND BAKING

DECORATING

WEIGHING AND MEASURING

Making pastries, desserts, and confectionery is equal parts art and science. Creativity, flair, and imagination are all important, but precisely weighing and measuring out each ingredient is imperative—even when very small quantities are being used, such as active raising agents and concentrated flavorings. Guessing the weight of any ingredient will rarely give the desired end result. To avoid such disappointment, weighing scales are an essential kitchen tool, just as they are in a science laboratory.

— Digital weighing scales
Modern digital weighing scales are efficient, lightweight, easy to store, and simple to wipe clean. While traditional mechanical or balance scales might look good in the kitchen, they are less accurate and leave more room for error.

— Measuring cups, cones, pitchers (jugs), and spoons
Essential for measuring liquids, from water to milk and cream. Some measuring cups or jugs allow you to convert one unit of measurement to another, while others show units commonly used in other countries, which is useful when trying to convert between the two.

— Weights and measures
Both imperial and metric measurements are given for every recipe in this book. Always follow one set of measurements throughout, not a combination of imperial and metric, as they are not interchangeable.

PREPARING AND MIXING

The successful preparation of any confectionery or dessert starts with a tried-and-tested recipe, good-quality ingredients, and all the necessary tools. First, you must weigh and measure out all the ingredients. Then you can set to work transforming them with the help of electric mixers, whisks, and blenders, as well as other simple yet indispensable small tools that are essential in any kitchen:

— Strainer (sieve)
Preferably one with a metal mesh. This is essential for sifting flour, cocoa, baking powder, and other powdered dry ingredients; sifting dry ingredients minimizes any lumps in a mixture but it also allows air to permeate the particles as they separate. A strainer (sieve) can also be used to dust confectioners' (icing) sugar or cocoa powder over desserts, although for this a fine-mesh strainer would be even better.

— Grater and vegetable peeler
Some graters have holes of different shapes and sizes, so they can be used for a variety of purposes, such as zesting citrus fruits (small holes) and shredding chocolate bars (larger, oblong holes); this can be useful if you don't have a specific grater for chocolate. Despite its name, a simple vegetable peeler can be used for many different purposes in the kitchen, and it can even prove useful for making chocolate shards, ribbons, and curls.

— Hand or electric whisk
Essential for beating eggs and whipping cream. Whisks are also more effective than a simple spoon for mixing and blending sauces, creams, and batters. An electric model is often faster and more efficient than a hand whisk; they are easy to use and usually come with a range of accessories to mix even dense mixtures to perfection.

— Immersion (stick) blender
A highly practical, handheld appliance that enables ingredients to be blended directly in a bowl or pan. The most classic ones have a blade for mixing, while others come with a whisk or a disk for whipping, and sometimes even a small hook accessory for mixing dough. Without doubt, it is an essential tool for any kitchen. It is best to choose one with a powerful motor, so it won't overheat with use, and with detachable accessories for easier cleaning.

— Kitchen thermometer
Preferably a digital one; this is a must-have item for any aspiring confectionery chef. For many recipes, the perfect end result relies on achieving and maintaining the correct temperature during the preparation and cooking of the ingredients. Tempering chocolate, caramelizing sugar, and melting ingredients in a bain-marie or double boiler are just some of the processes in which being just a few degrees out can make a difference. For each of these techniques, a particular kind of thermometer is required with its own characteristics and temperature scales: from simple immersion thermometers to digital probes, complete with a small display screen at one end and a metal thermal probe or skewer at the other.

— Mixer
A professional or semi-professional appliance able to work with a wide variety and large quantity of ingredients. Available as a stand mixer in its most substantial version,

with many accessories, this is your best option if you are a keen cook who wants a multitasking appliance. Medium-sized mixers are better suited for domestic use, and are more than capable of performing a range of tasks, thanks to their interchangeable attachments. For example, the rotary motion using the hook-shaped attachment is perfect for working with thicker doughs, such as bread. There is also a paddle attachment for working softer doughs, such as sponge cake batter. A whisk attachment can be used for whisking egg whites, cream, and meringue. Some models also have a cooking function. The choice of mixers in terms of power, size, range of attachments, and price is extensive. Instead of a stand mixer, a handheld mixer is a good option for anyone short on kitchen space.

— Spatula
Whether rubber or silicone, a spatula is an extremely flexible tool, which means it can scrape out even the smallest amounts of mixture from any awkward corners. It is also the tool of choice for incorporating whipped cream or egg whites into a mixture with no loss of volume. Metal spatulas—or palette knives—on the other hand, are used for filling, distributing, spreading, and leveling any cream, glaze, or frosting (icing) inside or on top of a cake or dessert. The angle formed by the blade and handle of a palette knife makes it particularly suited to spreading melted chocolate or chocolate glaze over a work surface or any base.

— Chocolate tempering machine
Although chocolate can easily be tempered on a marble work surface using common utensils—mixing bowl, saucepan, digital thermometer, and spatulas—enthusiasts will find a tempering machine to be an invaluable aid. These machines come in different sizes suited for both professional and amateur use, but all have a rotating bowl that is capable of melting and processing chocolate at the desired temperature—depending on the type of chocolate chosen—and keeping it at a certain temperature for a period of time, which can also be programmed.

SHAPING AND BAKING
Once the base mixture has been prepared, it is necessary to shape the dough or batter to transform it into its final form. This may be a tart, cake, muffin, or pudding, depending on the consistency of the base mixture and the type of cooking required. These are baking processes that require careful handling, as well as specific types of pans (tins) and molds.

— Baking sheets, pans (tins) and molds
Available in aluminum, as well as non-stick materials, they all have different characteristics. Therefore, the choice can be a subjective one. As for the minimum number of pans required, a round pan for tarts and other types of cake (8–10 inches/20–25 cm in diameter) is absolutely essential, with one loaf pan for loaf-shaped cakes and one Bundt pan for ring-shaped cakes. Springform pans or pans with a removable base make the unmolding of cakes exceptionally easy, and are very useful. Baking molds made of foil or corrugated, heat-resistant paper are also very practical as they are disposable.

— Pastry (piping) bag
This item is an icon for pastry enthusiasts. Once, these conical bags were made of paper or waxed cloth, but more recently disposable bags in lightweight transparent plastic have been preferred, as they are practical and hygienic. If you want to reduce your consumption of single-use plastics, reusable bags, made from coated cotton that can be washed are also readily available. Filled with cream, frosting (icing), dough, choux, or any other soft mixture, the bag is rolled or twisted at the top to close and then lightly squeezed until the contents are extruded through a narrow opening or piping tip (nozzle) at the bottom. Pastry bags are used for making cookies (biscuits), profiteroles, and meringues, as well as to fill and to decorate. A wide range of decorative effects can be achieved by fitting the bag with a piping tip. An array of different piping tips is available, from small to large, smooth or shaped.

— Pastry or cookie cutters
Available in metal or plastic, in various shapes and sizes, these cutters are used for punching out shapes from sheets of rolled-out dough to make cookies (biscuits) or decorations. Cutters can be smooth for a straight cut, scalloped for a wavy edge, or molded into novelty shapes. Cutters are also used to punch out pastry or fondant shapes to decorate tarts and cakes. As a piece of basic kitchen equipment, the round cutters sold in sets of various diameters are indispensable.

— Wire cooling rack
This is simply a wire cooling rack in the shape of a grid on which to rest pastries and cookies (biscuits) while they cool, and cakes when filling or decorating. When placed over a tray, it is also useful for collecting any excess frosting (icing), glaze, or crème.

— Rolling pin

Made of wood, or other materials, a rolling pin is essential for stretching and flattening doughs and pastries. Some rolling pins are made from marble or metal, as the cold material helps to keep the pastry cool. Others are hollow and can be filled with ice.

— Pastry brush

Very useful for soaking the bottom of desserts with flavored syrups and liqueurs, for brushing pastry surfaces with egg or milk to glaze them, and for greasing molds, baking sheets, and pans (tins) uniformly and without waste. Nowadays silicone brushes are preferred to natural bristles as they are more hygienic and practical—and without the inconvenience of it occasionally shedding a bristle.

— Silicone molds

Food-grade silicone molds are often more practical than metal pans as they don't always need to be buttered and dusted with flour. Thanks to the non-stick and flexible properties of the silicone material, removing cakes from them is easy and the shape will always be perfect. However, for an intricately shaped mold, such as for a Bundt cake, you may need to grease the mold to ensure the cake turns out cleanly. Silicone molds can be used at temperatures ranging from -40°F/-40°C to 536°F/280°C, so they can be transferred directly from the oven to the freezer, if necessary. They can be used in both the refrigerator and the freezer, in fan-assisted, convection and static temperature ovens, as well as in microwave ovens—but they must never be used in gas ovens.

— Polycarbonate molds

Less flexible than silicone molds, polycarbonate molds are particularly suitable for working with chocolate. Their ability to evenly distribute the heat of tempered chocolate and the transparency of the material, which allows you to see the formation of any air bubbles and the state of the chocolate as it cools, make them ideal for making bonbons, chocolate bars, Easter eggs, and nougats. However, for full spheres, small waffles, small cones, and complex 3-D figures, where unmolding is a delicate operation, it is best to use silicone molds.

DECORATING

The tradition of decorating desserts is an ancient one, but it was as recently as the eighteenth century when the pâtissier Antonin Carême turned it into a veritable art form. The simplest forms of decoration are chopped or sliced fruit, dried or candied fruit, crystallized sugar grains, or chocolate drops (available ready-made and resistant to melting). For decoration using chocolate, it is sufficient just to melt the chocolate then draw or write with it using a paper cone (see page 64) or a pastry (piping) bag fitted with a very small piping tip (nozzle).

— Chocolate tools

As in any art form, working with chocolate requires the use of specific tools, which are used for shaving, melting, mixing, molding and decorating. Some tools—or similar ones—can be found in an averagely equipped domestic kitchen, others are more specialized.

— Chocolate dipping forks

Mostly made of steel, these are essential for making and decorating bonbons. They are used to enrobe prepared fillings by dipping into previously tempered chocolate until coated. Because these small forks come in different shapes—triangular, teardrop-shaped, spiral, circular, 2-, 3-, and 4-pronged—they can be used to make a wide variety of decorative patterns on the surface of the chocolate.

— Piping tips or nozzles

These are additional and interchangeable accessories for use with pastry (piping) bags of frostings (icings), chocolate, cream and other toppings. Piping tips (nozzles) can be made of plastic or metal, and have openings in different shapes and sizes to create many different types of decoration, allowing you to personalize decorations.

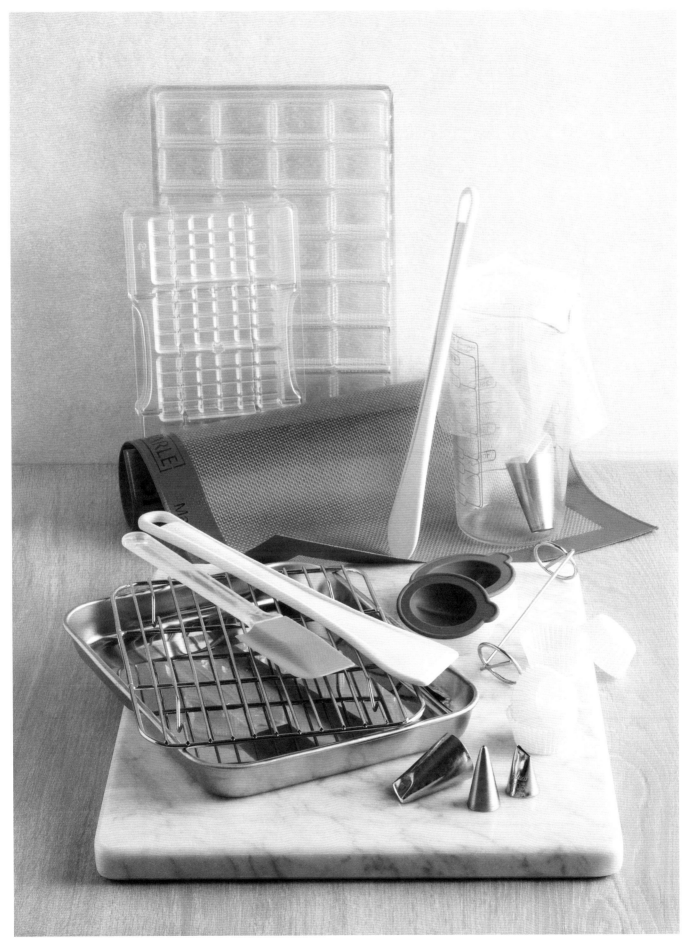

FOR THE BEST RESULTS

SIFTING

MIXING

WHIPPING

WHISKING

SIFTING
— Sifting flour

When you add flour to a mixture that must rise—thanks to the presence of a raising agent or whisked egg whites—the flour must always be sifted to ensure there are no lumps and to incorporate air, making the mixture lighter and more likely to achieve a good rise. Yeast, baking soda (bicarbonate of soda), or other powdered raising agents must always be sifted to eliminate small lumps and to evenly distribute them in the mixture.

MIXING
— Folding in

When you incorporate dry ingredients, such as flour or cocoa, into ingredients full of air, such as whisked egg whites or whipped cream, it is essential to add the sifted dry ingredients a little at a time and blend the mixture with a silicone spatula using circular movements from the bottom towards the top. This will prevent the air bubbles in the whipped mix from bursting; otherwise, you risk the mixture deflating and not rising as it should during baking, which will affect the final result. When blending mixtures with a silicone spatula, rotate the bowl in a clockwise direction and blend from the edge, as well as in the center of the bowl to avoid the formation of clumps.

WHIPPING
— Whipping cream

In all the recipes that follow, whipping cream always refers to fresh cream and never to long-life (UHT) cream. When whipping cream, it needs to be cold in order to get the best results; keep it at refrigerator temperature—that is, between 35°F/2°C and 39°F/4°C. It is even better still if the mixing bowl and electric whisk attachments have also been chilled in the refrigerator. Start whisking at a low speed then gradually increase to a faster speed. It is essential not to overwhip the cream—stop when the cream is firm but still smooth. If you go past this point, the cream becomes lumpy, curdles, and then separates into a liquid and a solid part, rendering it unusable. If you add sugar before you start whipping, the cream will not achieve the same volume. For best results, it is advisable to add the sugar towards the end once the cream is partially whipped.

WHISKING
— Whisking egg whites

Whether you whisk egg whites by hand or use an electric whisk or stand mixer, the temperature of the egg whites does not have an impact on the final result. If cold from the refrigerator, egg whites will take longer to whisk than those at room temperature, but at the end of the process the volume and stability will be the same in both cases. At a temperature of between 86°F/30°C and 122°F/50°C, which can be obtained by slightly warming the egg whites in a bain-marie or double boiler, they will whisk faster and incorporate more air. It is not advisable to add a pinch of salt to the egg whites: salt does make the egg whites foam at the start of the whisking process but then has a negative impact on the final result because, by removing water from the foam, it makes the fragile structure less stable. On the other hand, adding an acidic element—such as a few drops of lemon juice, vinegar, or cream of tartar—helps the whisked egg whites to achieve a more stable structure during cooking and a greater volume. The presence of any fat in the egg whites, caused by a drop of egg yolk or by using a bowl or whisk that is not completely grease-free, reduces the volume obtained at the end of the whisking process by up to two-thirds. When the egg whites are whisked with an electric whisk or a stand mixer, you must always start at a low speed, increasing it gradually to the maximum speed as the egg whites are whisked.

HOW TO READ THE RECIPES

BASE PREPARATIONS
AND MAIN RECIPES

PREPARATION, COOKING,
AND STORAGE TIMES

SERVINGS

INGREDIENTS AND EQUIPMENT

FURTHER ADVICE

BASE PREPARATIONS AND MAIN RECIPES

With every baking recipe it is essential to adopt a comprehensive, clear, and intuitive approach. This objective has been the driving force when devising all the recipes in this book, whereby the base preparations lay the foundation for the main recipes or finished dishes.

In the main recipes, the base preparations, and in some cases also the basic recipes that appear at the end of the book, are clearly referenced, including the relevant page number so you can find each one easily. In cases where the base preparation has been used without any variation in weight and ingredients, the main recipes will call for "1 quantity" or a simple multiple of the base preparation: for example, listed under ingredients will be "1 quantity of tempered chocolate" or "2 quantities of simple ganache." In all other cases, the precise weight of the base preparation is given; in these instances, you will need to prepare a sufficient quantity of the base recipe to achieve the weight needed.

In those base preparations that are later subject to significant changes in ingredients or weights when incorporated into a particular recipe, reference will be made to the basic procedure to be followed, and the relative ingredients and weights to be used for that recipe will be given.

PREPARATION, COOKING, AND STORAGE TIMES

Preparation times are calculated to exclude cooking times, unless the cooking phase requires the active presence of the person preparing it. The cooking time on the stove (hob) is the total of all the cooking times on the stove and the same applies to cooking time in the oven. For base preparations, the storage times in the refrigerator or freezer are those for the precooked dough or mix. For the other recipes, strict safety margins have been observed: when recipes include creams or crème, this results in shorter storage times.

SERVINGS

Almost all the main recipes serve between six and eight people. This is considered to be the most useful number of portions for a celebration cake or dessert. Some recipes serve ten people, particularly festive dishes, and substantial cakes and desserts, and those that can be stored in the refrigerator, freezer, or pantry and consumed later.

INGREDIENTS AND EQUIPMENT

With very rare exceptions, the ingredients and equipment required for each base preparation and main recipe have been listed in order of use. Where greater clarity is necessary, ingredients have been divided by preparation: "for the base," "for the custard," "for the glaze," "for decoration," etc. Each equipment list indicates what is needed for mixing, cutting, sifting, tempering, enrobing, etc. The quantities of ingredients needed for each recipe are given in imperial or metric measurements, or in volumetric cups. When measuring out your ingredients, do not mix and match but always follow a single set of measurements as the imperial, metric, and cups are not interchangeable.

FURTHER ADVICE

For every basic technique and for many recipes, there is a brief and useful tip or trick for saving time or for making a difficult step easier, to avoid the most common errors, and to vary a recipe.

STEP-BY-STEP TECHNIQUES

Melting

10 m   5 m

Difficulty: EASY

FOR THE MELTED CHOCOLATE
9 ounces/250 g dark, milk, white, or ruby chocolate

(For vegan/dairy-free, use dark chocolate with a cocoa content of at least 50%, and check the labeling)

EQUIPMENT NEEDED
Chopping board
Chef's knife
Bain-marie or double boiler
Silicone spatula

On a clean and dry chopping board, use a sharp chef's knife to finely chop the chocolate. Hold the knife firmly and always work from the corners, turning the bar around whenever a new edge is formed (1).

If you have a bain-marie or double boiler you can use this to gently melt the chopped chocolate, or you can assemble your own using a medium-sized saucepan and a heat-resistant metal or glass bowl which is large enough to fit snugly over the pan without touching the base. Transfer the chopped chocolate to the bowl (2).

Pour water into the saucepan to a depth of 2 inches/5 cm and bring to a gentle simmer. Place the heat-resistant bowl over the pan, making sure the base of the bowl does not touch the water to prevent the chocolate from overheating and burning (3).

Once the chocolate begins to melt, stir it gently with a silicone spatula, taking care not to incorporate air into the chocolate or to allow it to set on the sides of the bowl (4–5).

Alternatively, after chopping the chocolate, you can melt it in a microwave at 500W for 30 seconds. Remove the bowl from the microwave, stir the chocolate, and repeat until the chocolate has fully melted.

TIPS AND TRICKS
You can also finely chop the chocolate in a food processor. Before you do so, chill it in the refrigerator for at least 15 minutes then break it into pieces. The cold bar can also be shredded (grated). However, it does tend to melt during this process, so it is important to clear away any chocolate adhering to the grater with a brush. If you touch it with your hands, it will melt.

Tempering

10 m   5 m

Difficulty: ADVANCED

For Melting the chocolate:
  see page 38

FOR THE TEMPERED CHOCOLATE
9 ounces/250 g dark, milk, white, or ruby chocolate

(For vegan/dairy-free, use dark chocolate with a cocoa content of at least 50%, and check the labeling)

EQUIPMENT NEEDED
Bain-marie or double boiler
Kitchen thermometer
Marble board
Metal spatula or palette knife
Silicone spatula
Ladle (optional)

Melt the chocolate in a bain-marie or double boiler until it obtains a smooth and even consistency (see page 38). Constantly monitor the temperature with a kitchen thermometer (digital is best) and continue to heat the chocolate until it reaches 131°F/55°C for dark chocolate, 122°F/50°C for milk chocolate, 113°F/45°C for white and ruby chocolate (1).

Pour two-thirds of the melted chocolate onto a marble board, leaving the remainder in the bowl, and work it with a metal spatula or palette knife (2).

Continue to work with the spatula until the temperature drops to 82–84°F/28–29°C for dark chocolate, 80–82°F/27–28°C for milk chocolate, and 79–80°F/26–27°C for white and ruby chocolate (3).

Combine the tempered chocolate with the reserved chocolate in the bowl (4) and heat to 88–89.5°F/31–32°C for dark chocolate, 84–86°F/29–30°C for milk chocolate, and 82–84°F/28–29°C for white and ruby chocolate (5).

Use the tempered chocolate straight away and, if it cools down, bring it back up to this temperature again in the bain-marie.

Alternatively, after melting the chocolate, transfer a third to another bowl, set aside, and keep warm (6). Add a quarter of the initial weight in finely chopped chocolate to the remaining melted chocolate (7) and stir with a silicone spatula until it melts and reaches the temperatures indicated in step 3.

Add the reserved melted chocolate until it reaches the temperatures in step 5 (8). This type of tempering is called the seeding method.

TIPS AND TRICKS
The larger the quantity of chocolate you temper, the easier it is to control the temperature. A quantity of 9 ounces/250 g is easy to work, and any leftover chocolate can be stored to use later. Pour any remaining chocolate into an ice-cube tray and allow it to set, then transfer to a food storage bag, zip it closed, and store in the butter compartment of your refrigerator.

Enrobing

15 m   1 h 30 m

Difficulty: AVERAGE

For the Whipped Ganache:
    see page 78
For Tempering the chocolate:
    see page 40

FOR THE WHIPPED GANACHE
12 ounces/350 g 70% dark chocolate
8½ fl oz/1 cup/250 ml heavy (whipping) cream
2½ ounces/⅔ stick/70 g unsalted butter

FOR THE TEMPERED CHOCOLATE
9 ounces/250 g dark, milk, white, or ruby chocolate

EQUIPMENT NEEDED
Rectangular baking pan (tin)
Parchment paper
Palette knife
Marble board
Ladle
Chef's knife
Chocolate dipping fork
Toothpick
Acetate sheet or parchment paper

Line the baking pan (tin) with parchment paper. Place the Whipped Ganache in the pan and spread it out evenly using a palette knife to smooth the surface. Place in the refrigerator for at least 1 hour to harden then turn out of the pan onto a clean surface or marble board.

Pour enough of the tempered chocolate over the ganache base to cover it in a thin layer (1) and immediately spread it out evenly with a palette knife (2).

Heat the blade of a sharp knife under hot running water and cut out squares to use as bonbon fillings (3–4).

Place the ganache squares in the refrigerator to harden, then enrobe them by dipping each one in the remaining tempered chocolate, to coat.

One by one, insert the dipping fork into the ganache squares (5).

Dip them into the tempered chocolate (6), then lift the fork out and tap it on the edge of the bowl to remove any excess chocolate (7).

Use a toothpick to help remove the chocolate bonbon from the fork and place it on an acetate sheet or parchment paper to set.

VARIATION
This technique is used to make bonbons without using a mold. By using the same technique, you can enrobe dried fruit, nuts, and candied orange peel, for instance. Before the chocolate coating is dry, you can decorate the bonbons with chopped hazelnuts, walnuts, slivered almonds, or pistachios.

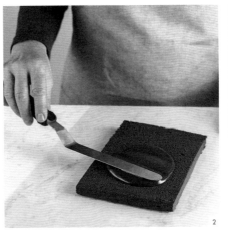

Chocolate shells: bonbons

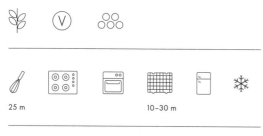

25 m   10–30 m

Difficulty: ADVANCED

For Tempering the chocolate:
  see page 40
For the Ganache for Bonbons and Truffles:
  see page 74

FOR THE BONBONS
10½ ounces/300 g dark, milk, white, or ruby chocolate,
  tempered
1 quantity of Ganache for Bonbons and Truffles, flavored,
  if desired

EQUIPMENT NEEDED
Polycarbonate chocolate bonbon mold
Cooling rack
Metal tray
Ladle
Metal spatula or palette knife
Disposable pastry (piping) bag or cone

AS USED IN
– Orange and Chili Chocolate Bonbons (page 208)
– Caramel-filled Chocolate Cups (page 210)
– White Chocolate Bonbons (page 214)
– Mint Ganache-filled Chocolate Cups (page 224)
– Chocolate Cups filled with Clementine Mousse (page 226)
– Dark Chocolate Bonbons (page 234)

Clean and thoroughly dry the polycarbonate mold and set it on a cooling rack over a metal tray. Fill the mold cavities to the brim with the tempered chocolate and set aside to cool until the chocolate begins to set but is still runny and soft (1).

Scrape the top of the mold with a metal spatula to level off and remove any excess chocolate (2).

Turn the mold upside down to pour out the excess chocolate from the cavities and scrape along the top of the mold again, to remove any smears (3).

Leave the chocolate to harden in the refrigerator for at least 10 minutes or about 30 minutes at room temperature. Fill a disposable pastry (piping) bag with the ganache and cut off the tip. Pipe the ganache into the chocolate shells until about three-quarters full. (4).

Pour tempered chocolate over the ganache filling to cover it fully (5), then clean the mold again by scraping with the spatula.

Leave the chocolates to harden then turn them out of the mold onto the work surface (6).

TIPS AND TRICKS
You can make decorations out of the remaining chocolate using camellia, rose, or plum leaves. After washing and drying the leaves well, dip them into the tempered chocolate and remove any excess by wiping the underside of the leaves against the rim of the bowl. Place the leaves, chocolate side up, on a sheet of parchment paper and refrigerate until the chocolate has hardened. Carefully peel the leaves from the chocolate, starting at the stem.

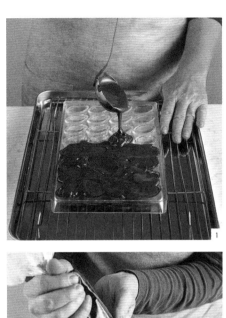

Chocolate shells: eggs

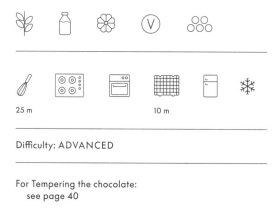

25 m   10 m

Difficulty: ADVANCED

For Tempering the chocolate:
   see page 40

FOR THE EGGS
14 ounces/400 g dark, milk, white, or ruby chocolate, tempered

(For vegan/dairy-free, use dark chocolate with a cocoa content of at least 50%, and check the labeling)

EQUIPMENT NEEDED
Polycarbonate chocolate egg mold
Ladle
Metal spatula
Palette knife

Clean and thoroughly dry the egg mold then use a ladle to fill it with plenty of the tempered chocolate. When the mold is about half filled, tilt it from front to back and side to side to distribute the chocolate around the edge of the cavities (1).

When the chocolate starts to set, but is still a little soft and runny, turn the mold upside down so the excess chocolate can drip out (2). This can be used for other recipes or stored for use later on (see Tips and Tricks page 40).

Scrape the top of the mold with a metal spatula to level off and remove any excess chocolate (3).

Place the mold in the refrigerator for 10 minutes for the chocolate to harden, then take it out, wait a few minutes, and turn it upside down on the work surface to unmold each half of the egg (4).

Heat a palette knife over a flame and run it around the inside edge of one of the egg halves to lightly warm and melt the chocolate (5).

Line up and gently hold both halves of the egg together until the chocolate hardens and seals the two halves together (6).

To make thicker eggs, repeat the first step until the desired thickness is achieved.

VARIATION
For a marbled effect, temper a batch of white and a batch of dark chocolate. Use a clean sponge to dab the inside of the mold cavities with a very thin layer of dark chocolate. Place the mold into the refrigerator to set well, then use a small ladle to pour the white chocolate into the cavities. Proceed with the method described above. The eggs will be two-toned.

Solid shapes: chocolate bars

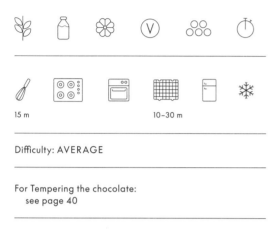

15 m   10–30 m

Difficulty: AVERAGE

For Tempering the chocolate:
    see page 40

FOR THE BARS
9 ounces/250 g dark, milk, white, or ruby chocolate,
    tempered

(For vegan/dairy-free, use dark chocolate with a cocoa
content of at least 50%, and check the labeling)

EQUIPMENT NEEDED
Disposable pastry (piping) bag or cone
Polycarbonate chocolate tablet mold
Metal spatula or palette knife

AS USED IN
– Chocolate Bars with Dried and Candied Fruit (page 232)

Fill a disposable pastry (piping) bag with the tempered chocolate and cut off the tip (1). Clean and thoroughly dry the polycarbonate mold then pipe the tempered chocolate into the mold until it is completely filled (2). Tap the mold lightly on the work surface to remove any air bubbles.

Scrape the top of the mold with a metal spatula to level off and remove any excess chocolate (3–4).

Leave the chocolate to harden in the refrigerator for at least 10 minutes or about 30 minutes at room temperature. Turn the mold upside down on the work surface to unmold the chocolate bars without breaking them (5).

HOW TO USE
Polycarbonate molds are particularly suitable for working with chocolate. Their ability to evenly distribute the heat of tempered chocolate and the transparency of the material, which allows you to see the formation of any air bubbles and the state of the chocolate as it cools, make them ideal for making bonbons, chocolate bars, Easter eggs, and nougats. However, for full spheres, small waffles, small cones, and complex 3-D figures, where unmolding is a delicate operation, it is best to use more flexible food-grade silicone molds.

Chocolate curls

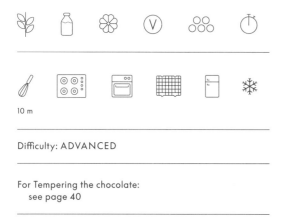

10 m

Difficulty: ADVANCED

For Tempering the chocolate:
see page 40

FOR THE CURLS
9 ounces/250 g dark, milk, white, or ruby chocolate,
tempered

(For vegan/dairy-free, use dark chocolate with a cocoa
content of at least 50%, and check the labeling)

EQUIPMENT NEEDED
Ladle
Marble board
Metal spatula or palette knife
Small round pastry cutter

AS USED IN
– Chocolate Charlotte with Rum, Banana, and Coconut
  (page 140)
– Dark Chocolate Baked Custard Torte (page 150)
– Black Forest Cupcakes (page 154)
– White Chocolate and Raspberry Tart (page 164)
– Baked Gianduja Custard (page 240)
– Chocolate Bavarois with Modica Chocolate
  (page 250)
– White Chocolate and Passion Fruit Mousse Cake
  (page 264)
– Ruby Chocolate and Roasted Plum Semifreddi
  (page 288)

Pour the tempered chocolate onto a clean, dry marble board (1) to facilitate the cooling process.

Use a metal spatula to spread the chocolate out to a thickness of ⅛ inch/3 mm (2–3) and continue to work it with the spatula until it has almost completely set and the surface of the chocolate becomes matt and even.

To make fans, start at the edge of the chocolate rectangle and use the spatula held at a 45-degree angle to shave off a strip of chocolate, while rotating the spatula outwards (4).

Use a small round pastry cutter to make chocolate curls by tilting the cutter at a 45-degree angle to the work surface and scraping it along the surface of the chocolate, forming thin curls on the inside edge of the cutter (5–6).

To make chocolate cigarette curls, hold the metal spatula at a 10-degree angle to the work surface and push it along the underside of the chocolate so it rolls up to form wide, compact curls (7).

For thin shavings, hold the spatula at a 10-degree angle to the work surface and scrape the chocolate more superficially than for cigarette curls (8).

VARIATION
There is a much simpler way to prepare chocolate curls for use in decorating cakes and frozen desserts, although it is less versatile. Place a block of chocolate kept at room temperature on a clean, dry chopping board. Hold it steady with one hand, and quickly shave the top of the block with a wide-mouth vegetable peeler held with the other hand.

Chocolate tuiles

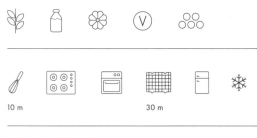

10 m 30 m

Difficulty: AVERAGE

For Tempering the chocolate:
   see page 40

FOR THE TUILES
9 ounces/250 g dark, milk, white, or ruby chocolate,
   tempered

(For vegan/dairy-free, use dark chocolate with a cocoa
content of at least 50%, and check the labeling)

EQUIPMENT NEEDED
Ladle
Disposable pastry (piping) bag or cone
2 × 4-inch/10-cm wide acetate sheets
Tablespoon
Tuile mold or baguette pan (tin)

AS USED IN
– Gianduja Pudding (page 254)

Fill a disposable pastry (piping) bag with the tempered chocolate and cut off the tip (1).

Pipe the chocolate onto one of the acetate sheets to form discs measuring ¾ inch/2 cm in diameter. Space the discs at least 1½ inches/4 cm apart so they do not touch each other while you work (2).

Cover the chocolate disks with the second acetate sheet (3).

Use the back of a tablespoon to lightly press the chocolate, forming flattened disks of uniform size (4).

Set aside until the chocolate has begun to set but is still malleable, then peel off the top acetate sheet (5).

Transfer the bottom acetate sheet to a tuile mold, chocolate side up, and leave to harden, then carefully peel each tuile from the acetate sheet (6).

TIPS AND TRICKS
If they are not for immediate use, the chocolate tuiles can be stored in the freezer for up to 3 months. Ideally, they should be kept separate by placing parchment paper between each one. Store inside a rigid container with a lid to prevent breakage.

Chocolate shards

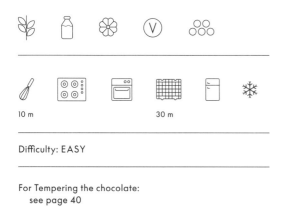

Difficulty: EASY

10 m   30 m

For Tempering the chocolate:
   see page 40

FOR THE SHARDS
9 ounces/250 g dark, milk, white, or ruby chocolate,
   tempered

(For vegan/dairy-free, use dark chocolate with a cocoa
content of at least 50%, and check the labeling)

EQUIPMENT NEEDED
Acetate sheets
Metal spatula or palette knife

AS USED IN
– Chocolate and Walnut Cake with Caramel (page 170)
– Mint Ganache-filled Chocolate Cups (page 224)
– Chocolate Cups filled with Clementine Mousse (page 226)
– White Chocolate and Hazelnut Mousse (page 238)
– Chocolate and Orange Ricotta Semifreddo Cake
   (page 282)

Pour the tempered chocolate onto an acetate sheet and spread it out to a thin layer with a metal spatula (1).

Set aside for 2 minutes to allow the chocolate to harden but without setting completely. Roll up the acetate sheet as tightly as required, depending on the size of the shards you want to make (2).

Leave the rolled chocolate to harden fully (3), then unroll the acetate sheet (4).

As it is detached from the acetate, the chocolate will shatter into thin, irregular shards that can be used to decorate the surface of cakes (5).

TIPS AND TRICKS
By adjusting the tightness of the roll, squeezing the roll once the chocolate has hardened, or varying the speed at which the acetate is unrolled, you can make shards of different sizes and shapes.

Chocolate strands

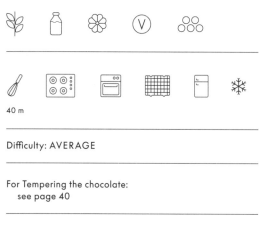

40 m

Difficulty: AVERAGE

For Tempering the chocolate:
  see page 40

FOR THE STRANDS
3½ ounces/100 g dark, milk, white, or ruby chocolate,
  tempered

(For vegan/dairy-free, use dark chocolate with a cocoa
content of at least 50%, and check the labeling)

EQUIPMENT NEEDED
Metal tray
Squeeze bottle or pastry (piping) bag
Metal spatula

AS USED IN
– Chocolate Cheesecake with Rhubarb Sauce (page 158)

Place a metal tray in the freezer to chill for 30 minutes.

Fill a squeeze bottle with the tempered chocolate (1) then pipe
a thin line of chocolate over the base of the chilled metal tray in
a continuous zigzag (2).

When the chocolate has set, but before it fully hardens, use a metal
spatula to push the lines of chocolate closer together on the tray.
First, loosen the strands from the tray at each end (3) then slide the
spatula along the entire length of the strands to loosen them fully
and push them together (4).

Cut the strands to the desired length with the spatula (5) and
remove them from the tray (6).

HOW TO USE
Depending on the size to which they are cut, chocolate strands
can be used to decorate the edge or surface of cakes, or individually
to decorate cookies (biscuits) and small pastries.

Chocolate lace collar

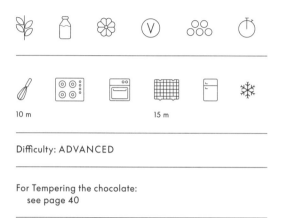

10 m   15 m

Difficulty: ADVANCED

For Tempering the chocolate:
   see page 40

FOR THE LACE COLLAR
3½ ounces/100 g dark, milk, white, or ruby chocolate,
   tempered

(For vegan/dairy-free, use dark chocolate with a cocoa
content of at least 50%, and check the labeling)

EQUIPMENT NEEDED
Ladle
Disposable pastry (piping) bag or cone
Acetate strip slightly wider than the height of the cake
   to be decorated and cut to the correct length to fit the
   cake's circumference

AS USED IN
– Almond Mousse Cake with Milk Chocolate Mousse Center
   (page 260)

Fill a disposable pastry (piping) bag with the tempered chocolate and cut off the tip. Pipe the chocolate over the entire length and height of the acetate strip in a circular motion to create irregular swirls. Go over the strip several times to give the decoration structure and strength (1).

When the chocolate has set but is still soft and malleable, position the acetate strip around the sides of the cake, making sure the chocolate-covered side is facing in and is in direct contact with the cake (2).

Gently press the chocolate lace collar to the sides of the cake with your fingers, then set aside to allow the chocolate to harden fully (3).

Carefully peel off the acetate strip (4) and place the cake in the refrigerator for 15 minutes.

TIPS AND TRICKS
For the chocolate lace collar to properly adhere to the cake, the cake must be glazed beforehand. It is not possible to attach the collar to an irregular and uneven surface, so make sure the edges are smooth and level. You can also use the pastry bag to pipe different patterns of varying thickness over the acetate strip. You can also make a solid collar, using a metal spatula or palette knife this time, to evenly spread the tempered chocolate over the acetate to a thickness of ⅛ inch/3mm. Then continue as described.

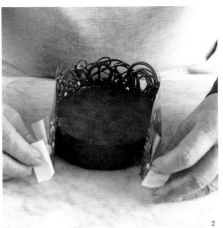

Chocolate batons

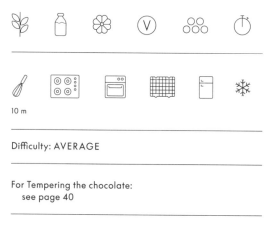

10 m

Difficulty: AVERAGE

For Tempering the chocolate:
  see page 40

FOR THE BATONS
7 ounces/200 g dark, milk, white, or ruby chocolate,
  tempered

(For vegan/dairy-free, use dark chocolate with a cocoa
content of at least 50%, and check the labeling)

EQUIPMENT NEEDED
Ladle
Large acetate sheet
Metal spatula
Small sharp knife

AS USED IN
– Milk Chocolate Chai Semifreddo (page 276)

Ladle the tempered chocolate onto a large acetate sheet (1) and spread it out with a metal spatula into a rectangle ⅛ inch/3 mm thick (2–3).

Before the chocolate sets, make indentations on the surface by gently pressing with the edge of the spatula to the width you wish the batons to be (4).

Cut the chocolate rectangle in half lengthwise (5).

When the chocolate has set but hasn't fully hardened, make individual batons by cutting along the indentations (6). Leave the chocolate to harden fully before peeling the batons off the acetate sheet.

TIPS AND TRICKS
The right time to create the indentations on the chocolate is when the chocolate is still soft but starting to set. The indentations will not remain if you try to make them while the chocolate is too soft, and it will be impossible once it has already hardened.

3-D ribbon decoration

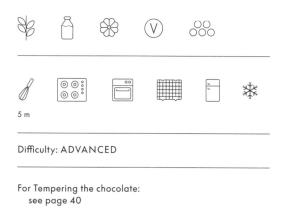

5 m

Difficulty: ADVANCED

For Tempering the chocolate:
   see page 40

FOR THE DECORATION
3½ ounces/100 g dark, milk, white, or ruby chocolate, tempered

(For vegan/dairy-free, use dark chocolate with a cocoa content of at least 50%, and check the labeling)

EQUIPMENT NEEDED
Large and small acetate sheets
Ladle
Palette knife
Comb scraper

AS USED IN
– Chocolate Pavlova (page 138)
– Triple Chocolate Cake (page 146)

Lay the smaller acetate sheet over the larger one and ladle the tempered chocolate over it (1).

Spread out the chocolate with a palette knife to a thickness of ⅛ inch/3 mm to cover the entire surface of the smaller sheet (2). Score it lengthwise with a comb scraper (3).

When the chocolate has begun to set, but is still soft and malleable, peel the small acetate sheet off the larger one using a palette knife to lift the sheet (4).

Holding the opposite corners of the acetate sheet with your fingertips (5), roll it up on a diagonal without allowing the chocolate to overlap (6).

Leave the chocolate to harden fully before carefully peeling off the acetate (7).

TIPS AND TRICKS
If the room temperature where you are working with chocolate is high, refrigerate the roll for 10 minutes to fully harden the chocolate. Peel off the acetate very carefully to avoid breaking the decoration.

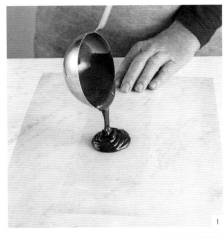

Decorating bonbons

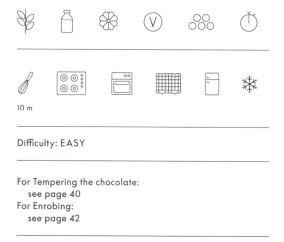

10 m

Difficulty: EASY

For Tempering the chocolate:
    see page 40
For Enrobing:
    see page 42

FOR DECORATING THE BONBONS
3½ ounces/100 g dark, milk, white, or ruby chocolate,
    tempered

(For vegan/dairy-free, use dark chocolate with a cocoa
content of at least 50%, and check the labeling)

EQUIPMENT NEEDED
Parchment paper
Sharp knife or scalpel
Scissors
Ladle
Selection of chocolate dipping forks

AS USED IN
– Dark Chocolate and Ginger Bonbons (page 220)
– Chocolate, Beer, and Acacia Honey Truffles (page 222)

For piped decorations, begin by making a paper cone. Take a rectangle of parchment paper that measures 13 ¾ × 17 ¾ inches/ 30 × 45 cm and fold it carefully along its diagonal so you have two triangles of the same size. Using a sharp knife or scalpel, cut the paper along the fold. Try to slide the sharp blade through the paper to get as clean a cut as possible. You can make a paper cone out of each triangle (1).

Take one of the paper triangles and hold it at the middle of the longest side between your thumb and index finger (2). Using your other hand, hold the point on the opposite side. The longer side of the triangle should be on your left. Curl the shorter corner on your right over the corner that is pointing towards you, so that it forms a cone. With your left hand wrap the longer corner on the left around the tip of the cone twice then join it together with the other two corners at the back of the cone (3).

If the bag still has an open tip at the front, you can close it by wiggling the inner and outer layers of paper back and forth, until the cone forms a small, sharp point.

Fold the corners at the open end into the inside of the cone twice to prevent it from unravelling (4–6).

At this point you can fill the paper cone with the tempered chocolate (7). Only ever half fill the paper cone, otherwise the contents will ooze out of the top when you squeeze on the cone to pipe your decorations. Close the top opening of the cone by folding the side with the seam over the plain side twice.

Using scissors, snip away the tip of the paper cone (8). Depending on the decorations you are piping, adjust the size of the opening at the tip of the cone. Keep the opening small when piping fine decorative lines (9) and make the opening larger when piping frostings (icings) and fillings.

Decorating bonbons
(cont.)

Other types of decoration can be achieved by using the appropriate dipping forks.

Once the bonbon is enrobed with the tempered chocolate, press a dipping fork with straight tines into the chocolate as it sets, but before it has fully hardened (10–11). For chocolate truffles, you can use a spiral fork to decorate, again, by pressing into the chocolate before it has fully set (12–13).

HOW TO USE
In the absence of a pastry (piping) bag or icing syringe, a paper cone is particularly suitable for creating small decorations and lettering. Pushing on the closed end at the top with your thumb extrudes the contents, while your other hand guides the tip to create the decorating.

10

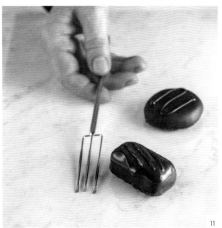

11

12

13

Chocolate modeling paste

20 m   5 m   4 h 30 m

Difficulty: AVERAGE

For Melting the chocolate:
  see page 38

FOR THE PASTE
9 ounces/250 g dark, milk, white, or ruby chocolate, melted
1 ounce/1½ tablespoons/30 g acacia honey
2 ounces/scant ½ cup/50 g confectioners' (icing) sugar

(For dairy-free, use dark chocolate with a cocoa content of
at least 50%, and check the labeling)

EQUIPMENT NEEDED
Mixing bowl
Silicone spatula
Plastic wrap (cling film)

Place the melted chocolate in a mixing bowl. Add the honey
and a tablespoon of warm water, and stir with a silicone spatula
until combined (1).

Gradually add the sugar, stirring continuously until a smooth
paste forms (2).

Transfer to a work surface or marble board and knead with your
hands for a few minutes (3).

Shape the paste into a disk, cover in plastic wrap (cling film), and
leave to rest in the refrigerator for 4 hours, followed by 30 minutes
at room temperature. Alternatively, leave at room temperature
for 12 hours.

Take a hazelnut-sized portion of the paste and flatten it into a thin
disk (4). Roll it into a cylinder to form the center of a rose (5).

Take another portion of the same size and shape into a thin disk.
Then wrap it like a petal around the center of the rose (6).

Flatten the top of the petal and turn it slightly outward (7), then
continue in the same way until you have an open rose (8).

VARIATION
You can also make chocolate modeling paste by using two parts
chocolate to one part glucose syrup. Melt the chocolate in
a bain-marie or double boiler until it reaches a temperature of
104°F/40°C, then stir in the glucose syrup and knead the resulting
paste on the work surface. Cover in plastic wrap and leave to
rest in the refrigerator for 30 minutes before making decorations.

Chocolate and cream glaze

10 m   8 m

Difficulty: EASY

For Melting the chocolate:
  see page 38

FOR THE GLAZE
5 ounces/150 g dark chocolate, melted
8½ fl oz/1 cup/250 ml heavy (whipping) cream
2¼ ounces/3 tablespoons/60 g acacia honey
2 ounces/½ stick/60 g unsalted butter, at room temperature

EQUIPMENT NEEDED
Mixing bowl
Measuring cup or jug
Small saucepan
Ladle
Silicone spatula
Kitchen thermometer
Immersion (stick) blender

AS USED IN
– Milk Chocolate and Macadamia Semifreddo (page 292)

Place the melted chocolate in a mixing bowl. Pour the cream into a small saucepan and add the honey (1). Place the pan over a moderate heat and stir until the honey has dissolved and the mixture comes to a boil. Pour a third of the cream and honey mixture into the melted chocolate and stir with a silicone spatula to combine (2).

Add the remaining cream, one half at a time, while stirring continuously (3). Continue to stir until the mixture cools to 104°F/40°C.

Cut the butter into small pieces, add to the mixture (4), and blend with an immersion (stick) blender to a smooth glaze (5).

TIPS AND TRICKS
To properly glaze a cake or pastry, place on a cooling rack set inside a parchment-lined, rimmed baking tray (pan). Pour the glaze over the cake, starting in the center and gradually spiraling toward the edges. Once the glazing is complete, tap the rack against the baking tray so any excess glaze drips off.

Chocolate and syrup glaze

5 m   10 m

Difficulty: EASY

For Melting the chocolate:
  see page 38

FOR THE GLAZE
5 ounces/150 g dark chocolate, melted
7 ounces/scant 1 cup/200 g superfine (caster) sugar

(For vegan/dairy-free, use dark chocolate with a cocoa
content of at least 50%, and check the labeling)

EQUIPMENT NEEDED
Bain-marie or double boiler
Measuring cup or jug
Small saucepan
Silicone spatula
Ladle

Keep the melted chocolate warm in a bain-marie or double boiler (1).

Pour 4 fl oz/ ½ cup/125 ml water into a small saucepan, add the sugar, and bring to a boil for 5 minutes, stirring often (2).

Add the boiling syrup to the melted chocolate in a thin stream while stirring continuously with a silicone spatula (3).

Continue to stir until the mixture is smooth and glossy, then use it immediately to glaze a cake or pastry.

HOW TO USE
This type of glaze should be used immediately after preparation, as it tends to form a skin on the surface. It is the typical glaze used on such cakes as Sacher torte, and on any desserts where a thin coating is appropriate.

 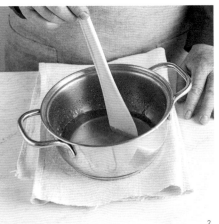 

Ganache for bonbons and truffles

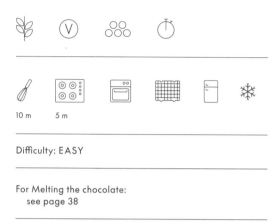

10 m   5 m

Difficulty: EASY

For Melting the chocolate:
  see page 38

FOR THE GANACHE
12 ounces/350 g 70% dark chocolate or 13 ounces/370 g
   60% dark chocolate or 1 pound/450 g milk, white, or
   ruby chocolate, melted
8½ fl oz/1 cup/250 ml heavy (whipping) cream
2½ ounces/⅔ stick/70 g unsalted butter

EQUIPMENT NEEDED
Mixing bowl
Measuring cup or jug
Small saucepan
Ladle
Silicone spatula
Kitchen thermometer
Immersion (stick) blender

AS USED IN
– Chocolate and Chili Tart (page 142)
– Orange and Chili Chocolate Bonbons (page 208)
– Ruby Chocolate and Ganache Lollipops (page 212)
– White Chocolate Bonbons (page 214)
– Sesame Brittle and Ganache Candies (page 218)
– Mint Ganache-filled Chocolate Cups (page 224)
– Praline Truffles (page 228)
– Dark Chocolate Bonbons (page 234)

Place the melted chocolate in a mixing bowl. Pour the cream into a small saucepan and place the pan over a moderate heat until it comes to a boil. Pour a third of the cream into the melted chocolate and stir with a silicone spatula to combine (1).

Add the remaining cream, one half at a time, while stirring continuously. Continue to stir until the mixture turns glossy and cools to 104°F/40°C (2).

Cut the butter into small pieces and stir into the mixture until melted, then blend the ganache with an immersion (stick) blender until smooth (3).

VARIATION
Finely chop the chocolate and place into a microwave-safe bowl. Add the cream and heat on the highest power setting for 1 minute. Stir until the chocolate has melted, then continue as for the basic technique.

Simple ganache

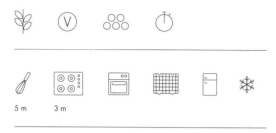

5 m   3 m

Difficulty: EASY

FOR THE GANACHE
12 ounces/350 g 70% dark chocolate or 13 ounces/370 g
   60% dark chocolate or 1 pound/450 g milk, white, or
   ruby chocolate
8½ fl oz/1 cup/250 ml heavy (whipping) cream

EQUIPMENT NEEDED
Chef's knife
Chopping board
Mixing bowl
Measuring cup or jug
Small saucepan
Silicone spatula

AS USED IN
– Triple Chocolate Cake (page 146)
– Gianduja Macarons (page 180)

Finely and evenly chop the chocolate and place in a mixing bowl. Pour the cream into a small saucepan and place the pan over a moderate heat until it is just below boiling point. Pour the hot cream over the chopped chocolate, a little at a time (1).

Use a silicone spatula to stir in the cream after each addition (2) until the ganache is glossy.

Continue to stir until the chocolate pieces have melted and the ganache is smooth (3).

HOW TO USE
The measures of chocolate and cream given for this basic technique make a thick ganache that sets more quickly because of the higher percentage of chocolate. If you want to use the ganache as a frosting (icing), use equal measures of chocolate and cream.

Whipped ganache

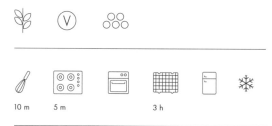

Difficulty: EASY

FOR THE GANACHE
9 ounces/250 g dark or milk chocolate
8½ fl oz/1 cup/250 ml heavy (whipping) cream

EQUIPMENT NEEDED
Chef's knife
Chopping board
Mixing bowl
Measuring cup or jug
Small saucepan
Silicone spatula
Electric whisk

AS USED IN
– Chocolate Pavlova (page 138)
– Dark Chocolate Baked Custard Torte (page 150)
– Cinnamon Cannoli with Ganache and Cocoa Beans
  (page 152)
– Double Chocolate, Coffee, and Elderberry Slice
  (page 160)

Finely and evenly chop the chocolate and place in a mixing bowl. Pour the cream into a small saucepan and place the pan over a moderate heat until it is just below boiling point. Pour the hot cream, a third at a time, over the chopped chocolate. Use a silicone spatula to stir in the cream after each addition until the mixture is smooth (1).

Set aside to cool then refrigerate the ganache for 3 hours until it has thickened.

Whip the ganache with an electric whisk (2), first on medium speed, increasing to high, until it becomes fluffy and changes to a lighter color (3).

If intended as a cake frosting (icing), use immediately, as it tends to harden if left in the refrigerator.

VARIATION
You can flavor the ganache with orange liqueur, or any liquor that goes well with the chocolate flavor, such as rum or sherry. Add 1¾ fl oz/3 tablespoons/50 ml to the quantities of cream and chocolate given in this recipe and stir well to incorporate.

Chocolate mousse
with raw eggs

20 m   5 m   12h   24 h

Difficulty: EASY

For Melting the chocolate:
  see page 38

FOR THE MOUSSE
10½ ounces/300 g 70% dark chocolate or 14 ounces/390 g
  milk, white, or ruby chocolate, melted
1 sheet (3 g) gelatin, if using milk, white, or ruby chocolate
5 fl oz/scant ⅔ cup/150 ml heavy (whipping) cream
3 egg yolks, at room temperature
6 egg whites
2 ounces/¼ cup/50 g superfine (caster) sugar

(For vegetarian, use dark chocolate)

EQUIPMENT NEEDED
Mixing bowl
Small bowl
Measuring cup or jug
Small saucepan
Silicone spatula
Strainer (sieve)
Hand whisk
Immersion (stick) blender
Electric whisk

Place the melted chocolate in a mixing bowl. If you are using milk, white, or ruby chocolate, soak the gelatin sheet in a small bowl of cold water for 10 minutes until it is completely rehydrated and soft, making sure it is fully immersed in the water.

Pour the cream into a small saucepan and place over a moderate heat to bring to a boil, then remove from the heat. If using gelatin, drain the sheet and squeeze it with your hands to remove as much water as possible. Add the gelatin to the cream and stir until it has completely dissolved.

Pour the cream through a strainer (sieve) and add a third to the melted chocolate. Mix with a silicone spatula then add the remaining cream, a half at a time, stirring continuously to combine.

Leave the mixture to cool to room temperature, then beat the egg yolks with a fork and stir into the mixture (1).

Stir with a hand whisk to incorporate (2), then blend with an immersion (stick) blender.

Use an electric whisk to whisk the egg whites with the sugar to soft peaks (3).

Add a third of the whisked egg whites to the chocolate mixture and gently fold in with the spatula taking care not to knock any air out of the mixture (4).

Fold in the remaining whisked egg whites, a half at a time, until the mousse is smooth (5).

Refrigerate for at least 12 hours before serving and store in the refrigerator for no longer than 24 hours.

TIPS AND TRICKS
If the yolks are at a lower temperature than that of the chocolate mixture, the mousse will set too quickly and become lumpy, uneven, and unusable. Take the eggs out of the refrigerator for at least 4 hours before use.

Chocolate mousse
with Italian meringue

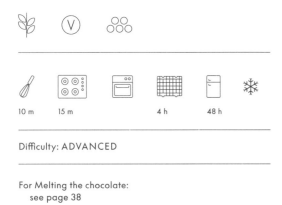

10 m   15 m   4 h   48 h

Difficulty: ADVANCED

For Melting the chocolate:
   see page 38

FOR THE MOUSSE
9 ounces/250 g 70% dark chocolate
½ ounce/2 teaspoons/10 g unsalted butter
3 eggs, at room temperature
2 ounces/¼ cup/50 g superfine (caster) sugar

EQUIPMENT NEEDED
Chef's knife
Chopping board
Bain-marie or double boiler
Measuring cup or jug
Silicone spatula
Mixing bowl
Hand whisk
Small saucepan
Kitchen thermometer
Electric whisk

AS USED IN
– Chocolate Charlotte with Rum, Banana, and Coconut
  (page 140)

Finely chop the dark chocolate and melt in a bain-marie or double boiler with 2 fl oz/¼ cup/60 ml water (1).

Stir in the butter until completely melted (2). Remove the bowl from the bain-marie and leave the mixture to cool to room temperature.

Separate the egg yolks into a mixing bowl, beat with a hand whisk, then incorporate the melted chocolate (3).

Transfer the mixture back to the bain-marie and cook over a very low heat for 3 minutes while stirring continuously with a silicone spatula (4). Remove the bowl from the bain-marie and leave the mixture to cool to room temperature.

Pour 2 fl oz/¼ cup/60 ml water into a small saucepan, add the sugar, and set over a low heat until the sugar dissolves, then increase the heat to moderate and bring the syrup to a temperature of 250°F/121°C (5).

Meanwhile, whisk the egg whites in a clean, dry bowl with an electric whisk on medium speed until soft peaks form. When the syrup is ready, remove from the heat and very slowly drizzle the hot syrup around the sides of the bowl into the whisked egg whites, whisking continuously to incorporate (6).

Gently fold a third of the meringue into the chocolate mixture using the spatula and taking care not to knock any air out of the mixture (7–8). Fold in the remaining meringue until just combined, do not overmix. Refrigerate for at least 4 hours before serving, and store in the refrigerator for no longer than 24 hours.

MISTAKES TO AVOID
Whisk the egg whites with the boiling syrup only until the mixture has cooled. Whisking them longer than this time will turn the egg whites very stiff, making them difficult to fold into the chocolate mixture.

Chocolate mousse with water

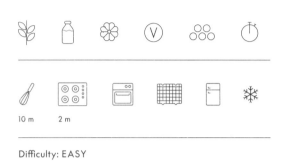

10 m   2 m

Difficulty: EASY

FOR THE MOUSSE
12 ounces/350 g chocolate of your choice

(For vegan/dairy-free, use dark chocolate with a cocoa content of at least 50%, and check the labeling)

EQUIPMENT NEEDED
Chef's knife
Chopping board
Mixing bowl
Measuring cup or jug
Small saucepan
Silicone spatula
Cold bain-marie
Electric whisk

Finely and evenly chop the chocolate and place in a mixing bowl. Pour 14 fl oz/1¾ cups/420 ml water into a small saucepan and bring to a boil. Pour the boiling water over the chopped chocolate, stirring with a silicone spatula until smooth (1), then place the mixing bowl into a cold bain-marie (2).

Continue to stir with the spatula until the chocolate takes on a creamy consistency (3).

Remove the bowl from the cold bain-marie and whisk with an electric whisk until a fluffy mousse forms (4). Serve immediately.

HOW TO USE
This is a very intensely flavored mousse, but it cannot be stored. It should be served immediately as is, although it can be decorated and enhanced with whipped cream, if desired.

Eggless chocolate mousse

10 m   5 m   6 h   24 h

Difficulty: EASY

For Melting the chocolate:
   see page 38

FOR THE MOUSSE
5 ounces/150 g 60% dark chocolate, melted
1 sheet (3 g) gelatin
12½ fl oz/1½ cups/370 ml heavy (whipping) cream

EQUIPMENT NEEDED
Mixing bowls
Measuring cup or jug
Small saucepan
Silicone spatula
Strainer (sieve)
Kitchen thermometer
Electric whisk

AS USED IN
– Almond Mousse Cake with Milk Chocolate Mousse Center
  (page 260)

Place the melted chocolate in a mixing bowl. Soak the gelatin sheet in a small bowl of cold water for 10 minutes until it is completely rehydrated and soft, making sure it is fully immersed in the water.

Pour 4 fl oz/½ cup/120 ml of the cream into a small saucepan and place over a moderate heat to bring to a boil. Drain the sheet of gelatin and squeeze it with your hands to remove as much water as possible. Add the gelatin to the cream and stir over a low heat until it has completely dissolved (1).

Pour a third of the cream at a time through a strainer (sieve) into the melted chocolate, stirring continuously with a silicone spatula (2). Transfer the mixture to a clean mixing bowl and set aside to cool, checking the temperature regularly with a thermometer.

Meanwhile, whip the remaining cream with an electric whisk until firm, but still smooth. When the chocolate mix reaches 95°F/35°C, gently fold in the whipped cream (3).

Refrigerate for at least 6 hours before serving, and store in the refrigerator for no longer than 24 hours.

TIPS AND TRICKS
You can replace the gelatin of animal origin with ⅒ ounce/3 g agar-agar. Add it to the cold cream, bring to a boil, stir with a whisk, and cook over a very low heat for about 1 minute. Then add it to the cream as above.

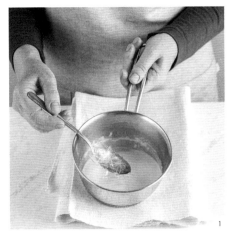  

Chocolate pastry cream

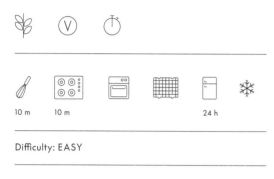

10 m   10 m   24 h

Difficulty: EASY

For Melting the chocolate:
  see page 38

FOR THE CREAM
3 ounces/85 g 70% chocolate or 3½ ounces/95 g
   60% chocolate, melted
2 egg yolks
1 ounce/2½ tablespoons/30 g superfine (caster) sugar
½ ounce/10 g rice starch
8 fl oz/scant 1 cup/220 ml whole (full-fat) milk
1¾ fl oz/scant ¼ cup/50 ml heavy (whipping) cream
1 vanilla bean (pod)

EQUIPMENT NEEDED
Mixing bowls
Electric whisk
Hand whisk
Measuring cup or jug
Saucepans
Paring knife
Ladle
Silicone spatula
Immersion (stick) blender
Plastic wrap (cling film)

Place the melted chocolate in a mixing bowl. In a separate bowl, beat the egg yolks with the sugar using an electric whisk until pale and fluffy, then stir in the rice starch using a hand whisk (1).

Pour the milk and cream into a small saucepan. Split the vanilla bean (pod) lengthwise with a sharp paring knife, scrape out the seeds and add them to the pan (2).

Heat the milk and cream until just below boiling point then drizzle into the egg yolk mixture while stirring with a hand whisk (3).

Transfer the pastry cream to a saucepan and cook over a low heat, stirring continuously, until it comes to a simmer and thickens (4).

Add a third of the pastry cream at a time to the melted chocolate while stirring with a silicone spatula (5).

Blend the chocolate cream with an immersion (stick) blender until smooth then cover with plastic wrap (cling film), ensuring the wrap touches the surface of the cream to prevent a skin from forming. Set aside to cool before use, and store in the refrigerator for no longer than 24 hours.

TIPS AND TRICKS
Even after covering the pastry cream with plastic wrap in direct contact with the surface of the cream, it is still possible for small lumps to form. If this happens, blend the cream for a few seconds with an immersion blender until it is smooth again.

Chocolate crémeux

20 m   10 m   12 h   48 h

Difficulty: EASY

For Melting the chocolate:
  see page 38

FOR THE CRÉMEUX
6½ ounces/190 g 70% dark chocolate or 7 ounces/210 g
  60% dark chocolate or 9 ounces/250 g milk chocolate or
  225 g white or ruby chocolate, melted
2 sheets (6 g) gelatin
5 egg yolks
2 ounces/¼ cup/50 g superfine (caster) sugar
17 fl oz/2 cups/500 ml whole (full-fat) milk

EQUIPMENT NEEDED
Bain-marie or double boiler
Mixing bowls
Hand or electric whisk
Measuring cup or jug
Small saucepan
Kitchen thermometer
Ladle
Immersion (stick) blender
Silicone spatula
Plastic wrap (cling film)

AS USED IN
– Double Chocolate, Coffee, and Elderberry Slice
  (page 160)

Keep the melted chocolate warm in a bain-marie or double boiler. Soak the gelatin sheets in a small bowl of cold water for 10 minutes until completely rehydrated and soft, making sure they are fully immersed in the water. In a mixing bowl, beat the egg yolks with the sugar using a hand or electric whisk (1).

Pour the milk into a small saucepan and warm over a moderate heat but do not bring to a boil. Add the hot milk to the egg yolk mix and cook, stirring, in a bain-marie until the resulting crème anglaise reaches 185°F/85°C or is thick enough to coat the back of a spoon (2).

Drain the sheets of gelatin and squeeze them with your hands to remove as much water as possible. Add the gelatin to the cream and stir until completely dissolved (3).

Transfer the cream to a clean bowl and blend with an immersion (stick) blender. Add the cream to the melted chocolate, a third at a time, (4), using a silicone spatula to mix in the middle of the bowl in a circular motion.

Blend again with the immersion blender until thick and smooth (5).

Cover the crémeux with plastic wrap (cling film) ensuring the wrap touches the surface of the cream to prevent a skin from forming. Set aside to cool (6).

Refrigerate for at least 12 hours before use and store for no longer than 48 hours.

TIPS AND TRICKS
You can also cook the crème anglaise over direct heat and not in a bain-marie. In this case, the cream must not come to a boil and you must watch it closely as it cooks, until the temperature reaches 185°F/85°C. Although this is faster than the bain-marie method, it requires care and attention.

Chocolate pâte à bombe

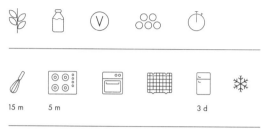

15 m   5 m   3 d

Difficulty: AVERAGE

FOR THE PÂTE À BOMBE
5 egg yolks
2 ounces/¼ cup/50g superfine (caster) sugar
8¾ ounces/240 g 70% dark chocolate
3¾ fl oz/scant ½ cup/110 ml boiling water

EQUIPMENT NEEDED
Bain-marie or double boiler
Hand whisk
Kitchen thermometer
Mixing bowls
Electric whisk
Chef's knife
Chopping board
Measuring cup or jug
Silicone spatula
Immersion (stick) blender

AS USED IN
– Milk Chocolate Chai Semifreddo (page 276)
– Ruby Chocolate and Roasted Plum Semifreddi (page 288)

Place the yolks in the bowl of a bain-marie or double boiler, add the sugar and mix with a hand whisk (1). Heat the mixture in a bain-marie until it reaches 140°F/60°C, then transfer to a bowl and beat with an electric whisk until it cools to 77°F/25°C (2).

Finely chop the chocolate and place in a bowl. Add the boiling water, and stir with a silicone spatula until melted (3).

Blend with an immersion (stick) blender (4) then stir continuously until the temperature of the chocolate falls to 104°F/40°C.

Fold in the beaten egg yolk mixture (5).

HOW TO USE
Pâte à bombe is typically used in traditional pastry making as a base for making spoon desserts, such as mousses, semifreddi, and parfaits. Cooking the yolks prevents any risk associated with eating raw eggs.

THE RECIPES

SIMPLE CAKES AND TARTS

GIANDUJA CAKE

Torta gianduia

30 m	5 m	50 m	10 m	3 d	60 d

Difficulty: EASY

For Melting the chocolate:
see page 38

TO SERVE 8

FOR THE CAKE
7 ounces/200 g 60% dark chocolate
7 ounces/1½ cups/200 g roasted hazelnuts
7 ounces/scant 1 cup/200 g superfine (caster) sugar
7 ounces/1¾ sticks/200 g unsalted butter, at room
   temperature
4 eggs
¾ ounce/scant ¼ cup/20 g type "00" flour or all-purpose
   (plain) flour
Pinch of salt
1 teaspoon lemon juice
Unsweetened cocoa powder, for dusting
Chopped hazelnuts, for decorating

EQUIPMENT NEEDED
7-inch/18-cm round springform pan (tin)
Parchment paper
Chef's knife
Chopping board
Bain-marie or double boiler
Food processor
Mixing bowls
Electric whisk
Strainer (sieve)
Silicone spatula
Cooling rack
Fine-mesh strainer (sieve)

Preheat the oven to 375°F/190°C/170°C Fan/Gas 5 and line the springform pan (tin) with parchment paper.

Finely chop and melt the chocolate in a bain-marie or double boiler. Grind the hazelnuts with 2 ounces/¼ cup/50 g of the sugar to a fine powder in a food processor.

Place the butter in a mixing bowl with the remainder of the sugar and beat together using an electric whisk until pale and fluffy. Separate the eggs and add the yolks to the mix, one at a time, alternating with a tablespoon of the sifted flour. Add the remaining flour, a pinch of salt, the ground hazelnuts, and melted chocolate and mix with a silicone spatula to combine.

Place the egg whites in a grease-free bowl and add the lemon juice. Whisk the egg whites to soft peaks with an electric whisk then gently fold into the batter using the spatula.

Pour the batter evenly into the springform pan and bake in the preheated oven for 20 minutes. Lower the temperature to 350°F/180°C/160°C Fan/Gas 4 and continue to bake for a further 30 minutes. Remove from the oven and rest for 10 minutes, then remove from the pan and leave to cool completely on a cooling rack. Serve cold dusted with cocoa powder and decorated with a few hazelnuts, as desired.

TIPS AND TRICKS
Adding sugar to the hazelnuts before grinding in a food processor prevents them from turning into a paste, because the sugar absorbs the oil released by the nuts.

CHOCOLATE CUSTARD PIE WITH AVOCADO CRUST

Crostata con frolla all'avocado e crema al cioccolato

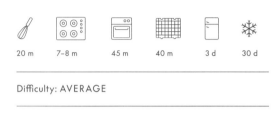

| 20 m | 7–8 m | 45 m | 40 m | 3 d | 30 d |

Difficulty: AVERAGE

TO SERVE 6–8

FOR THE BASE
3½ ounces/100 g very ripe avocado pulp
8 ounces/1¾ cups/230 g type "00" flour or all-purpose
   (plain) flour, plus extra for dusting
1 teaspoon baking powder
2½ ounces/⅔ cup/70 g unsweetened cocoa powder
3 ounces/⅓ cup/80 g superfine (caster) sugar
Pinch of salt

FOR THE CUSTARD
2 egg yolks
2 ounces/¼ cup/50 g superfine (caster) sugar
½ ounce/4 teaspoons/10 g type "00" flour or all-purpose
   (plain) flour
½ ounce/10 g rice starch
8½ fl oz/1 cup/250 ml whole (full-fat) milk
4 fl oz/½ cup/120 ml heavy (whipping) cream
1 level teaspoon ground cinnamon
7 ounces/200 g 70% dark chocolate

FOR THE DECORATION
Confectioners' (icing) sugar

EQUIPMENT NEEDED
Mixing bowls
Immersion (stick) blender
Food processor
Strainer (sieve)
Plastic wrap (cling film)
Electric whisk
Silicone spatula
Measuring cup or jug
Saucepan
Hand whisk
Chef's knife
Chopping board
Rolling pin
7-inch/18-cm round pie pan (tin)
Palette knife
Cooling rack
Fine-mesh strainer (sieve)

Preheat the oven to 350°F/180°C/160°C Fan/Gas 4.

Place the avocado in a mixing bowl and blend with an immersion (stick) blender to a creamy consistency. Transfer to a food processor, add the sifted flour, baking powder, cocoa powder, sugar, and a pinch of salt, and blend until the resulting dough sticks to the blades. Shape and flatten the dough into a disk, cover in plastic wrap (cling film), and leave to rest in the refrigerator for 30 minutes.

To make the custard, place the egg yolks and sugar in a bowl and beat with an electric whisk until pale and fluffy. Add the sifted flour and rice starch, and mix with a silicone spatula to combine. Pour the milk and cream into a saucepan, add the cinnamon and heat. Drizzle the warm milk into the egg and flour mix, stirring continuously with a hand whisk to incorporate. Transfer back to the saucepan and cook over a low heat, stirring often, until the custard thickens.

Finely chop the chocolate and add to the pan, stirring until melted, then blend with an immersion blender to a smooth consistency. Pour the custard into a bowl and cover with plastic wrap ensuring the wrap touches the surface of the custard to prevent a skin from forming. Set aside to cool.

Lightly dust a clean work surface with flour and roll out the dough to a thickness of ⅛ inch/3 mm. Transfer to the pie pan (tin). Line the pan with the dough, pressing down on the base and sides, and trimming off the excess dough with a small sharp knife. Prick the base with a fork, fill the pie crust with the custard, and level with a palette knife. Roll out the leftover dough to a thickness of ⅛ inch/3 mm and cut into strips ¾ inch/2 cm wide. Weave them over the top of the custard, attaching them to the edge of the crust.

Bake the pie on a low shelf in the preheated oven for 45 minutes. Remove from the oven and rest for 10 minutes, then remove from the pan and leave to cool on a cooling rack. Dust the pie with confectioners' (icing) sugar, if desired, and serve.

CHOCOLATE AND GINGER BROWNIE CUPCAKES

Tortine brownie allo zenzero

20 m	5 m	20 m		48 h	30 d

Difficulty: EASY

For Melting the chocolate:
see page 38

TO SERVE 6

FOR THE CUPCAKES
6 ounces/1½ sticks/170 g unsalted butter, at room
temperature, plus extra for greasing
3 ounces/⅔ cup/80 g type "00" flour or all-purpose (plain)
flour, plus extra for dusting
8 ounces/220 g 70% dark chocolate
4 ounces/½ cup/120 g superfine (caster) sugar
3 eggs
Pinch of salt
2 ounces/50 g candied (crystallized) ginger, cut into
small dice
Unsweetened cocoa powder, for dusting

EQUIPMENT NEEDED
6 × 3-inch/8-cm round smooth tartlet pans (tins)
Strainer (sieve)
Chef's knife
Chopping board
Bain-marie or double boiler
Mixing bowl
Hand whisk
Silicone spatula
Cooling rack
Fine-mesh strainer (sieve)

Preheat the oven to 350°F/180°C/160°C Fan/Gas 4 and grease
the tartlet pans (tins) with butter and a dusting of flour.

Finely chop the chocolate and place in the bowl of a bain-marie
or double boiler. Add the butter and sugar and gently heat, stirring
often, until the chocolate has melted and the ingredients are
combined. Remove the bowl from the bain-marie and set aside
to cool.

Break the eggs into a mixing bowl and beat lightly with a hand
whisk, then add to the chocolate mix, stirring with a silicone
spatula. Add the sifted flour, a pinch of salt, and 1 ounce/30 g
of the candied (crystallized) ginger, stirring to combine.

Pour the batter into the prepared tartlet pans and bake in the
preheated oven for 20 minutes until a crust forms on the surface.
Remove from the oven and leave the cupcakes to cool in the
pans, then transfer to a cooling rack and dust with cocoa powder.
Decorate with the remaining ginger, as desired.

MISTAKES TO AVOID
It is extremely important to watch the cupcakes closely as they
bake because the temperature can vary from oven to oven. They
must remain soft; if they are cooked for too long they will become
too hard. They will firm up as they cool, but remain soft and
gooey when eaten.

RUBY CHOCOLATE AND STRAWBERRY CHEESECAKE

Cheesecake ai cioccolato ruby e fragole

20 m   8 m   6 h 20 m   48 h

Difficulty: EASY

For Melting the chocolate:
   see page 38

TO SERVE 8

FOR THE CHEESECAKE
3½ ounces/scant 1 stick/100 g unsalted butter
1 unwaxed lemon
7 ounces/200 g graham crackers or digestive biscuits
14 ounces/3⅓ cups/400 g spreadable cream cheese,
   at room temperature
2 ounces/¼ cup/50 g superfine (caster) sugar
Pinch of salt
9 ounces/260 g ruby chocolate
7 fl oz/scant 1 cup/200 ml heavy (whipping) cream
5 ounces/½ cup/150 g sugar-free strawberry preserve (jam)
3½ ounces/100 g fresh strawberries, halved

EQUIPMENT NEEDED
7-inch/18-cm round springform pan (tin)
Parchment paper
Acetate strip, a little wider than the height of the
   springform pan
Bain-marie or double boiler
Zester
Silicone spatula
Food processor
Electric whisk
Mixing bowls
Chef's knife
Chopping board
Measuring cup or jug
Juicer
Fine-mesh strainer (sieve)
Chocolate grater

Line the base of the springform pan (tin) with parchment paper and the sides with the acetate strip.

Place the butter in the bowl of a bain-marie or double boiler and heat gently until melted. Grate the zest from the lemon, add to the melted butter and stir with a silicone spatula to combine. Place the graham crackers or digestive biscuits in a food processor and blend to a fine crumb. Drizzle over the melted butter and blend again to coat the crumbs evenly. Cover the bottom of the pan with the cookie (biscuit) crumb base and press it down firmly with the back of a spoon. Chill in the refrigerator for 20 minutes.

Meanwhile, use an electric whisk to whip the cream cheese with the sugar and a pinch of salt until fluffy. Reserve ½ ounce/10 g of the ruby chocolate for decoration and finely chop the remainder. Place the chopped chocolate in the bowl of the bain-marie and melt, then fold into the cream cheese mixture with the spatula.

Whip the cream until firm then fold into the cream cheese mixture. Pour half the mix over the chilled crust then spread 3½ ounces/⅓ cup/100 g of the strawberry preserve (jam) over the center. Pour the remaining cream cheese mixture on top and chill in the refrigerator for at least 6 hours.

Transfer the cheesecake from the springform pan to a serving platter. Add the strained juice of ½ lemon to the remaining preserve to loosen, and spread on top of the cheesecake. Decorate with the strawberries, and shred (grate) over the remaining ruby chocolate.

MISTAKES TO AVOID
Before use, keep the cream cheese at room temperature for a few hours so it blends perfectly with the melted ruby chocolate. If the cream cheese is too cold, the chocolate risks setting, which would lead to the formation of small lumps.

MARBLED BUNDT CAKE WITH GIANDUJA GLAZE

Ciambella marmorizzata con glassa al gianduia

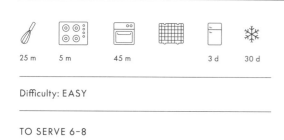

25 m   5 m   45 m   3 d   30 d

Difficulty: EASY

TO SERVE 6–8

FOR THE CAKE
7 ounces/1¾ sticks/200 g unsalted butter, at room
    temperature, plus extra for greasing
12 ounces/2¾ cups/350 g type "00" flour or all-purpose
    (plain) flour, plus extra for dusting
7 ounces/1⅔ cups/200 g confectioners' (icing) sugar
Pinch of salt
3 eggs
6¼ fl oz/¾ cup/180 ml whole (full-fat) milk
2¼ ounces/generous ½ cup/60 g unsweetened
    cocoa powder

FOR THE GLAZE
3½ ounces/100 g gianduja chocolate
2½ fl oz/⅜ cup/80 ml heavy (whipping) cream

EQUIPMENT NEEDED
8-inch/20-cm round Bundt pan (tin)
Strainer (sieve)
Mixing bowls
Hand or electric whisk
Silicone spatula
Measuring cup or jug
Cooling rack
Chef's knife
Chopping board
Saucepan

Preheat the oven to 350°F/180°C/160°C Fan/Gas 4 and grease the Bundt pan (tin) with butter and a dusting of flour.

Place the butter in a mixing bowl with the confectioners' (icing) sugar and a pinch of salt. Beat together with a hand or electric whisk until fluffy and creamy. Add the eggs, one at a time, alternating with a tablespoon of the sifted flour. Mix in the remaining flour and the milk. Divide the batter into two equal parts and place in separate bowls. Add the sifted cocoa powder to one bowl and stir until fully combined.

Fill the Bundt pan with a tablespoon of batter at a time, alternating between the two colored batters. Place in the preheated oven and bake for about 45 minutes until golden, risen, and springy to the touch. Turn out the cake onto a cooling rack and leave to cool completely.

To make the glaze, finely chop the chocolate. Pour the cream into a saucepan and place over a moderate heat until hot but not boiling. Remove from the heat, add the chocolate, and stir until the chocolate has melted. Leave to cool, then pour over the cake, and serve.

TIPS AND TRICKS
To divide the batter into equal parts, take two identical bowls, weigh them, fill them with the batter, and weigh them again. Adjust the amount of batter in each until they weigh the same.

BREAD AND CHOCOLATE PUDDING
Pudding di pane e cioccolato

20 m   5 m   1 h   20 m   48 h   30 d

Difficulty: EASY

For Melting the chocolate:
    see page 38

TO SERVE 6

FOR THE PUDDING
3½ ounces/100 g 70% dark chocolate
1½ fl oz/3 tablespoons/40 ml whole (full-fat) milk
4 ounces/1 stick/120 g unsalted butter, at room temperature
3½ ounces/scant ½ cup/100 g superfine (caster) sugar
1 egg
3 ounces/⅔ cup/80 g type "00" flour or all-purpose
    (plain) flour
½ teaspoon baking powder
3 ounces/1 cup/80 g fresh bread crumbs
Pinch of salt
Confectioners' (icing) sugar, for dusting
Vanilla gelato, to serve

EQUIPMENT NEEDED
Chef's knife
Chopping board
Bain-marie or double boiler
Mixing bowls
Hand whisk
Silicone spatula
Strainer (sieve)
Electric whisk
34-fl oz/1-liter capacity pudding mold
Kitchen foil
Steamer or high-sided oven tray
Fine-mesh strainer (sieve)

Preheat the oven (if using) to 300°F/150°C/130°C Fan/Gas 2.

Finely chop the chocolate and place in the bowl of a bain-marie or double boiler. Add the milk and gently heat in the bain-marie, stirring from time to time, until the chocolate has melted. Remove from the heat. In a separate bowl, use a hand whisk to beat 3½ ounces/scant 1 stick/100 g of the butter with the superfine (caster) sugar until smooth and fluffy, then mix in the cooled chocolate.

Separate the egg and place the white in a separate, grease-free bowl; set aside. Stir the yolk into the chocolate mixture, then add the sifted flour, baking powder, bread crumbs, and a pinch of salt. Mix with a silicone spatula to combine. Whisk the egg whites to soft peaks with the electric whisk and gently fold into the batter.

Grease the pudding mold with the remaining butter, fill with the batter, and cover with kitchen foil. Steam the pudding in the preheated oven, or bake in a bain-marie, for about an hour.

Test if the pudding is ready by inserting a wooden toothpick in the center, which should come out clean and dry. Leave the pudding to rest for 20 minutes, then turn out onto a serving platter. Serve warm dusted with confectioners' (icing) sugar and accompanied with vanilla gelato.

TIPS AND TRICKS
Steaming or baking in a bain-marie gives the pudding a soft and moist consistency. Lightly warm any leftover pudding before serving.

WHITE CHOCOLATE, LIME, AND COCONUT BUNDT CAKE

Ciambella al cioccolato bianco, lime e cocco

| 20 m | 10 m | 1 h | 5 m | 48 h | 30 d |

Difficulty: EASY

For Melting the chocolate:
   see page 38

TO SERVE 6–8

FOR THE CAKE
4 ounces/1 stick/120 g unsalted butter, at room temperature,
   plus extra for greasing
11 ounces/generous 2½ cups/320 g type "00" flour or
   all-purpose (plain) flour, plus extra tor dusting
7 ounces/200 g white chocolate
8½ fl oz/1 cup/240 ml coconut milk
Grated zest of 2 unwaxed limes
4 egg whites
Pinch of salt
2 level teaspoons baking powder
4 ounces/½ cup/120 g superfine (caster) sugar

FOR THE DECORATION
2 ounces/50 g white chocolate
1 ounce/30 g fresh coconut flesh
Grated zest of 1 unwaxed lime

EQUIPMENT NEEDED
8-inch/20-cm round Bundt pan (tin)
Strainer (sieve)
Chef's knife
Chopping board
Mixing bowls
Measuring cup or jug
Small saucepan
Zester
Silicone spatula
Food processor
Cooling rack
Bain-marie or double boiler
Coarse grater

Preheat the oven to 350°F/180°C/160°C Fan/Gas 4 and grease the Bundt pan (tin) with butter and a dusting of flour.

Finely chop the chocolate and place in a bowl. Pour the coconut milk into a small saucepan, add the lime zest, and heat to a simmer over a moderate heat. Remove from the heat and drizzle into the chocolate while stirring with a silicone spatula until the chocolate has fully melted. Set aside to rest for 5 minutes.

Meanwhile, lightly beat the egg whites with a fork. Add the beaten egg whites and a pinch of salt to the coconut chocolate mix, and stir to combine. Cut the butter into small cubes. Place the sifted flour, baking powder, sugar, and butter in a food processor, and blend until the mixture resembles fine bread crumbs.

With the food processor running, add the coconut chocolate mixture and continue to blend for 2–3 minutes until smooth. Pour the batter into the Bundt pan and bake in the preheated oven for 1 hour until golden, risen, and springy to the touch. Turn out the cake onto a cooling rack and leave to cool completely.

To decorate, finely chop the white chocolate and melt in a bain-marie or double boiler. Use a spoon to drizzle the melted chocolate in parallel lines across the width of the cake. Use a coarse grater to shred (grate) the coconut and sprinkle over the cake with the lime zest to finish.

TIPS AND TRICKS
To decorate more uniformly with the white chocolate, use a squeeze bottle or pastry (piping) bag fitted with a small plain piping tip (nozzle) filled with the melted chocolate.

MOIST CHESTNUT AND CHOCOLATE CAKE

Dolce morbido di castagne e cioccolato

20 m   5 m   30 m   4 h   48 h   30 d

Difficulty: EASY

For Melting the chocolate:
  see page 38

TO SERVE 6–8

FOR THE CAKE
9 ounces/250 g chestnut cream
2½ fl oz/⅜ cup/80 ml whole (full-fat) milk
6¼ ounces/1⅔ sticks/180 g unsalted butter,
  at room temperature
4¾ ounces/140 g milk chocolate
3 eggs
1 ounce/2½ tablespoons/30 g superfine (caster)
  sugar
Pinch of salt
1 ounce/¼ cup/30 g type "00" flour or all-purpose
  (plain) flour
Unsweetened cocoa powder, for dusting

EQUIPMENT NEEDED
8-inch/20-cm round springform pan (tin)
Parchment paper
Measuring cup or jug
Saucepan
Silicone spatula
Chef's knife
Chopping board
Bain-marie or double boiler
Mixing bowls
Electric whisk
Strainer (sieve)
Fine-mesh strainer (sieve)
Vegetable peeler

Preheat the oven to 350°F/180°C/160°C Fan/Gas 4 and line the springform pan (tin) with parchment paper.

Place the chestnut cream and milk in a saucepan, stir to combine, and warm over a very low heat, stirring often with a silicone spatula. Cut the butter into small cubes and finely chop 4 ounces/120 g of the chocolate. Melt the chocolate with the butter in a bain-marie or double boiler, stirring until creamy.

Separate the eggs and use an electric whisk to beat the yolks with the sugar and a pinch of salt until pale and fluffy. Add the melted butter and chocolate mixture, the warmed chestnut milk, and the sifted flour, and whisk to combine.

Whisk the egg whites to soft peaks and gently fold into the batter. Pour the batter into the springform pan and bake in the preheated oven for 30 minutes. Remove from the oven and leave to cool in the pan, then carefully transfer to a plate and chill in the refrigerator for 4 hours.

Immediately before serving, dust with cocoa powder and decorate as desired with the remaining chocolate, shaved into chocolate curls with a vegetable peeler and sprinkled over the top.

VARIATION
As an alternative to chestnut cream, you can use the same weight in boiled chestnuts pureed in a food processor and diluted with warm milk to a creamy, jam-like consistency. In this case, increase the amount of sugar to 2½ ounces/⅓ cup/80 g.

TORTA CAPRESE (FLOURLESS CAKE) WITH PISTACHIOS

Caprese ai pistacchi

| 20 m | 5 m | 35 m | 10 m | 48 h | 30 d |

Difficulty: EASY

For Melting the chocolate:
  see page 38

TO SERVE 8

FOR THE CAKE
4 ounces/1 stick/120 g unsalted butter, at room temperature
4 ounces/120 g 60% dark chocolate
4¾ ounces/1 cup/140 g pistachio nuts, shelled and peeled
¾ ounce/20 g potato starch
4 eggs
3½ ounces/scant 1 cup/100 g confectioners' (icing) sugar
½ ounce/1 heaping tablespoon/15 g unsweetened
  cocoa powder
Pinch of salt

EQUIPMENT NEEDED
9-inch/23-cm square baking pan (tin)
Parchment paper
Chef's knife
Chopping board
Bain-marie or double boiler
Food processor
Mixing bowls
Electric whisk
Strainer (sieve)
Silicone spatula
Cooling rack

Preheat the oven to 350°F/180°C/160°C Fan/Gas 4 and line the baking pan (tin) with parchment paper.

Cut the butter into small cubes and finely chop the chocolate. Melt the chocolate with the butter in a bain-marie or double boiler. Place 4 ounces/¾ cup/120 g of the pistachios in a food processor, add the potato starch, and blend to a powder.

Separate the eggs and use an electric whisk to beat the yolks with half the sugar until pale and fluffy. Add the sifted cocoa powder, a pinch of salt, the pistachio and starch powder, and the chocolate and butter mixture, and mix with a silicone spatula to combine.

Whisk the egg whites to soft peaks with the remaining sugar and gently fold into the batter. Pour the batter into the baking pan and bake on the middle shelf of the preheated oven for about 35 minutes. Remove from the oven and leave to cool in the pan for 10 minutes. Turn out the cake onto a cooling rack and leave to cool completely.

Place the remaining pistachios in the food processor, blend to a powder, and sprinkle over the cake to finish.

VARIATION
If you love a more intense chocolate flavor, you can substitute the one listed in the recipe with 72% dark chocolate.

MOIST CHOCOLATE AND ORANGE CAKE

Torta morbida al profumo di arancia

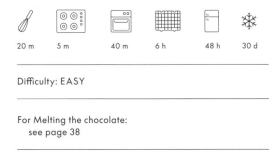

20 m   5 m   40 m   6 h   48 h   30 d

Difficulty: EASY

For Melting the chocolate:
    see page 38

TO SERVE 8

FOR THE CAKE
3½ ounces/scant 1 stick/100 g unsalted butter,
    at room temperature
7 ounces/200 g 80% dark chocolate
4 eggs, at room temperature
3½ ounces/scant ½ cup/100 g superfine (caster) sugar
Pinch of salt
Grated zest of 1 unwaxed orange
Unsweetened cocoa powder, for dusting
1½ ounces/40 g candied orange peel

EQUIPMENT NEEDED
9 × 3-inch/23 × 8-cm loaf pan (tin)
Parchment paper
Chef's knife
Chopping board
Bain-marie or double boiler
Mixing bowls
Electric whisk
Zester
Silicone spatula
Fine-mesh strainer (sieve)

Preheat the oven to 325°F/160°C/140°C Fan/Gas 3 and line the loaf pan (tin) with parchment paper.

Cut the butter into small cubes and finely chop the chocolate. Melt the chocolate with the butter in a bain-marie or double boiler. Set aside to cool to room temperature.

Separate the eggs and use an electric whisk to beat the yolks with half the sugar until pale and fluffy. Add a pinch of salt, the cooled chocolate, and the orange zest, and mix with a silicone spatula to combine.

Whisk the egg whites to soft peaks with the remaining sugar and gently fold into the batter.

Pour the batter into the loaf pan and bake in the preheated oven for 40 minutes. Remove from the oven and leave to cool in the pan, then chill in the refrigerator for at least 6 hours.

When ready to serve, transfer the cake from the pan to a serving plate, dust with cocoa powder, and decorate as desired with thinly sliced candied orange peel.

TIPS AND TRICKS
As it bakes, a thin and crispy crust forms on the top of the cake and gives it texture. If you prefer a more moist cake, you can remove the crust once the cake has cooled.

CHOCOLATE MUG CAKES

Torta in tazza al cioccolato

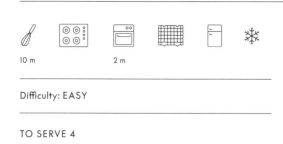

10 m   2 m

Difficulty: EASY

TO SERVE 4

FOR THE CAKES
1 vanilla bean (pod)
3½ ounces/¾ cup/100 g type "00" flour or all-purpose
    (plain) flour
2¼ ounces/generous ½ cup/60 g unsweetened
    cocoa powder
4 ounces/½ cup/120 g superfine (caster) sugar
4 eggs
7 fl oz/scant 1 cup/200 ml whole (full-fat) milk
5½ fl oz/⅔ cup/160 ml sunflower oil
Pinch of salt
5½ ounces/160 g milk chocolate
Confectioners' (icing) sugar, for dusting

EQUIPMENT NEEDED
Paring knife
Strainer (sieve)
Mixing bowl
Hand or electric whisk
Measuring cup or jug
Chef's knife
Chopping board
4 × mugs with 7 fl oz/200 ml capacity
Microwave oven
Fine-mesh strainer (sieve)

Use a sharp paring knife to split the vanilla bean (pod) lengthwise and scrape out the seeds. Sift the flour with the cocoa powder into a mixing bowl, add the vanilla seeds and the sugar, and mix with a hand or electric whisk to combine. Add the eggs, milk, oil, and a pinch of salt and whisk until a smooth batter has formed.

Finely chop the chocolate, stir into the batter, then divide the batter equally between the four mugs. Cook in the microwave oven on the highest power setting for 2 minutes. Remove from the microwave and leave to cool, then dust with confectioners' (icing) sugar, and serve.

VARIATION

If you like pistachios or hazelnuts, pour half the batter into the mug and add a teaspoon of unsweetened pistachio or hazelnut paste to the center, then cover with the remaining batter and cook as instructed.

CHOCOLATE, BEER, AND ORANGE CAKE

Torta di cioccolato alla birra e arancia

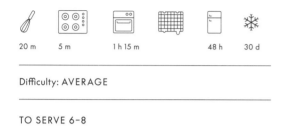

20 m   5 m   1 h 15 m   48 h   30 d

Difficulty: AVERAGE

TO SERVE 6–8

FOR THE CAKE
2 ounces/60 g 60% dark chocolate
4 ounces/1 stick/120 g unsalted butter
6 fl oz/¾ cup/170 ml porter
Grated zest of 1 unwaxed orange
2 large eggs
2 ounces/¼ cup/60 g sour cream
Pinch of salt
7 ounces/1⅔ cups/200 g type "00" flour or all-purpose
   (plain) flour
1½ ounces/⅓ cup/40 g unsweetened cocoa powder
1 teaspoon baking soda (bicarbonate of soda)
2 ounces/¼ cup/50 g superfine (caster) sugar

FOR THE TOPPING
8½ fl oz/1 cup/250 ml heavy (whipping) cream
1 ounce/¼ cup/30 g confectioners' (icing) sugar
Unsweetened cocoa powder, for dusting
1½ ounces/40 g candied orange peel

EQUIPMENT NEEDED
7-inch/18-cm round springform pan (tin)
Parchment paper
Chef's knife
Chopping board
Mixing bowls
Measuring cup or jug
Saucepan
Zester
Silicone spatula
Hand whisk
Strainer (sieve)
Electric whisk

Preheat the oven to 350°F/180°C/160°C Fan/Gas 4 and line the springform pan (tin) with parchment paper.

Finely chop the chocolate and place in a mixing bowl. Cut the butter into small cubes. Pour the beer into a saucepan, add the butter and orange zest, and bring to a boil. Remove from the heat and drizzle the mixture into the chocolate, stirring continuously with a silicone spatula, until the chocolate has melted and is incorporated.

Leave the mixture to cool to room temperature. Beat the eggs, then add to the cooled mixture with the sour cream and a pinch of salt, and mix together with a hand whisk. In a separate bowl, combine the sifted flour, cocoa powder, baking soda (bicarbonate of soda), and sugar. Pour in the liquid mixture, beating with a whisk to prevent lumps forming.

Pour the batter into the springform pan and bake in the preheated oven for 1 hour 15 minutes. Remove from the oven and leave to cool in the pan, then transfer to a serving dish to cool completely.

When ready to serve, use an electric whisk to whip the cream with the confectioners' (icing) sugar until firm, adding the sugar towards the end once the cream is partially whipped. Top the cake with the whipped cream, dust with a little cocoa powder, and decorate with candied orange peel cut into julienne strips.

MISTAKES TO AVOID
Always sift cocoa powder before adding it to batters as it often contains small lumps that do not dissolve, even when mixed with other ingredients.

PEAR AND CHOCOLATE CRUMBLE

Crumble di pere e cioccolato

20 m   45 m   40 m   48 h   60 d

Difficulty: EASY

For the Chocolate Gelato:
see page 272

TO SERVE 6–8

FOR THE CRUMBLE
3 ounces/⅔ cup/80 g raisins
1¾ fl oz/3 tablespoons/50 ml sherry or other dessert wine
4 Decana pears
5 ounces/¾ cup/150 g brown sugar
3½ ounces/100 g 80% dark chocolate
3½ ounces/scant 1 stick/100 g cold unsalted butter
4 ounces/1 cup/120 g type "00" flour or all-purpose
(plain) flour
3½ ounces/1 cup/100 g rolled oats
1 heaped teaspoon ground cinnamon
Pinch of salt
Chocolate Gelato, to serve

EQUIPMENT NEEDED
Mixing bowls
Measuring cup or jug
Paring knife
Chopping board
Silicone spatula
Chef's knife
10-inch/24-cm round baking dish
Strainer (sieve)

Soak the raisins in hot water for 10 minutes, then drain and combine with the sherry in a mixing bowl. Peel, core, and cut the pears into wedges. Add to the bowl with a third of the brown sugar, stir, and leave to steep for 30 minutes.

Meanwhile, coarsely chop the chocolate.

Preheat the oven to 400°F/200°C/180°C Fan/Gas 6 and lightly grease the baking dish with a little of the butter.

Arrange the pear wedges inside the baking dish and sprinkle over the chocolate. Cut the remaining butter into small cubes. Place the sifted flour, oats, remaining sugar, cinnamon, a pinch of salt, and the butter in a mixing bowl. Working quickly to ensure the ingredients do not become too warm, rub everything together using your fingertips until it resembles coarse bread crumbs. Do not overwork it or you will end up with a smooth dough instead of a crumb texture.

Spread the crumble evenly over the pears and bake in the pre-heated oven for about 45 minutes when the crumble should be lightly golden and the fruit soft. Leave to cool a little and serve, warm or cold, as desired, with Chocolate Gelato.

MISTAKES TO AVOID
While baking this fruit crumble, juice from the pears may drip from the dish. To prevent any juice from falling to the bottom of the oven, burning, and smoking, line the oven rack under the dish with kitchen foil. The crumble will usually be done when the juice of the fruit starts to bubble out around the edges.

CHOCOLATE AND ALMOND MILK CAKE

Cake di cioccolato al latte di mandorle

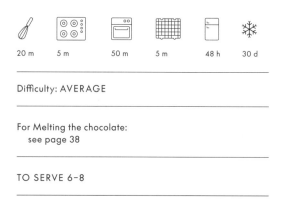

20 m 5 m 50 m 5 m 48 h 30 d

Difficulty: AVERAGE

For Melting the chocolate:
  see page 38

TO SERVE 6–8

FOR THE CAKE
3¾ ounces/1 stick/110 g unsalted butter, at room temperature
5 ounces/⅔ cup/150 g superfine (caster) sugar
2½ ounces/⅔ cup/70 g unsweetened cocoa powder
½ teaspoon baking powder
1 teaspoon baking soda (bicarbonate of soda)
4 eggs
5½ ounces/1¼ cups/160 g type "00" flour or all-purpose (plain) flour
Pinch of salt
6¼ fl oz/¾ cup/180 ml unsweetened almond milk

FOR THE GLAZE
5 ounces/150 g white chocolate
2 tablespoons/30 ml whole (full-fat) milk
½ ounce/2 teaspoons/10 g unsalted butter, at room temperature
¾ ounce/20 g 60% dark chocolate, shredded (grated)

EQUIPMENT NEEDED
9 × 3-inch/23 × 8-cm loaf pan (tin)
Parchment paper
Mixing bowls
Electric whisk
Strainer (sieve)
Silicone spatula
Measuring cup or jug
Cooling rack
Chef's knife
Chopping board
Bain-marie or double boiler
Chocolate grater

Preheat the oven to 350°F/180°C/160°C Fan/Gas 4 and line the loaf pan (tin) with parchment paper.

Place the butter in a mixing bowl with the sugar and beat together with an electric whisk until fluffy and creamy. Add the sifted cocoa powder, baking powder, and baking soda (bicarbonate of soda), and continue to beat at low speed. Add one egg and 1 tablespoon of the sifted flour, and mix with a silicone spatula to combine, then add the remaining eggs and flour in the same way. Add a pinch of salt and stir, then add the almond milk, continuing to stir until it is fully combined.

Pour the batter into the loaf pan and bake in the preheated oven for 50 minutes. The cake is ready when a skewer inserted into the center comes out clean. Remove from the oven and leave to cool in the pan for 5 minutes, then turn out onto a cooling rack and leave to cool completely.

To make the glaze, finely chop the white chocolate and place it in the bowl of a bain-marie or double boiler with the milk and butter. Gently heat, stirring, until the chocolate melts and the mixture becomes smooth. Pour the warm glaze over the cake and sprinkle with shredded (grated) dark chocolate. Allow the shredded (grated) chocolate to melt in the heat of the glaze, then set aside until the chocolate hardens before serving.

TIPS AND TRICKS
If you want your cake to look more striking, leave the chocolate glaze to cool before sprinkling with dark chocolate shavings.

WHITE CHOCOLATE AND MANGO TARTLETS

Tartellette al cioccolato bianco e mango

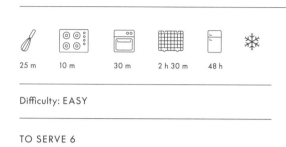

25 m 10 m 30 m 2 h 30 m 48 h

Difficulty: EASY

TO SERVE 6

FOR THE TARTLETS
3 ounces/¾ stick/80 g unsalted butter
6¼ ounces/180 g ginger cookies (biscuits)
7 ounces/200 g white chocolate
10 fl oz/1¼ cups/300 ml heavy (whipping) cream
4–5 sprigs of mint, plus extra to decorate
2 eggs
¾ ounce/20 g superfine (caster) sugar
Pinch of salt
1 ripe mango
Grated zest of 1 unwaxed lime

EQUIPMENT NEEDED
Round, square, and rectangular tartlet pans (tins) (3 inch/
    8 cm round, 2½ × 2½ inch/6 × 6 cm, and 2 × 3 inch/
    5 × 8 cm, respectively)
Parchment paper
Bain-marie or double boiler
Food processor
Chef's knife
Chopping board
Heat-resistant bowl
Measuring cup or jug
Saucepan
Strainer (sieve)
Silicone spatula
Zester

Preheat the oven to 340°F/170°C/150°C Fan/Gas 3 and line the bottom of the tartlet pans (tins) with parchment paper.

Place the butter in the bowl of a bain-marie or double boiler and heat gently until melted. Place the cookies (biscuits) in a food processor and blend to a fine crumb. Drizzle over the melted butter and blend again to coat the crumbs evenly. Cover the bottom and sides of the tartlet pans with the crumb base and press it down firmly with the back of a teaspoon. Chill in the refrigerator for 30 minutes.

Meanwhile, finely chop the chocolate and place in a heat-resistant bowl. Pour the cream into a saucepan, add the mint, and bring to a simmer over a moderate heat. Remove from the heat, cover with a lid, and set aside to cool.

Once cool, pour the cream through a strainer (sieve) and return to the pan. Reheat the cream, then pour it into the chopped chocolate. Stir with a silicone spatula until the chocolate has melted, then set aside to cool. Beat the eggs in a small bowl, then add to the chocolate cream with the sugar and a pinch of salt. Stir to combine.

Divide the cream equally between the prepared tart crusts and bake in the preheated oven for 30 minutes. Remove from the oven and leave to cool in the pans, then refrigerate for 2 hours.

Wash and dry the mango, then pit, peel, and thinly slice the flesh. Remove the tartlets from the pans, arrange on a serving platter, and decorate with mango slices, the lime zest, and sprigs of mint.

TIPS AND TRICKS
If you find that lumps have formed in the cream after cooling, restore its velvety consistency by blending with an immersion (stick) blender.

SPICED CHOCOLATE, APPLE, AND WALNUT CAKE

Torta speziata di cioccolato, mele e noci

25 m   10 m   50 m   15 m   48 h

Difficulty: EASY

TO SERVE 8

FOR THE CAKE
3 ounces/⅔ cup/80 g raisins
2 ounces/½ cup/50 g walnut kernels
4 ounces/120 g 60% dark chocolate
1 pound/450 g Golden Delicious apples
    (10 ounces/270 g pureed)
3¾ ounces/1 stick/110 g unsalted butter, at room
    temperature
5 ounces/⅔ cup/150 g superfine (caster) sugar
2 eggs
2½ ounces/⅔ cup/70 g unsweetened cocoa powder
9 ounces/2 cups/260 g type "00" flour or all-purpose
    (plain) flour
2 level teaspoons baking powder
2 teaspoons ground cinnamon
Pinch of grated nutmeg
½ teaspoon ground ginger
Pinch of salt

FOR THE DECORATION
1 Royal Gala apple
¾ ounce/1½ tablespoons/20 g unsalted butter
¾ ounce/⅛ cup/20 g brown sugar
1 teaspoon lemon juice

EQUIPMENT NEEDED
7 × 9-inch/18 × 23-cm baking pan (tin)
Parchment paper
Mixing bowls
Chef's knife
Chopping board
Saucepan
Immersion (stick) blender
Hand or electric whisk
Silicone spatula
Strainer (sieve)
Cooling rack

Preheat the oven to 350°F/180°C/160°C Fan/Gas 4 and line the baking pan (tin) with parchment paper.

Soak the raisins in warm water for 15 minutes then drain and squeeze to remove excess moisture, and set aside. Coarsely chop the walnuts and finely chop the chocolate. Peel and dice the apples and place in a saucepan with 4 tablespoons water. Cook, covered, until very soft. Increase the heat and allow the cooking liquid to evaporate completely. Puree with an immersion (stick) blender and set aside to cool.

To make the decoration, quarter and core the Royal Gala apple. Halve each quarter lengthwise, then halve each wedge again crosswise. Cook the apple pieces with the butter, brown sugar, and lemon juice for 5 minutes until cooked through and caramelized. Set aside.

Place the butter in a mixing bowl with the sugar and beat together with a hand or electric whisk until light and fluffy. Beat the eggs in a separate bowl, then add to the butter and sugar mix with the pureed apple. Stir with a silicone spatula to combine. Add 2 ounces/scant ½ cup/50 g of the sifted cocoa powder, the flour, and baking powder and stir to combine. Add the spices, raisins, walnuts, chocolate, and a pinch of salt. Stir to combine.

Pour the batter into the baking pan and bake in the preheated oven for 50 minutes. The cake is ready when a skewer inserted into the center comes out clean. Remove from the oven, then turn out onto a cooling rack and leave to cool completely.

Cut into squares, top each one with a caramelized apple piece, and serve.

CHOCOLATE AND RASPBERRY CAKE

Torta di cioccolato e lamponi

20 m   5 m   50 m   10 m   48 h   30 d

Difficulty: EASY

TO SERVE 6–8

FOR THE CAKE
3½ ounces/scant 1 stick/100 g unsalted butter
8 ounces/220 g 60% dark chocolate
6 fl oz/¾ cup/170 ml coffee
4½ ounces/⅔ cup/140 g superfine (caster) sugar
6¼ ounces/1½ cups/180 g type "00" flour or all-purpose
   (plain) flour
1½ ounces/⅓ cup/40 g unsweetened cocoa powder
1 teaspoon baking powder
Pinch of salt
2 eggs
7 ounces/scant 1⅔ cups/200 g fresh raspberries
½ ounce/10 g potato starch
Confectioners' (icing) sugar, for dusting (optional)

EQUIPMENT NEEDED
8-inch/20-cm round springform pan (tin)
Parchment paper
Chef's knife
Chopping board
Mixing bowls
Measuring cup or jug
Saucepan
Silicone spatula
Strainer (sieve)
Hand whisk
Immersion (stick) blender
Cooling rack
Fine-mesh strainer (sieve)

Preheat the oven to 350°F/180°C/160°C Fan/Gas 4 and line the springform pan (tin) with parchment paper.

Cut the butter into small cubes. Finely chop the chocolate and place in a bowl. Pour 5 fl oz/scant ⅔ cup/150 ml water into a saucepan, then add the coffee, sugar, and butter. Place over a low heat until the butter and sugar have melted, then pour the mixture over the chocolate, a third at a time, stirring with a silicone spatula until the chocolate has melted. Set aside to cool.

Sift the flour, cocoa powder, and baking powder into a bowl. Mix to combine and add a pinch of salt. Drizzle the chocolate mixture into the dry ingredients, mixing with a hand whisk to combine. Beat the eggs in a separate bowl, then add and blend the batter mix with an immersion (stick) blender.

Pour half of the batter into the springform pan and sprinkle with three-quarters of the raspberries dredged in the potato starch. Carefully pour in the remaining batter and bake in the preheated oven for 50 minutes. Remove from the oven and rest in the pan for 10 minutes, then remove from the pan and place on a cooling rack to cool completely. Decorate with the remaining raspberries and dust with confectioners' (icing) sugar, if desired.

TIPS AND TRICKS
It is very important that the hot liquid be added to the chopped chocolate gradually in order to melt the chocolate and become fully incorporated.

ELABORATE DESSERTS

CHOUX WREATHS WITH HAZELNUT CREAM AND BRITTLE

Profiterole alla nocciola con briciole di croccante

| 40 m | 20 m | 35 m | 1 h | 24 h | 60 d |

Difficulty: ADVANCED

For the Choux Pastry for Choux Wreaths:
    see page 319
For Melting the chocolate:
    see page 38

TO SERVE 8–10

FOR THE CHOUX WREATHS
1 quantity Choux Pastry for Choux Wreaths, made
    according to the basic recipe

FOR THE FILLING
3 ounces/scant ⅔ cup/80 g roasted hazelnuts
5 ounces/150 g 60% dark chocolate
½ vanilla bean (pod)
2 ounces/scant ½ cup/50 g confectioners' (icing) sugar
½ ounce/1 heaping tablespoon/10 g unsweetened
    cocoa powder
2 tablespoons/25 ml sunflower oil
20 fl oz/2½ cups/600 ml heavy (whipping) cream

FOR THE HAZELNUT BRITTLE
¾ ounce/⅙ cup/20 g roasted hazelnuts
5 ounces/⅔ cup/150 g superfine (caster) sugar

FOR THE CHOCOLATE SAUCE
5 ounces/150 g 85% dark chocolate
2½ ounces/scant ⅓ cup/70 g superfine (caster) sugar
2½ ounces/scant ¼ cup/70 g acacia honey
1½ ounces/⅓ cup/40 g unsweetened cocoa powder

EQUIPMENT NEEDED
2 baking sheets
Parchment paper
Pastry (piping) bags
½-inch/1-cm plain piping tip (nozzle)
Chef's knife
Chopping board
Saucepans
Silicone spatula
Rolling pin
Strainer (sieve)
Measuring cup or jug
Hand whisk
Squeeze bottle or disposable pastry bag
Food processor
Bain-marie or double boiler
Paring knife
Mixing bowls
Electric whisk
Large star piping tip (nozzle)
Serrated knife

Preheat the oven to 400°F/200°C/180°C Fan/Gas 6, line two baking sheets with parchment paper, and fit a pastry (piping) bag with a plain piping tip (nozzle).

Fill the pastry bag with the Choux Paste and pipe apricot-sized mounds, spaced about ½ inch/1 cm apart, in a circle on each of the baking sheets. Dip your finger in cold water and smooth the surface of the choux paste. Bake the wreaths in the preheated oven for 35 minutes, then turn off the oven, leave the door slightly ajar, and rest for a further 30 minutes.

To make the hazelnut brittle, coarsely chop the hazelnuts. Place the sugar in a small saucepan and cook to a golden caramel, add the coarsely chopped hazelnuts, and stir with a silicone spatula to combine. Lay a sheet of parchment paper over a work surface and pour the caramel onto the center of the paper. Cover with a second sheet of paper and use a rolling pin to roll out the caramel into a thin layer. Take care not to burn yourself as the caramel will be very hot. Leave the caramel to cool and harden fully, then remove the parchment paper and crush into small pieces.

To make the chocolate sauce, finely chop the 85% dark chocolate. Place the sugar, honey, sifted cocoa powder, and 7 fl oz/scant 1 cup/200 ml water in a saucepan and stir with a hand whisk. Bring to a boil and cook for 1 minute, then add the chopped chocolate and stir with the spatula until the chocolate has melted. Transfer the sauce to a bowl, leave to cool, then fill the squeeze bottle with the sauce and refrigerate for 30 minutes.

To make the filling, grind the hazelnuts to a paste in a food processor. Finely chop the 60% dark chocolate and melt in a bain-marie or double boiler. Split the vanilla bean (pod) lengthwise, using a sharp paring knife, and scrape out the seeds. Place 1 ounce/¼ cup/30 g of the confectioners' (icing) sugar, the sifted cocoa powder, vanilla seeds, oil, and melted dark chocolate in the food processor and blend until the mixture is smooth and creamy. In a separate, clean mixing bowl, whip the cream and remaining sugar with an electric whisk, then fold the whipped cream into the hazelnut mixture using the spatula. Fit a pastry bag with a star piping tip. Cut the choux wreathes across the center into two equal layers and fill by piping with the hazelnut cream to sandwich the two layers together. Arrange the wreaths on serving plates and pour the chocolate sauce over. Sprinkle with the crushed hazelnut brittle and serve.

CHOCOLATE AND STRAWBERRY CAKE

Torta di cioccolato e fragole

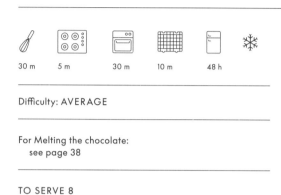

30 m	5 m	30 m	10 m	48 h	

Difficulty: AVERAGE

For Melting the chocolate:
   see page 38

TO SERVE 8

FOR THE CAKE
4 eggs
5½ ounces/160 g 60% dark chocolate
3½ ounces/scant 1 stick/100 g unsalted butter
1 ounce/¼ cup/30 g type "00" flour or all-purpose
   (plain) flour
Pinch of salt
5½ ounces/scant ¾ cup/160 g superfine (caster) sugar
9 ounces/1¼ cups/250 g fresh strawberries
¾ ounce/2 tablespoons/20 g confectioners' (icing) sugar
½ ounce/½ tablespoon/10 g acacia honey

EQUIPMENT NEEDED
8-inch/20-cm round springform pan (tin)
Parchment paper
Mixing bowls
Chef's knife
Chopping board
Bain-marie or double boiler
Strainer (sieve)
Silicone spatula
Electric whisk
Cooling rack
Immersion (stick) blender
Fine-mesh strainer

Preheat the oven to 350°F/180°C/160°C Fan/Gas 4 and line the springform pan (tin) with parchment paper.

Separate the eggs and place the whites in a clean, grease-free mixing bowl. Finely chop the chocolate, cut the butter into small cubes, and melt together in a bain-marie or double boiler. Leave to cool to room temperature, then add the egg yolks, sifted flour, a pinch of salt, and the superfine (caster) sugar, and mix with a silicone spatula to combine. Whisk the egg whites to soft peaks using an electric whisk, then fold, a little at a time, into the batter.

Fill the springform pan with the batter and bake in the preheated oven, on the middle shelf, for 30 minutes. Remove from the oven and leave to cool in the pan for 10 minutes, then transfer to a cooling rack to cool completely. Hollow out the center of the cake, starting 1¼ inches/3 cm from the edge and leaving a depth of about 2 inches/4 cm from the bottom. Set aside the offcuts of cake.

Wash and hull 3½ ounces/½ cup/100 g of the strawberries, place in a bowl with half the confectioners' (icing) sugar and 2 tablespoons water and blend with an immersion (stick) blender to make a sauce.

Chop up the offcuts of the chocolate cake, stir into the strawberry sauce so that it soaks up the sauce, and return it to the hollowed-out center of the cake, packing it down lightly with a spoon. Dust the cake with the remaining confectioners' sugar.

Wash and hull the remaining strawberries. Halve, drizzle with honey, and arrange on the cake immediately before serving.

TIPS AND TRICKS
Before removing the hull from the strawberries, it is important to wash and then dry them with paper towels. This prevents any water from coming into contact with their flesh and altering their flavor.

CHOCOLATE PAVLOVA

Pavlova al cioccolato

30 m   5 m   1 h   3 h   24 h

Difficulty: ADVANCED

For the French Meringue:
    see page 321
For the Whipped Ganache:
    see page 78
For the 3-D Chocolate Ribbon:
    see page 62

TO SERVE 8–10

FOR THE MERINGUE
4 egg whites
8 ounces/1 cup/220 g superfine (caster) sugar
½ ounce/1 heaping tablespoon/15 g unsweetened
    cocoa powder

FOR THE WHIPPED GANACHE
3½ ounces/100 g 70% dark chocolate
17 fl oz/2 cups/500 ml heavy (whipping) cream

FOR THE DECORATION
White, milk, and ruby chocolate
3-D Chocolate Ribbon

EQUIPMENT NEEDED
Baking sheet
Parchment paper
Bain-marie or double boiler
Stand mixer fitted with whisk attachment or
    electric whisk and bowl
Strainer (sieve)
Silicone spatula
Palette knife
Chef's knife
Chopping board
Measuring cup or jug
Saucepan
Mixing bowl
Electric whisk
Chocolate grater

Preheat the oven to 300°F/150°C/130°C Fan/Gas 1 and line the baking sheet with parchment paper.

Place the egg whites in the clean, grease-free bowl of a bain-marie or double boiler and heat for 2–3 minutes. Whisk the egg whites in a stand mixer fitted with a whisk attachment, or use a mixing bowl and electric whisk. Gradually add the sugar, 1 tablespoon at a time, while continuing to whisk. Whisk the meringue for about 10 minutes until stiff and glossy peaks form.

Gently fold in the sifted cocoa powder, using a silicone spatula. Spread the meringue onto the lined baking sheet, using a palette knife. Build up the sides to leave a well about 7 inches/18 cm in diameter in the center.

Lower the oven temperature to 210°F/120°C/100°C Fan/Gas ¼ and bake the meringue for 1 hour. Leave to cool in the oven with the door closed.

Finely chop the chocolate for the ganache. Pour the cream into a saucepan and bring to a simmer. Remove from the heat, add the chocolate, and stir until the chocolate has melted. Pour into a mixing bowl and chill the ganache in the refrigerator for 3 hours.

When ready to serve, whip the ganache with an electric whisk until it turns pale and fluffy. Fill the center of the pavlova with the whipped ganache and decorate by shredding (grating) over the three types of chocolate. Top with the 3-D Chocolate Ribbon.

MISTAKES TO AVOID
Chocolate meringue is much more fragile than plain meringue. Take great care when transferring it to the serving dish and filling it.

CHOCOLATE CHARLOTTE WITH RUM, BANANA, AND COCONUT

Charlotte con cioccolato al rum, banane e cocco

| 40 m | 5 m | 8 m | 4 h 15 m | 24 h | 60 d |

Difficulty: ADVANCED

For the Chocolate Savoy Sponge:
  see page 318
For the Chocolate Mousse with Italian Meringue:
  see page 82
For the Chocolate Curls:
  see page 50

TO SERVE 8

FOR THE CHOCOLATE SAVOY SPONGE
4 eggs
½ vanilla bean (pod)
3 ounces/⅓ cup/80 g superfine (caster) sugar
2 ounces/scant ½ cup/50 g type "00" flour or all-purpose (plain) flour
¾ ounce/2 heaping tablespoons/20 g unsweetened cocoa powder

FOR THE FILLING
2½ ounces/scant ⅓ cup/70 g superfine (caster) sugar
1½ fl oz/3 tablespoons/40 ml rum
2 medium bananas
¾ ounce/scant ¼ cup/20 g desiccated coconut
1 quantity Chocolate Mousse with Italian Meringue

FOR THE DECORATION
7 fl oz/scant 1 cup/200 ml heavy (whipping) cream
1 ounce/¼ cup/30 g confectioners' (icing) sugar
Chocolate Curls
1 ounce/30 g fresh coconut

EQUIPMENT NEEDED
10 × 12½-inch/26 × 32-cm rectangular baking pan (tin)
Parchment paper
Mixing bowls
Paring knife
Electric whisk
Silicone spatula
Strainer (sieve)
7-inch/18-cm round × 4-inch/10-cm deep springform pan (tin)
Measuring cup or jug
Saucepan
4-inch/10-cm-wide acetate strip, the same length as the circumference of the springform pan
Palette knife
Coarse grater

To make the Savoy sponge, preheat the oven to 350°F/180°C/160°C Fan/Gas 4 and line the rectangular baking pan (tin) with parchment paper.

Separate the eggs and place the whites in a clean, grease-free mixing bowl. Split the vanilla bean (pod) lengthwise with a sharp paring knife and scrape out the seeds. In a separate bowl, beat the egg yolks with the vanilla seeds and sugar until pale and fluffy. Whisk the egg whites to soft peaks using an electric whisk, then fold into the beaten egg yolk mixture, using a silicone spatula. Sift the flour and cocoa powder into a mixing bowl and add to the mixture, a third at a time, folding in using the silicone spatula.

Pour the batter into the rectangular baking pan and bake in the preheated oven for 8 minutes. Remove from the oven and leave to cool completely in the pan. Cut out a disk of sponge cake using the base of the springform pan as a template, and cut two long strips of sponge the same width as the height of the sides of the springform pan.

To make the filling, pour 1½ fl oz/3 tablespoons/40 ml water in a saucepan, add the sugar, and bring to a boil to make a syrup. Leave to cool then add the rum. Peel and slice the bananas and add to the pan, then leave to steep in the syrup for at least 15 minutes.

Line the base of the springform pan with parchment paper and the sides with the acetate strip. Cover the base with the sponge disk and the sides with the sponge strips. Drain the banana slices and form a layer over the sponge disk at the bottom of the pan, then sprinkle over the desiccated coconut. Cover with the Chocolate Mousse with Italian Meringue, level the surface with a palette knife, and place the pan in the refrigerator for 4 hours.

When ready to serve, remove the charlotte from the pan and transfer to a serving plate. Pour the cream into a clean mixing bowl, add the confectioners' (icing) sugar, and whip with an electric whisk. Spoon the whipped cream over the chocolate mousse and decorate the top with Chocolate Curls and coarsely shredded (grated) fresh coconut.

CHOCOLATE AND CHILI TART

Tarte al cioccolato e peperoncino

30 m	15 m	21 m	2 h 30 m	48 h	60 d

Difficulty: AVERAGE

For the Classic Pie Dough (Shortcrust Pastry):
  see page 314
For the Ganache for Bonbons and Truffles:
  see page 74
For Melting the chocolate:
  see page 38

TO SERVE 8

FOR THE TART CRUST
3½ ounces/scant 1 stick/100 g cold unsalted butter
7 ounces/1⅔ cup/200 g type "00" flour or all-purpose
  (plain) flour, plus extra for dusting
2 ounces/scant ½ cup/50 g confectioners' (icing) sugar
Pinch of salt
1 egg
1 egg yolk

FOR THE GANACHE
7 ounces/200 g 70% dark chocolate
8½ fl oz/1 cup/250 ml heavy (whipping) cream
1 pinch of chili powder
¾ ounce/1½ tablespoons/20 g cold unsalted butter

FOR THE DECORATION
2 fresh red chilies (chillies)
1½ ounces/3 heaping tablespoons/40 g superfine
  (caster) sugar

EQUIPMENT NEEDED
Chef's knife
Chopping board
Food processor
Plastic wrap (cling film)
Bain-marie or double boiler
Measuring cup or jug
Silicone spatula
Immersion (stick) blender
Parchment paper
Rolling pin
8-inch/20-cm round fluted tart pan (tin)
Pie weights or dried beans
Saucepan
Cooling rack

To make the tart crust, cut the butter into small cubes. Place the flour, confectioner's (icing) sugar, butter, and a pinch of salt in a food processor and blend until the mixture resembles fine crumbs. Add the whole egg and extra yolk and blend for a few more seconds until the dough (pastry) sticks to the blades. Cover in plastic wrap (cling film) and rest for 30 minutes.

To make the ganache, finely chop the chocolate and place in the bowl of a bain-marie or double boiler. Add the cream and chili powder and melt. Add the butter and stir with a silicone spatula until the butter has melted. If necessary, blend for a few seconds with an immersion (stick) blender to incorporate.

Preheat the oven to 350°F/180°C/160°C Fan/Gas 4.

Soak a sheet of parchment paper in water, then squeeze to remove excess water and set aside. On a lightly floured work surface, roll out the dough into a disk with a thickness of ⅛ inch/3 mm. Carefully lift the dough over the tart pan (tin), gently pressing it down on the base and sides of the pan, then cut away any excess dough that is overhanging the pan. Prick the base with a fork, cover with the damp sheet of parchment paper, and fill the crust with dried beans or pie weights. Blind bake the crust in the preheated oven for 15 minutes.

Remove the paper and beans or weights and continue to bake for a further 5–6 minutes. Remove from the oven and leave to cool completely in the pan, then fill the crust with the ganache and chill the tart in the refrigerator for at least 2 hours.

Meanwhile, clean the chilies for the decoration, remove the stem, deseed, and cut lengthwise into strips. Place the sugar and 1½ fl oz/ 3 tablespoons/40 ml water in a saucepan and bring to a boil. Add the chili strips and cook for 7–8 minutes until translucent. Remove from the syrup, drain, and leave to dry on a cooling rack. When ready to serve, remove the tart from the pan onto a serving plate, and decorate the tart with the chili strips.

MOIST CHOCOLATE CAKE
Tortino al fondente

30 m   3 m   35 m   10 m   3 d

Difficulty: AVERAGE

TO SERVE 8

FOR THE CAKE
3½ ounces/scant 1 stick/100 g unsalted butter,
   plus extra for greasing
7 ounces/200 g 60% dark chocolate
4 eggs
8 ounces/1 cup/225 g superfine (caster) sugar
2 ounces/scant ½ cup/50 g type "00" flour or all-purpose
   (plain) flour
Pinch of salt
Heavy (whipping) cream, to serve
Unsweetened cocoa powder, for dusting

EQUIPMENT NEEDED
7-inch/18-cm round springform pan (tin)
Chocolate grater
Bain-marie or double boiler
Mixing bowls
Electric whisk
Strainer (sieve)
Silicone spatula
Palette knife
Measuring cup or jug

Preheat the oven to 325°F/160°C/140°C Fan/Gas 3 and grease the springform pan (tin) with butter.

Coarsely shred (grate) the chocolate with a chocolate grater. Melt the butter in a bain-marie or double boiler. Separate the eggs and place the whites in a clean, grease-free mixing bowl. In a separate bowl, beat the egg yolks with 7 ounces/scant 1 cup/200 g of the sugar using an electric whisk until pale and fluffy. Add the melted butter, shredded (grated) chocolate, 1½ ounces/⅓ cup/40 g of the sifted flour, and a pinch of salt, mixing with a silicone spatula to combine. Whisk the egg whites to soft peaks with the electric whisk and fold into the batter using the spatula.

Mix the remaining sugar and flour together and dust over the greased springform pan in an even layer. Fill the pan with the batter, using a palette knife to level the surface, and bake in the preheated oven for 35 minutes.

Remove the cake from the oven and rest in the pan for 10 minutes, then remove from the pan and transfer to a serving platter. Leave to cool completely.

When ready to serve, pour the cream into a mixing bowl and whip to soft peaks using an electric whisk. Dust the cake with a little cocoa powder and serve with the whipped cream on the side.

TIPS AND TRICKS
If you do not have a specialized chocolate grater, you can use a grater with medium or large holes. Chill the chocolate bar in the refrigerator for 30 minutes before shredding (grating), and prevent heating the chocolate with your hands by holding the bar between a sheet of parchment paper.

TRIPLE CHOCOLATE CAKE

Torta ai tre cioccolati

1 h   15 m   1 h 10 m   1 h 50 m   3 d   60 d

Difficulty: ADVANCED

For Melting the chocolate:
    see page 38
For the Simple Ganache:
    see page 76
For the 3-D Chocolate Ribbons:
    see page 62

TO SERVE 8

FOR THE CAKE
3½ ounces/100 g 70% dark chocolate
5 ounces/1⅓ sticks/150 g unsalted butter
8½ fl oz/1 cup/240 ml whole (full-fat) milk
10½ ounces/1⅓ cups/300 g superfine (caster) sugar
8 ounces/1¾ cups/220 g self-rising (self-raising) flour
7 ounces/1⅔ cups/200 g type "00" flour or all-purpose
    (plain) flour
2 ounces/½ cup/50 g unsweetened cocoa powder
1 level teaspoon baking soda (bicarbonate of soda)
4 eggs
Pinch of salt
1¼ fl oz/2½ tablespoons/35 ml sunflower oil
1 vanilla bean (pod)
1½ ounces/40 g white chocolate
3½ ounces/generous ½ cup/100 g dark chocolate chips

FOR THE BUTTERCREAM
6¼ ounces/180 g milk chocolate
10½ ounces/2⅔ sticks/300 g unsalted butter, at room
    temperature
1 pound/3½ cups/450 g confectioners' (icing) sugar
2 tablespoons/30 ml whole (full-fat) milk

FOR THE SIMPLE GANACHE
7 ounces/200 g 70% dark chocolate
7 fl oz/scant 1 cup/200 ml heavy (whipping) cream

FOR THE DECORATION
3-D Chocolate Ribbons

To make the cake, preheat the oven to 325°F/160°C/140°C Fan/ Gas 3 and line both springform pans (tins) with parchment paper.

For the two chocolate sponge layers, finely chop the dark chocolate and cut 3½ ounces/scant 1 stick/100 g of the butter into small cubes. Pour 5½ fl oz/⅔ cup/160 ml of the milk into a saucepan, add the dark chocolate and 7 ounces/scant 1 cup/200 g of the sugar. Place over a low heat until the chocolate and butter have melted. Stir with a hand whisk, transfer to a mixing bowl, and set aside to cool.

Sift together 5 ounces/1¼ cups/150 g of the self-rising (self-raising) flour, 4 ounces/1 cup/120 g of the type "00" flour, the cocoa powder, and ⅔ teaspoon baking soda (bicarbonate of soda). Add to the melted butter and chocolate mixture, and stir with a silicone spatula to incorporate. Beat two eggs in a small bowl, then add to the mixture with a pinch of salt, and 1½ tablespoons/20 ml of the oil, stirring with the spatula to incorporate.

Pour the batter into the lined springform pans and bake in the preheated oven for 35 minutes. Remove from the oven and rest the cakes in the pans for 10 minutes, then remove from the pans and transfer to a cooling rack to cool completely. Clean one of the springform pans and line it with parchment paper.

For the vanilla sponge layer, split the vanilla bean (pod) lengthwise with a sharp paring knife and scrape out the seeds. Finely chop the white chocolate. Heat the remaining milk in a saucepan with the white chocolate, the remaining butter, and the remaining sugar. Stir until the chocolate and butter have melted and the mixture is smooth. Transfer to a bowl and set aside to cool.

Sift together the remaining flours with the remaining baking soda. Add to the melted butter and white chocolate mixture, and stir with a silicone spatula to incorporate. Beat the remaining two eggs in a small bowl with the vanilla seeds, then add to the mixture with the remaining oil, stirring with the spatula to incorporate. Fold in the chocolate chips.

Pour the batter into the lined springform pan and bake in the preheated oven for 35 minutes. Remove from the oven and rest the cake in the pan for 10 minutes, then remove from the pan and transfer to a cooling rack to cool completely.

EQUIPMENT NEEDED
2 × 7-inch/18-cm round springform pans (tin)
Parchment paper
Chef's knife
Chopping board
Measuring cup or jug
Saucepan
Hand whisk
Mixing bowls
Strainer (sieve)
Silicone spatula
Cooling rack
Paring knife
Bain-marie or double boiler
Electric whisk
Palette knife
Rimmed baking tray (pan)

Image on page 148

To make the buttercream, finely chop the milk chocolate and melt in a bain-marie or double boiler. Place the butter in a mixing bowl and beat with an electric whisk, gradually incorporating the confectioners' (icing) sugar until creamy. Add the melted milk chocolate, and the milk, and whisk until smooth. Place one of the dark chocolate sponges on a cooling rack and spread the top with about one-sixth of the buttercream, using a palette knife. Place the vanilla sponge layer on top, spread with another one-sixth of the buttercream, and finish with the second dark chocolate sponge layer. Spread the remaining buttercream over the sides and top of the assembled cake and chill for 1 hour in the refrigerator.

Make the Simple Ganache following the basic technique, using the ingredient quantities specified opposite.

Place the cooling rack with the cake over a rimmed baking tray (pan) and glaze the cake with the ganache, pouring it over the top and allowing it to drip down the sides. Gently tap the cooling rack against the baking tray so any excess glaze drips off. Refrigerate the cake for 30 minutes, then decorate with the 3-D Chocolate Ribbons.

DARK CHOCOLATE BAKED CUSTARD TORTE

Torta con crema cotta al cioccolato fondente

1 h   15 m   1 h 5 m   4 h   48 h   60 d

Difficulty: ADVANCED

For the Classic Pie Dough (Shortcrust Pastry):
  see page 314
For the Whipped Ganache:
  see page 78
For the Chocolate Curls:
  see page 50

TO SERVE 8–10

FOR THE BASE
10½ ounces/300 g Classic Pie Dough (Shortcrust Pastry)

FOR THE SPONGE
¾ ounce/scant ¼ cup/25 g type "00" flour or all-purpose
  (plain) flour, plus extra for dusting
3 egg whites
4 ounces/½ cup/120 g superfine (caster) sugar
4 egg yolks
1 ounce/¼ cup/30 g unsweetened cocoa powder
¾ ounce/25 g potato starch
1 teaspoon unsalted butter

FOR THE CUSTARD
10 ounces/280 g 70% dark chocolate
6¼ fl oz/¾ cup/180 ml whole (full-fat) milk
3 ounces/⅓ cup/80 g superfine (caster) sugar
1 large egg
2 large egg yolks
12 fl oz/1⅔ cups/380 ml heavy (whipping) cream

FOR THE WHIPPED GANACHE
10 fl oz/1¼ cups/300 ml heavy (whipping) cream
7 ounces/200 g milk chocolate

FOR THE MIRROR GLAZE
3 sheets (9 g) gelatin
6½ ounces/185 g gianduja
3 ounces/⅓ cup/80 g superfine (caster) sugar
3½ ounces/⅓ cup/100 g condensed milk

FOR THE DECORATION
Chocolate Curls made with milk chocolate

To make the base, preheat the oven to 325°F/160°C/140°C Fan/Gas 3 and line the baking sheet with parchment paper.

On a lightly floured work surface, roll out the dough (pastry) to a thickness of ¼ inch/5 mm and shape into a 10 × 4-inch/24 × 10-cm rectangle. Place on the lined baking sheet, prick with a fork, and bake in the preheated oven for 15 minutes. Remove from the oven and leave to cool completely, then trim the edges with a serrated knife to straighten them.

To make the sponge, preheat the oven to 400°F/200°C/180°C Fan/Gas 6 and line the rectangular baking pan (tin) with parchment paper.

Place the egg whites in the bowl of a bain-marie or double boiler and whisk with an electric whisk until they begin to foam. Continue whisking while slowly adding the sugar until soft peaks form. Remove the bowl from the bain-marie, beat the egg yolks in a small bowl, and add them to the whisked egg whites, folding them in with a silicone spatula. Sift together the flour, cocoa powder, and potato starch and add to the mixture. Melt the butter in the bain-marie and add that to the mixture. Mix with a silicone spatula to incorporate all the ingredients.

Pour the batter into the baking pan (tin) and bake in the preheated oven for 8 minutes. Remove from the oven and leave in the pan to cool completely, then remove from the pan and trim the edges with a serrated knife to straighten them.

To make the baked custard, preheat the oven to 300°F/150°C/130°C Fan/Gas 1. Clean and line the rectangular baking pan with parchment paper.

Finely chop the chocolate and place in a mixing bowl. Pour the milk into a separate bowl, and add the sugar, eggs, and extra egg yolks. Pour the cream into a saucepan and bring to a simmer. Remove from the heat and pour into the chocolate, stirring with a silicone spatula until the chocolate has melted. Add the milk and egg mixture and stir to incorporate. Pour the custard into the lined baking pan and bake in the preheated oven for 40 minutes. Remove from the oven and leave in the pan to cool to room temperature, then freeze for 2–3 hours until frozen.

Make the Whipped Ganache following the basic technique, using the ingredient quantities specified.

Baking sheet
Parchment paper
Rolling pin
Serrated knife
10 × 4-inch/24 × 10-cm rectangular baking pan (tin)
Bain-marie or double boiler
Electric whisk
Silicone spatula
Strainer (sieve)
Mixing bowls
Chef's knife
Chopping board
Measuring cup or jug
Saucepan
Immersion (stick) blender
Cooling rack
Baking tray
Pastry (piping) bag
½-inch/1-cm plain piping tip (nozzle)

Image on page 149

To make the mirror glaze, soak the gelatin sheets in a small bowl of cold water for 10 minutes until they are completely rehydrated and soft, making sure they are fully immersed in the water. Finely chop the gianduja chocolate. Pour 2½ fl oz/5 tablespoons/75 ml water into a saucepan, add the sugar and condensed milk, and bring to a boil. Drain the sheets of gelatin and squeeze them with your hands to remove as much water as possible. Add the gianduja and gelatin and stir until the gelatin has completely dissolved, then blend with an immersion (stick) blender. Set aside to cool to room temperature.

To assemble the torte, spread the pastry with two-thirds of the Whipped Ganache and arrange the sponge on top. Transfer the frozen baked custard from the pan to a cooling rack set over a baking tray, and cover with the mirror glaze. Allow the glaze to set before placing the baked custard on top of the sponge layer. Leave the torte to stand at room temperature for 1 hour, or until the baked custard is soft.

Fit a pastry (piping) bag with the plain piping tip (nozzle) and fill with the remaining ganache. Finish the torte by piping the ganache over the top and decorating with the Chocolate Curls.

CINNAMON CANNOLI WITH GANACHE AND COCOA BEANS

Cannoli alla cannella con ganache e fave di cacao

40 m	15 m	8 m	1 h		60 d

Difficulty: ADVANCED

For the Whipped Ganache:
  see page 78

TO SERVE 8

FOR THE CANNOLI SHELLS
1½ fl oz/3 tablespoons/40 ml whole (full-fat) milk
1½ ounces/2 tablespoons/40 g acacia honey
3 ounces/scant ½ cup/80 g brown sugar
1 teaspoon ground cinnamon
2¼ ounces/½ stick/60 g unsalted butter
3 ounces/⅔ cup/80 g type "00" flour or all-purpose (plain) flour
2 egg whites

FOR THE SAUCE
3½ ounces/scant ½ cup/100 g superfine (caster) sugar
1 teaspoon ground cinnamon
3½ fl oz/scant ½ cup/100 ml boiling water

FOR THE FILLING
1 quantity Whipped Ganache
½ ounce/10 g roasted cocoa beans

TO SERVE
7 fl oz/scant 1 cup/200 ml heavy (whipping) cream

EQUIPMENT NEEDED
Measuring cup or jug
Saucepans
Hand whisk
Baking sheet
Parchment paper
¾-inch/2-cm stainless steel cannoli forms
Silicone spatula
Mortar and pestle
Disposable pastry (piping) bag or cone
Electric whisk

To make the cannoli shells, pour the milk into a saucepan, add the honey, sugar, cinnamon, and butter, and bring to a boil. Remove from the heat, add the flour, all at once, stirring continuously with a hand whisk, then add the egg whites. Stir to incorporate, leave to cool to room temperature, then rest the paste in the refrigerator for 1 hour.

Preheat the oven to 325°F/160°C/140°C Fan/Gas 3 and line the baking sheet with parchment paper.

Use a spoon to spread a thin layer of paste to form rectangles measuring 3 × 4 inches/7 × 11 cm on the lined baking sheet. Bake in the preheated oven for 8 minutes, then remove from the oven and leave to rest until just cool enough to handle. Line the cannoli forms with parchment paper and, starting with the short end, roll the rectangles around the forms. Leave to cool completely, then pull the forms out.

To make the caramel sauce, place the sugar in a saucepan with 1¾ fl oz/3 tablespoons/50 ml water, and the cinnamon, and cook to an amber caramel. Pour in the boiling water, stir with a silicone spatula until the caramel has melted, and cook to a syrupy consistency. Leave to cool to room temperature then set aside in the refrigerator.

Make the Whipped Ganache following the basic technique, using the ingredient quantities specified. Finely crush the cocoa beans in a mortar and pestle. Fill a disposable pastry (piping) bag with the ganache and cut off the tip. Pipe the ganache into the cannoli shells until completely filled, then dip the ends in the crushed cocoa beans. Pour the cream into a mixing bowl and whip to stiff peaks with an electric whisk. Arrange the cannoli on individual serving plates, with whipped cream on the side and the caramel sauce drizzled over, and serve.

TIPS AND TRICKS
If you buy raw cocoa beans, you can roast them yourself in a skillet (frying pan) over a moderate heat until the thin skin covering them begins to crackle and their aroma is released.

BLACK FOREST CUPCAKES

Tortine Foresta Nera

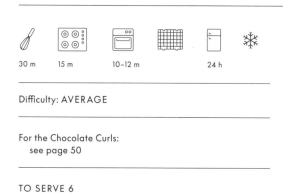

| 30 m | 15 m | 10–12 m | | 24 h | |

Difficulty: AVERAGE

For the Chocolate Curls:
  see page 50

TO SERVE 6

FOR THE CUPCAKES
2½ ounces/⅔ stick/75 g unsalted butter,
  plus extra for greasing
1 ounce/¼ cup/30 g type "00" flour or all-purpose
  (plain) flour, plus extra for dusting
1 vanilla bean (pod)
3 eggs
1 ounce/2½ tablespoons/30 g superfine (caster) sugar
1½ ounces/⅓ cup/40 g unsweetened cocoa powder

FOR THE DECORATION
6 cherries
1 ounce/2½ tablespoons/30 g superfine (caster) sugar
5 fl oz/scant ⅔ cup/150 ml heavy (whipping) cream
Chocolate Curls made with 70% dark chocolate

EQUIPMENT NEEDED
12-cup mini muffin pan (tin)
Saucepan
Paring knife
Mixing bowls
Electric whisk
Strainer (sieve)
Silicone spatula
Cooling rack
Skimmer
Measuring cup or jug
Disposable pastry (piping) bag or cone

Preheat the oven to 350°F/180°C/160°C Fan/Gas 4 and grease the muffin pan (tin) with butter and a dusting of flour.

Melt the butter in a saucepan over a very low heat. Split the vanilla bean (pod) lengthwise, using a sharp paring knife, and scrape out the seeds. Break the eggs into a mixing bowl, add the vanilla seeds and sugar, and beat together for 5 minutes with an electric whisk until very light and fluffy.

Sift the cocoa powder and flour together into a bowl, then fold into the beaten egg mixture, a little at a time, using a silicone spatula. Drizzle the melted butter into the mixture and stir to incorporate. Fill the muffin pan with the batter and bake in the preheated oven for 10–12 minutes, until cooked through .

Remove from the oven and leave the cupcakes to cool to room temperature, then remove from the pan and transfer to a cooling rack to cool completely.

Meanwhile, pit the cherries, place in a saucepan with the sugar and a tablespoon of water, and cook for 3–4 minutes. Remove the cherries with a skimmer and drain in a strainer (sieve), collecting the cooking syrup.

Prick the cupcakes with a wooden toothpick and drizzle over the cherry cooking syrup so that it soaks into the cakes. Pour the cream into a mixing bowl and whip with an electric whisk until firm. Fill a disposable pastry (piping) bag with the whipped cream and cut off the tip. Pipe whipped cream on top of each cupcake, top with the Chocolate Curls and the cherries, and serve.

VARIATION
When cherries are out of season, use amarena (morello) cherries from a jar, but thin their syrup with a little cold water to make it runnier. You can substitute candied chestnuts for the cherries, in which case, soak the cupcakes with a little rum.

PEAR AND CHOCOLATE TARTE TATIN

Tatin di pere e cioccolato

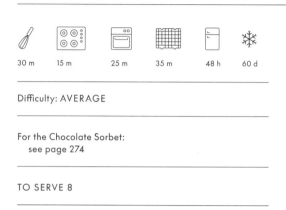

30 m	15 m	25 m	35 m	48 h	60 d

Difficulty: AVERAGE

For the Chocolate Sorbet:
    see page 274

TO SERVE 8

FOR THE TART CRUST
3¼ ounces/¾ stick/90 g cold unsalted butter
4 ounces/1 cup/125 g type "00" flour or all-purpose
    (plain) flour, plus extra for dusting
½ ounce/1 heaping tablespoon/15 g unsweetened
    cocoa powder
¾ ounce/4 teaspoons/20 g superfine (caster) sugar
Pinch of salt
1 large egg yolk

FOR THE FILLING
5 Williams pears
1½ ounces/40 g 70% dark chocolate
2¼ ounces/½ stick/60 g unsalted butter
2 ounces/scant ⅓ cup/50 g brown sugar

TO SERVE
Chocolate Sorbet

EQUIPMENT NEEDED
Chef's knife
Chopping board
Food processor
Strainer (sieve)
Plastic wrap (cling film)
Melon baller
Chocolate grater
8-inch/20-cm round heavy-bottomed baking pan (tin)
    or tarte Tatin pan
Rolling pin

Cut the butter into small cubes. Place the sifted flour and cocoa powder in a food processor, add the sugar and a pinch of salt and blend until the mixture resembles fine bread crumbs. Add the egg yolk and blend again until the resulting dough (pastry) sticks to the blades. Shape the dough into a disk, cover in plastic wrap (cling film), and rest in the refrigerator for at least 30 minutes.

Peel and halve the pears, remove the core with a melon baller, and cut each half into two wedges. Shred (grate) the chocolate. Place the butter into the baking pan (tin) and add the brown sugar. Melt on the stove (hob) over a low heat until the sugar turns golden. Arrange the pears in the pan in a flower pattern with the core side up and cook on the stove for 10 minutes. Remove from the heat and sprinkle with shredded (grated) chocolate, then set aside to cool.

Preheat the oven to 375°F/190°C/170°C Fan/Gas 5.

On a floured work surface, roll out the dough into a circle the same diameter as the pan. Carefully lift and drape the dough over the pears. Tuck the dough in around the edges of the pan and prick the surface with a fork. Bake the tart in the preheated oven for 25 minutes. Remove from the oven and rest the tart for 5 minutes, then invert onto a serving plate. Serve warm with the Chocolate Sorbet.

TIPS AND TRICKS
Instead of shredding (grating) the chocolate and sprinkling over the pears, you can cut it into as many chunks as there are pear segments and place a piece in each cavity where the core has been removed.

CHOCOLATE CHEESECAKE WITH RHUBARB SAUCE

Cheesecake al cioccolato con salsa di rabarbaro

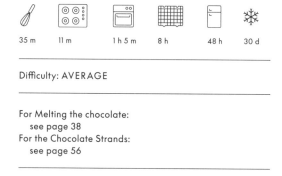

| 35 m | 11 m | 1 h 5 m | 8 h | 48 h | 30 d |

Difficulty: AVERAGE

For Melting the chocolate:
  see page 38
For the Chocolate Strands:
  see page 56

TO SERVE 8

FOR THE CHEESECAKE
3½ ounces/scant 1 stick/100 g unsalted butter,
  plus extra for greasing
7 ounces/200 g chocolate shortbread cookies (biscuits)
5 ounces/150 g 70% dark chocolate
1 pound/2 cups/450 g spreadable cream cheese,
  at room temperature
4 ounces/½ cup/120 g superfine (caster) sugar
¾ ounce/2 tablespoons/20 g cornstarch (cornflour)
Pinch of salt
4¾ ounces/generous ½ cup/140 g sour cream
2 eggs
1 egg yolk

FOR THE SAUCE
7 ounces/200 g rhubarb
3 ounces/⅓ cup/80 g sugar

FOR THE DECORATION
Chocolate Strands

EQUIPMENT NEEDED
8-inch/20-cm round springform pan (tin)
Parchment paper
Bain-marie or double boiler
Food processor
Chef's knife
Chopping board
Mixing bowls
Electric whisk
Fine-mesh strainer (sieve)
Saucepan
Immersion (stick) blender
Decorating spoon

Preheat the oven to 350°F/180°C/160°C Fan/Gas 4 and line the base of the springform pan (tin) with parchment paper.

Melt the butter in a bain-marie. Place the cookies (biscuits) in a food processor and blend to a fine crumb. Drizzle over the melted butter and blend again to coat the crumbs evenly. Cover the bottom of the springform pan with the cookie crumb base and press it down firmly with the bottom of a glass. Bake the cheesecake base in the preheated oven for 10 minutes, remove from the oven, and set aside in the pan to cool to room temperature. Lower the oven temperature to 325°F/160°C/140°C Fan/Gas 3.

Finely chop the chocolate and melt in a bain-marie. Place the cream cheese in a mixing bowl and whisk using an electric whisk until fluffy. Gradually add the sugar, chocolate, sifted cornstarch (cornflour), and a pinch of salt and whisk to combine. Add the sour cream, eggs, and the extra egg yolk and whisk for a few more seconds. Grease the sides of the cool springform pan with butter.

Pour the cream cheese mixture over the cheesecake base and bake in the preheated oven for 10 minutes, then lower the temperature to 230°F/110°C/90°C Fan/Gas ¼ and continue to bake for a further 45 minutes. Turn off the oven and leave the cheesecake to cool to room temperature inside, then chill for 8 hours in the refrigerator.

To make the rhubarb sauce, clean the rhubarb stalks by removing any strings, then cut into chunks and place in a saucepan with the sugar and 2 tablespoons water. Cook over a moderate heat for 5–6 minutes until very soft. Leave to cool, then puree with an immersion (stick) blender.

Fill the decorating spoon with rhubarb sauce and rest the tip of the spoon on an individual serving plate. When the sauce has partially run down the tip, slide it against the plate to create a crescent shape with the sauce. Arrange a slice of cheesecake on the plate and decorate with Chocolate Strands.

DOUBLE CHOCOLATE, COFFEE, AND ELDERBERRY SLICE

Barrette ai due cioccolati, caffè e sambuco

1 h   6 m   8 m   16 h   3 d

Difficulty: ADVANCED

For the dark Chocolate Crémeux:
   see page 90
For the Whipped Ganache:
   see page 78

TO SERVE 10

FOR THE ALMOND SPONGE
¾ ounce/¼ stick/25 g unsalted butter
2 eggs
2¼ ounces/½ cup/65 g confectioners' (icing) sugar
3 egg whites
¾ ounce/5 teaspoons/25 g superfine (caster) sugar
2¼ ounces/scant ⅔ cup/65 g almond meal (ground almonds)
¾ ounce/scant ¼ cup/25 g type "00" flour or all-purpose (plain) flour
¾ ounce/2 heaping tablespoons/20 g unsweetened cocoa powder
3½ fl oz/scant ½ cup/100 ml elderberry syrup
1 quantity Chocolate Crémeux made with dark chocolate

FOR THE WHITE CHOCOLATE WHIPPED GANACHE
8½ fl oz/1 cup/250 ml heavy (whipping) cream
10 coffee beans, finely crushed
4¾ ounces/140 g white chocolate

FOR THE MIRROR GLAZE
4 sheets (12 g) gelatin
5½ ounces/scant ¾ cup/160 g superfine (caster) sugar
2½ ounces/scant ¾ cup/75 g unsweetened cocoa powder
3¼ fl oz/6 tablespoons/90 ml heavy (whipping) cream

FOR THE DECORATION
4 tablespoons superfine (caster) sugar
10 almonds

Make the Whipped Ganache following the basic technique, using the ingredient quantities specified, flavoring the cream with finely crushed coffee beans, then straining, before adding to the chocolate.

To make the almond sponge, preheat the oven to 430°F/220°C/200°C Fan/Gas 8 and line the baking pan (tin) with parchment paper.

Melt the butter in a bain-marie or double boiler. Break the whole eggs into a mixing bowl, add the confectioners' (icing) sugar, and beat together with an electric whisk until light and fluffy. Place the egg whites in a separate grease-free bowl and whisk to soft peaks, gradually incorporating the superfine (caster) sugar. Add half the almond meal (ground almonds) to the egg yolk mixture and stir with a silicone spatula to combine, then fold in half the whisked egg whites. Fold in the remaining almond meal and whisked egg whites. Sift the flour together with the cocoa powder and fold into the mixture, then add the melted butter and stir to incorporate.

Pour the batter into the baking pan and bake in the preheated oven for 8 minutes. Remove from the oven and leave to cool a little. Cut the sponge horizontally into three layers, peel off the parchment paper, and leave to cool completely.

Dilute the elderberry syrup with 3½ fl oz/scant ½ cup/100 ml water. Place one of the cake layers on a baking sheet and drizzle over some of the elderberry syrup so that it soaks into the sponge. Whip the ganache with an electric whisk and spread half over the cake layer using a palette knife. Place a second cake layer over the ganache and drizzle with more syrup. Spread the remaining ganache over the second cake layer, and place the third layer of cake over the ganache. Finally, spread the Chocolate Crémeux over the top and freeze for 12 hours.

To make the mirror glaze, soak the gelatin sheets in a small bowl of cold water for 10 minutes until they are completely rehydrated and soft, making sure they are fully immersed in the water. Pour 3½ fl oz/scant ½ cup/100 ml water into a saucepan, add the sugar, sifted cocoa powder, and cream, and bring to a boil. Cook for 1 minute, then remove from the heat. Drain the sheets of gelatin and squeeze them with your hands to remove as much water as possible. Add the gelatin to the saucepan and stir until completely dissolved. Pour the mixture through a strainer (sieve) and set aside to cool to room temperature.

EQUIPMENT NEEDED
24 × 18-cm baking pan (tin)
Parchment paper
Bain-marie or double boiler
Mixing bowls
Electric whisk
Silicone spatula
Strainer (sieve)
Serrated knife
Measuring cup or jug
Baking sheet
Palette knife
Saucepan
Cooling rack
Rimmed baking tray (pan)

Image on page 162

Place the frozen cake on a cooling rack set over a rimmed baking tray, and pour over the mirror glaze, allowing the excess to drain into the tray. Transfer to the refrigerator and chill for 4 hours.

When ready to serve, place the sugar in a small saucepan and cook to an amber caramel. Dip the almonds in the caramel one at a time, taking care as the caramel will be very hot. Transfer to a sheet of parchment paper and leave until the caramel hardens. Remove the cake from the refrigerator, cut into individual slices, and decorate each slice with a candied almond.

VARIATION
For a simpler version of the slice, leave each element as a separate layer—a thicker cake base, whipped ganache center, and topped with the chocolate crémeux and mirror glaze.

WHITE CHOCOLATE AND RASPBERRY TART

Tarte al cioccolato bianco e lamponi

40 m   15 m   26 m   30 m   48 h   60 d

Difficulty: AVERAGE

For the Classic Pie Dough (Shortcrust Pastry):
see page 314
For the Chocolate Curls:
see page 50

TO SERVE 8

FOR THE TART CRUST
3¾ ounces/1 stick/110 g cold unsalted butter
6¼ ounces/1½ cups/180 g type "00" flour or all-purpose (plain) flour
1½ ounces/⅓ cup/40 g unsweetened cocoa powder
2 ounces/¼ cup/50 g superfine (caster) sugar
Pinch of salt
1 egg
17 fl oz/2 cups/500 ml chilled water

FOR THE CUSTARD
3⅓ sheets (10 g) gelatin
17 fl oz/2 cups/500 ml whole (full-fat) milk
6 egg yolks
1 ounce/2½ tablespoons/30 g superfine (caster) sugar
1 ounce/¼ cup/30 g type "00" flour or all-purpose (plain) flour
1 ounce/30 g potato starch
4¾ ounces/140 g white chocolate

FOR THE DECORATION
7 ounces/scant 1⅔ cups/200 g fresh raspberries
Chocolate Curls made with white chocolate

To make the tart crust, cut the butter into small cubes. Sift the flour and cocoa powder into a mixing bowl, then place in a food processor. Add the sugar, butter, and a pinch of salt and blend until the mixture resembles fine bread crumbs. Add the egg and cold water and blend for a few more seconds until the resulting dough (pastry) covers the blades. Form the dough into a disk, cover with plastic wrap (cling film), and rest in the refrigerator for at least 30 minutes.

To make the custard, soak the gelatin sheets in a small bowl of cold water for 10 minutes until they are completely rehydrated and soft, making sure they are fully immersed in the water. Pour the milk into a saucepan and bring to a simmer, then remove from the heat. Place the egg yolks in a mixing bowl with the sugar and beat with an electric whisk until pale and fluffy. Sift the flour together with the potato starch, and add to the egg yolk mix, stirring with a silicone spatula. Drizzle the milk into the bowl and stir to combine. Return the mixture to the saucepan and cook the custard over a low heat for 7–8 minutes until it thickens.

Finely chop the white chocolate. Drain the sheets of gelatin and squeeze them with your hands to remove as much water as possible. Remove the custard from the heat and add the gelatin and chocolate, stirring until the gelatin has completely dissolved and the chocolate has melted.

Preheat the oven to 350°F/180°C/160°C Fan/Gas 4.

Soak a sheet of parchment paper in water, then squeeze to remove excess water and set aside. Roll out the dough on a lightly floured work surface into a rectangle with a thickness of ⅛ inch/3 mm. Carefully lift the dough over the tart pan (tin), gently pressing it down on the base and sides of the pan, then cut away the excess dough that is overhanging the pan. Prick the base with a fork, cover with the damp sheet of parchment paper, and fill the crust with dried beans or pie weights.

EQUIPMENT NEEDED
Chef's knife
Chopping board
Strainer (sieve)
Mixing bowls
Food processor
Measuring cup or jug
Plastic wrap (cling film)
Saucepans
Electric whisk
Silicone spatula
Parchment paper
Rolling pin
4 x 11-inch/10 × 28-cm rectangular fluted tart pan (tin)
Pie weights or dried beans

Image on page 163

Blind bake the crust in the preheated oven for 20 minutes. Remove the parchment paper and beans or weights and continue to bake for a further 5–6 minutes.

Leave the tart crust to cool completely, then remove from the pan and fill with the custard. Decorate with fresh raspberries and the white Chocolate Curls.

CHOCOLATE AND PISTACHIO VERTICAL CAKE

Torta arrotolata di cioccolato e pistacchio

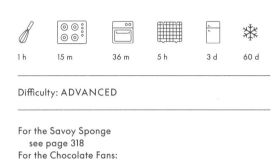

1 h   15 m   36 m   5 h   3 d   60 d

Difficulty: ADVANCED

For the Savoy Sponge
   see page 318
For the Chocolate Fans:
   see page 50

TO SERVE 10

FOR THE SAVOY SPONGE
4 ounces/1 stick/120 g unsalted butter
12 eggs
12¼ ounces/scant 1⅔ cups/360 g superfine (caster) sugar
Pinch of salt
8¾ ounces/1 cup/240 g self-rising (self-raising) flour
4 ounces/1¼ cups/120 g pistachio flour

FOR THE BUTTERCREAM
7 ounces/200 g 60% dark chocolate
7 ounces/1¾ sticks/200 g unsalted butter
14 ounces/3¼ cups/400 g confectioners' (icing) sugar
7 fl oz/scant 1 cup/200 ml heavy (whipping) cream

FOR THE DECORATION
1½ ounces/⅓ cup/40 g chopped pistachio nuts
Chocolate Fans made with 60% dark chocolate

EQUIPMENT NEEDED
8 x 12-inch/20 × 30-cm rectangular baking pan (tin)
Parchment paper
Bain-marie or double boiler
Stand mixer fitted with whisk attachment or electric whisk
   and bowl
Strainer (sieve)
Chef's knife
Chopping board
Saucepan
Mixing bowl
Palette knife

Preheat the oven to 350°F/180°C/160°C Fan/Gas 4 and line the baking pan (tin) with parchment paper.

Melt one-third of the butter in a bain-marie or double boiler. Break four of the eggs into the bowl of a stand mixer fitted with whisk attachment, or use a mixing bowl and electric whisk. Add one-third of the sugar and a pinch of salt to the bowl, and beat until very pale, and fluffy. Add one-third of the flour, sifted, one-third of the pistachio flour and the melted butter, and mix to combine.

Pour the batter into the baking pan, level the surface, and bake in the preheated oven for 12 minutes. Remove from the oven and invert the pan onto a sheet of parchment paper. Peel off the parchment from the sponge, so that it is no longer attached to it, and replace it back on top of the sponge. Starting with the short side of the sponge towards you, roll up the sponge while still warm, holding it sandwiched between the two sheets of parchment paper. Set aside to cool completely.

Repeat the process described above with the remaining ingredients to make two more sponge rectangles, but allow them to cool without rolling them up.

To make the buttercream, finely chop the chocolate. Place the butter, confectioners' (icing) sugar, cream, and chocolate in a saucepan and place over a low heat until the butter and chocolate have melted and the mixture is glossy and smooth. Transfer to a bowl and set aside to cool to room temperature, then chill in the refrigerator for 1 hour until it has the desired consistency for spreading.

Unroll the rolled-up sponge, remove the parchment paper, and use a palette knife to spread with a thin layer of buttercream. Roll up the sponge again, without using parchment paper. Spread one of the two remaining sponge rectangles with buttercream and wrap it around the rolled sponge, starting at the outer edge, to create a larger roll. Repeat with the third rectangle, then stand the roll upright on a serving plate. Spread the entire surface of the cake with the remaining buttercream, and decorate, as desired, with the chopped pistachios and Chocolate Fans, and chill in the refrigerator for 4 hours before serving.

If you want to make a shorter cake, cut the sponge rectangles in half lengthwise.

SACHER TORTE SQUARES

Sacher torte in versione mignon

40 m	8 m	25 m	1 h 5 m	3 d	60 d

Difficulty: ADVANCED

For Melting the chocolate:
see page 38

TO SERVE 8

FOR THE TORTE SQUARES
1 vanilla bean (pod)
4¾ ounces/1¼ sticks/140 g unsalted butter,
at room temperature
3½ ounces/scant 1 cup/100 g confectioners' (icing) sugar
Pinch of salt
6 eggs
8 ounces/230 g 60% dark chocolate
4¾ ounces/generous 1 cup/140 g type "00" flour or
all-purpose (plain) flour
3½ ounces/⅓ cup/100 g apricot jelly (jam)
5 ounces/⅔ cup/150 g superfine (caster) sugar
4 dried apricots

EQUIPMENT NEEDED
Mini brownie pan (tin) with 8 × 2-inch/6-cm square cavities
Parchment paper
Paring knife
Mixing bowls
Electric whisk
Chef's knife
Chopping board
Bain-marie or double boiler
Silicone spatula
Strainer (sieve)
Cooling rack
Saucepans
Serrated knife
Measuring cup or jug
Baking tray (pan)
Pastry brush

Preheat the oven to 340°F/170°C/150°C Fan/Gas 3 and line the mini brownie pan (tin) with parchment paper.

Split the vanilla bean (pod) lengthwise with a sharp paring knife and scrape out the seeds. Place the butter in a mixing bowl and beat with an electric whisk until creamy. Add the confectioners' (icing) sugar, a pinch of salt, and the vanilla seeds and beat together with the butter. Separate the eggs and place the egg whites in a clean, grease-free bowl; set aside. Add the yolks, one at a time, to the creamed butter, beating each one into the mixture before adding the next.

Finely chop the chocolate and melt 4 ounces/130 g in a bain-marie or double boiler. Reserve the remaining chopped chocolate. Leave the melted chocolate to cool to room temperature, then incorporate into the mixture, stirring with a silicone spatula. Using an electric whisk, whisk the egg whites to soft peaks and fold into the mixture, then fold in the sifted flour.

Pour the batter into the lined brownie pan and bake in the preheated oven for 25 minutes. Remove from the oven and rest in the pan for 5 minutes, then remove from the pan and transfer to a cooling rack to cool completely.

Place the apricot jelly (jam) in a small saucepan to warm slightly. Cut the mini cakes in half horizontally, spread the bottom half with some of the apricot jelly, and reassemble. Spread jelly over the top and sides of the cakes, reserving a little jelly to glaze the apricots.

Pour 2 ½ fl oz/⅜ cup/80 ml water into a saucepan, add the superfine (caster) sugar and bring to a boil. Remove from the heat, add the reserved chopped chocolate, and stir until the chocolate has melted. Leave the glaze to cool, stirring often to prevent a skin forming on the surface. Place the mini cakes on a cooling rack set over a baking tray (pan) and pour the glaze over the cupcakes to cover the top and sides.

Cut each dried apricot in half and brush with a little of the warmed apricot jelly. Decorate each Sacher torte square with a glazed apricot. Leave to stand for about 1 hour, for the glaze to harden, then serve.

CHOCOLATE AND WALNUT CAKE WITH CARAMEL

Torta di cioccolato e noci dal cuore di caramello

40 m   5 m   40 m   24 h

Difficulty: AVERAGE

For Melting the chocolate:
   see page 38
For the Chocolate Shards:
   see page 54

TO SERVE 8–10

FOR THE SPONGE
5 ounces/1½ cups/150 g walnut kernels
5 ounces/⅔ cup/150 g superfine (caster) sugar
Pinch of salt
9 ounces/250 g 60% dark chocolate
4 ounces/1 stick/120 g unsalted butter
5 eggs
1 egg white

FOR THE CARAMEL SAUCE
1½ ounces/⅓ stick/40 g unsalted butter
5 ounces/⅔ cup/150 g superfine (caster) sugar
4 fl oz/½ cup/120 ml heavy (whipping) cream

FOR THE DECORATION
7 fl oz/scant 1 cup/200 ml heavy (whipping) cream
½ ounce/1 heaping tablespoon/10 g unsweetened
   cocoa powder
¾ ounce/scant ¼ cup/20 g walnut kernels
Chocolate Shards made with dark chocolate

EQUIPMENT NEEDED
Chef's knife
Chopping board
Saucepans
Measuring cup or jug
Silicone spatula
9-inch/22-cm round springform pan (tin)
Parchment paper
Food processor
Bain-marie or double boiler
Mixing bowl
Electric whisk
Pastry (piping) bag
Ribbon piping tip (nozzle)
Fine-mesh strainer (sieve)

To make the caramel sauce, cut the butter into small cubes. Place the sugar in a saucepan with 3 tablespoons water and place over a low heat until the sugar melts, then increase the heat to high. When the sugar is cooked to an amber caramel, remove from the heat and gradually add the cream and butter, stirring with a silicone spatula until the sauce thickens. Leave to cool.

To make the sponge, preheat the oven to 350°F/180°C/160°C Fan/Gas 4 and line the springform pan (tin) with parchment paper.

Place the walnuts, sugar, and a pinch of salt in a food processor and blend to a fine powder. Finely chop the chocolate and cut the butter into small cubes, then melt together in a bain-marie or double boiler. Add the walnut and sugar mixture into the melted chocolate and stir with a silicone spatula to combine.

Separate the eggs and place the egg whites in a clean, grease-free mixing bowl. Add the egg yolks to the chocolate walnut mixture and mix to incorporate. Whisk all the egg whites to soft peaks with an electric whisk, then fold into the batter with the silicone spatula. Pour half the batter into the springform pan, cover with the caramel sauce, then fill with the remaining batter. Bake in the preheated oven for 40 minutes.

Remove from the oven and leave the cake to cool completely in the pan, then transfer to a serving plate. Pour the cream into a mixing bowl and whip to soft peaks with the electric whisk. Fit a pastry (piping) bag with a ribbon piping tip (nozzle) and fill with the whipped cream. Pipe a series of wavy lines over the top of the cake, then dust with cocoa powder and sprinkle with chopped walnuts. Decorate with Chocolate Shards to finish.

COOKIES AND BAKES

CHOCOLATE PISTACHIO COOKIES WITH SALT FLAKES

Biscotti cioccolato, pistacchio e fiocchi di sale

20 m   10–12 m   4 h 5 m   3 d

Difficulty: EASY

TO SERVE 8–10

FOR THE COOKIES
10 ounces/2½ sticks/280 g unsalted butter,
    at room temperature
6¼ ounces/1½ cups/180 g confectioners' (icing) sugar
Pinch of salt
11 ounces/generous 2½ cups/320 g type "00" flour or
    all-purpose (plain) flour, plus extra for dusting
2¼ ounces/generous ½ cup/60 g unsweetened cocoa
    powder
½ teaspoon baking soda (bicarbonate of soda)
5 ounces/generous 1 cup/150 g chopped pistachio nuts,
    plus extra for decorating
3½ ounces/100 g 60% dark chocolate
1 large egg white
Sea salt flakes, for sprinkling

EQUIPMENT NEEDED
Baking sheet
Parchment paper
Mixing bowls
Electric whisk
Strainer (sieve)
Food processor
Silicone spatula
Plastic wrap (cling film)
Chef's knife
Cookie (biscuit) stamp
Cooling rack

Preheat the oven to 350°F/180°C/160°C Fan/Gas 4 and line the baking sheet with parchment paper.

Place the butter in a mixing bowl, add the confectioners' (icing) sugar, and beat together with an electric whisk until fluffy, then add a pinch of salt. In a separate bowl, sift together the flour, cocoa powder, and baking soda (bicarbonate of soda), then gradually add the dry ingredients to the butter mix until incorporated. Place 3½ ounces/¾ cup/100 g of the chopped pistachios and the chocolate in a food processor and blend until very finely chopped. Add the egg white, pistachios, and chocolate to the mixture, stirring with a silicone spatula to combine.

Divide the dough into four equal portions. On a lightly floured work surface, shape each portion of dough into a cylinder measuring 2 inches/5 cm in diameter. Cover each cylinder in plastic wrap (cling film) and rest in the refrigerator for at least 4 hours.

Remove the plastic wrap and cut the cylinders into slices ¼ inch/ 5 mm thick. Arrange the cookies (biscuits), flat side down, on the lined baking sheet, spacing them about 1¼ inches/3 cm apart to allow for them to spread during baking. Press each cookie with a cookie stamp.

Sprinkle the cookies with the remaining chopped pistachios and a few salt flakes and bake in the preheated oven for 10–12 minutes. Remove from the oven and rest on the baking sheet for 5 minutes, then transfer to a cooling rack to cool completely. Decorate with a few chopped pistachios and sea salt flakes.

MISTAKES TO AVOID
Before chopping in a food processor, chill the chocolate in the freezer for 15 minutes then cut into small pieces with a knife to prevent it from heating and sticking to the blades.

CHOCOLATE AND GINGER MUFFINS WITH YOGURT

Muffin allo yogurt con cioccolato al latte e zenzero

| 20 m | 5 m | 20 m | 15 m | 48 h | 60 d |

Difficulty: EASY

TO SERVE 8

FOR THE MUFFINS
3 ounces/⅔ stick/80 g unsalted butter
2 eggs
3 ounces/⅓ cup/80 g superfine (caster) sugar
9 ounces/1 cup/250 g whole-milk Greek yogurt
Pinch of salt
10 ounces/2¼ cups/280 g type "00" flour or all-purpose
   (plain) flour
1 level teaspoon baking powder
1 ounce/¼ cup/30 g unsweetened cocoa powder
6¼ ounces/180 g milk chocolate
2 ounces/50 g candied (crystallized) ginger

EQUIPMENT NEEDED
Muffin pan (tin)
Paper baking cups (cases)
Chef's knife
Chopping board
Bain-marie or double boiler
Mixing bowl
Electric whisk
Strainer (sieve)
Silicone spatula
Cooling rack

Preheat the oven to 350°F/180°C/160°C Fan/Gas 4 and line the muffin pan (tin) with baking cups (cases).

Cut the butter into small cubes and melt in a bain-marie or double boiler. Break the eggs into a mixing bowl, add the sugar, and beat with an electric whisk until pale and fluffy. Add the yogurt, a pinch of salt, and the melted butter, and mix to combine. Sift in the flour, baking powder, and cocoa powder and briefly mix with a silicone spatula, just enough to incorporate the dry ingredients and without overworking the mixture.

Finely chop the milk chocolate and cut 1½ ounces/40 g of the candied (crystallized) ginger into very small cubes. Add to the batter and briefly mix to incorporate. Fill each baking cup two-thirds full with the batter and bake the muffins in the preheated oven for 20 minutes, or until a toothpick inserted in the center comes out clean. Remove the muffins from the oven and rest in the pan for 15 minutes, then transfer to a cooling rack to cool completely. Decorate with the remaining candied ginger.

TIPS AND TRICKS
When combining the muffin ingredients, mix them only long enough for the ingredients to be incorporated. Otherwise the baked muffins will be too firm.

CHOCOLATE CRACKLE COOKIES

Biscotti craquelé

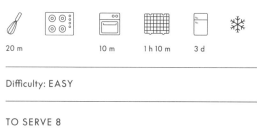

20 m   10 m   1 h 10 m   3 d

Difficulty: EASY

TO SERVE 8

FOR THE COOKIES
2 fl oz/¼ cup/60 ml sunflower oil
6 ounces/¾ cup/170 g superfine (caster) sugar
2¼ ounces/generous ½ cup/60 g unsweetened
    cocoa powder
2 large eggs
6¼ ounces/1½ cups/180 g type "00" flour or all-purpose
    (plain) flour
1 teaspoon baking powder
Pinch of salt
3 ounces/scant ⅔ cup/80 g confectioners' (icing) sugar

EQUIPMENT NEEDED
Baking sheet
Parchment paper
Measuring cup or jug
Mixing bowls
Fine-mesh strainer (sieve)
Hand or electric whisk
Silicone spatula
Plastic wrap (cling film)
Small tray
Cooling rack

Preheat the oven to 375°F/190°C/170°C Fan/Gas 5 and line the baking sheet with parchment paper.

Pour the oil into a mixing bowl, add the superfine (caster) sugar and sifted cocoa powder, and mix with a hand or electric whisk. Add the eggs, one at a time, continuing to whisk, to incorporate.

Sift the flour and baking powder into a separate bowl and add a pinch of salt. Add the wet mixture to the dry ingredients and stir with a silicone spatula until you have a smooth and soft dough. Cover the bowl with plastic wrap (cling film), transfer to the refrigerator, and rest for 1 hour.

Sift the confectioners' (icing) sugar into a small tray. Take a heaped teaspoon of the dough and roll with your hands into a ball. Roll in the confectioners' sugar to coat and place on the lined baking sheet, spacing them about 1¼ inches/3 cm apart to allow for them to spread during baking. Repeat until all the dough has been used.

Bake the cookies (biscuits) in the preheated oven for 10 minutes. Remove from the oven and rest on the baking sheet for 10 minutes, then transfer to a cooling rack to cool completely.

TIPS AND TRICKS
If you only have sweetened cocoa at home, reduce the 6 ounces/ ¾ cup/170 g superfine (caster) sugar to 4 ounces/½ cup/120 g.

GIANDUJA MACARONS

Macaron al cioccolato gianduia

40 m   7 m   12–15 m   1 h 30 m   3 d   180 d

Difficulty: ADVANCED

For the Simple Ganache
    see page 76

TO SERVE 8

FOR THE MACARONS
3½ ounces/100 g Simple Ganache made with gianduja
4 ounces/1⅓ cups/130 g almond meal (ground almonds)
¾ ounce/scant ¼ cup/25 g unsweetened cocoa powder
5 ounces/1¼ cups/150 g confectioners' (icing) sugar
5 ounces/⅔ cup/150 g superfine (caster) sugar
3 egg whites

EQUIPMENT NEEDED
Baking sheet
Parchment paper
Strainer (sieve)
Food processor
Measuring cup or jug
Saucepan
Stand mixer fitted with whisk attachment or
    electric whisk and bowl
Kitchen thermometer
Silicone spatula
Pastry (piping) bag
½-inch/1-cm plain piping tip (nozzle)
Disposable pastry bag or cone

Preheat the oven to 300°F/150°C/130°C Fan/Gas 2 and line the baking sheet with parchment paper. Place the Simple Ganache in the refrigerator to chill for 1 hour.

Place the almond meal (ground almonds), and the sifted cocoa powder and confectioners' (icing) sugar in a food processor and blend together. Pour 17 fl oz/2 cups/500 ml water into a saucepan, add the superfine (caster) sugar, and bring to a boil.

Place the egg whites in the bowl of a stand mixer fitted with a whisk attachment or use a mixing bowl and electric whisk and whisk until soft peaks form. Cook the syrup until it reaches a temperature of 250°F/121°C, then slowly drizzle the boiling syrup into the whisked egg whites, whisking continuously to incorporate. Continue to whisk until the meringue has cooled to room temperature, then fold in the almond, cocoa powder, and confectioners' sugar mixture, using a silicone spatula.

Fit a pastry (piping) bag with a plain piping tip (nozzle), fill with the meringue mix, and pipe mounds measuring 1¼ inch/3 cm in diameter on the lined baking sheet. Set aside for 30 minutes for the macaron shells to dry out and form a skin, then bake in the preheated oven for 12–15 minutes, until set. Remove from the oven and leave on the baking sheet to cool completely, then peel away from the parchment paper. Fill a disposable pastry bag with the ganache and cut off the tip. Pipe the ganache onto the flat side of half the macarons, then place another macaron shell on top to sandwich the two halves together.

CHOCOLATE AND PEANUT CUPCAKES

Cupcake al cioccolato e arachidi

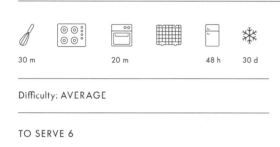

30 m   20 m   48 h   30 d

Difficulty: AVERAGE

TO SERVE 6

FOR THE CUPCAKES
4 fl oz/½ cup/120 ml whole (full-fat) milk
1 teaspoon lemon juice
3½ ounces/¾ cup/100 g type "00" flour or all-purpose
  (plain) flour
1½ ounces/⅓ cup/40 g unsweetened cocoa powder
1 teaspoon baking powder
½ teaspoon baking soda (bicarbonate of soda)
Pinch of salt
2 large eggs
4 ounces/½ cup/120 g superfine (caster) sugar
2½ fl oz/⅜ cup/80 ml sunflower oil

FOR THE FROSTING (ICING)
1 vanilla bean (pod)
3¾ ounces/1 stick/115 g unsalted butter, at room
  temperature
7 ounces/1⅔ cups/210 g confectioners' (icing) sugar
¾ ounce/2 heaping tablespoons/20 g unsweetened
  cocoa powder
1 fl oz/5 teaspoons/25 ml whole (full-fat) milk
1½ ounces/40 g peanut butter

FOR THE DECORATION
1½ ounces/¼ cup/40 g roasted and salted peanuts

EQUIPMENT NEEDED
Muffin pan (tin)
Paper baking cups (cases)
Measuring cup or jug
Strainer (sieve)
Mixing bowls
Electric whisk
Silicone spatula
Cooling rack
Paring knife
Chopping board
Pastry (piping) bag
Ribbon piping tip (nozzle)

Preheat the oven to 350°F/180°C/160°C Fan/Gas 4 and line the muffin pan (tin) with baking cups (cases).

Mix the milk with a teaspoon of lemon juice. Sift the flour, cocoa powder, baking powder, and baking soda (bicarbonate of soda) into a mixing bowl. Add a pinch of salt and mix to combine. Break the eggs into a separate bowl, add the sugar and oil, and beat together using an electric whisk. Add half the beaten egg mixture to the dry ingredients, then add half the sour milk, and whisk to incorporate.

Add the remaining egg mixture and sour milk and mix using a silicone spatula for just long enough to incorporate the ingredients without overworking the batter. Fill each baking cup two-thirds full with the batter and bake in the preheated oven for 20 minutes, or until a toothpick inserted in the center comes out clean. Remove the cupcakes from the pan and transfer to a cooling rack to cool completely.

To make the frosting (icing), split the vanilla bean (pod) lengthwise using a sharp paring knife and scrape out the seeds. Place the butter in a mixing bowl and beat using an electric whisk until creamy. Add the confectioners' (icing) sugar, sifted cocoa powder, and milk and beat for a few seconds to combine. Add the peanut butter and vanilla seeds and beat on medium speed for 2 minutes. Fit a pastry (piping) bag with a ribbon piping tip (nozzle), fill with the frosting, and decorate the cupcakes. Coarsely chop the peanuts, sprinkle over the frosting, and serve.

CHOCOLATE SHORTBREAD COOKIES

Shortbread al cioccolato

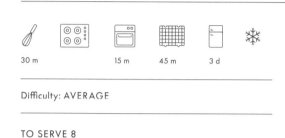

30 m   15 m   45 m   3 d

Difficulty: AVERAGE

TO SERVE 8

FOR THE COOKIES
9 ounces/2 cups/250 g type "00" flour or all-purpose
   (plain) flour
4 ounces/1 cup/120 g confectioners' (icing) sugar
2 ounces/½ cup/50 g unsweetened cocoa powder
7 ounces/1¾ sticks/200 g cold unsalted butter
Pinch of salt

FOR THE ROYAL ICING
9 ounces/2 cups/250 g confectioners' (icing) sugar
1 egg white
A few drops of lemon juice

EQUIPMENT NEEDED
Baking sheet
Parchment paper
Mixing bowls
Strainer (sieve)
Chef's knife
Chopping board
Food processor
Plastic wrap (cling film)
Rolling pin
2½-inch/6-cm round pastry cutter
Cooling rack
Electric whisk
Pastry (piping) bag
⅟₁₆-inch/2-mm plain piping tip (nozzle)

Preheat the oven to 325°F/160°C/140°C Fan/Gas 3 and line the baking sheet with parchment paper.

Sift the flour, confectioners' (icing) sugar, and cocoa powder together in a bowl. Cut the butter into small cubes. Place the dry ingredients in a food processor, add a pinch of salt, and the butter and blend together until the resulting dough forms a ball. Cover in plastic wrap (cling film) and rest in the refrigerator for 30 minutes.

Roll out the dough between two sheets of parchment paper to a thickness of about ½ inch/1 cm and freeze for 15 minutes. Remove the top parchment sheet and cut out cookies (biscuits) with the cookie cutter. Place on the lined baking sheet and bake in the preheated oven for 15 minutes. Remove from the oven and transfer to a cooling rack to cool completely.

To make the royal icing, place the confectioners' sugar, egg white, and a few drops of lemon juice in a mixing bowl and whisk with an electric whisk until smooth and thick. Fit a pastry (piping) bag with a plain tip (nozzle) and fill with the icing. Decorate the cookies with the royal icing as desired, set aside for the icing to dry, then serve.

TIPS AND TRICKS
When making a dark shortbread dough with cocoa powder, do not flour the work surface. Instead, roll out the dough between two sheets of parchment paper to prevent the dough from turning gray. Alternatively, dust the work surface with flour, but remember to remove all the flour from the dough with a pastry brush.

CHOCOLATE AND CINNAMON MADELEINES

Madeleine al cioccolato profumate alla cannella

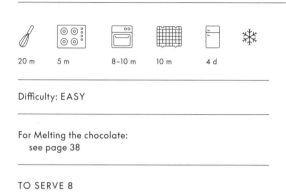

20 m   5 m   8–10 m   10 m   4 d

Difficulty: EASY

For Melting the chocolate:
    see page 38

TO SERVE 8

FOR THE MADELEINES
4 ounces/1 stick/120 g unsalted butter,
    plus extra for greasing
3½ ounces/100 g 54% dark chocolate
2 eggs
3½ ounces/scant ½ cup/100 g superfine (caster) sugar
3 ounces/⅔ cup/80 g type "00" flour or all-purpose
    (plain) flour
1 level teaspoon baking powder
1 teaspoon ground cinnamon
Pinch of salt
Confectioners' (icing) sugar, for dusting (optional)

EQUIPMENT NEEDED
Madeleine pan (tin)
Chef's knife
Chopping board
Bain-marie or double boiler
Mixing bowl
Electric whisk
Strainer (sieve)
Silicone spatula
Cooling rack
Fine-mesh strainer (sieve)

Preheat the oven to 410°F/210°C/190°C Fan/Gas 7 and grease the madeleine pan (tin) with butter.

Finely chop the chocolate and cut the butter into small cubes. Melt together in a bain-marie or double boiler, then set aside to cool to room temperature.

Break the eggs into a mixing bowl, add the superfine (caster) sugar, and beat using an electric whisk until light and fluffy. Add the sifted flour, baking powder, cinnamon, and a pinch of salt and mix together using a silicone spatula. Add the chocolate and butter mixture and gently fold the mixture to incorporate.

Fill the madeleine pan with batter to two-thirds full, rest for 10 minutes, then bake in the preheated oven for 8–10 minutes, until cooked through. Leave the madeleines to cool in the pan for a few minutes before transferring to a cooling rack to cool completely. Dust with confectioners' (icing) sugar before serving, if desired.

VARIATION
You can make these madeleines even more chocolatey by dipping their plain side in 3½ ounces/100 g melted 60% dark chocolate, then leaving it to harden at room temperature before serving.

COOKIES WITH MASCARPONE AND BLUEBERRIES

Biscottini al cioccolato al latte con mascarpone e mirtilli

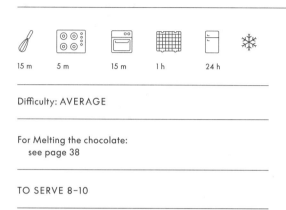

15 m   5 m   15 m   1 h   24 h

Difficulty: AVERAGE

For Melting the chocolate:
  see page 38

TO SERVE 8-10

FOR THE COOKIES
2 ounces/55 g milk chocolate
4 ounces/1 stick/120 g unsalted butter, at room temperature
2 ounces/scant ½ cup/50 g golden superfine (caster) sugar
Pinch of salt
1 egg yolk
3½ ounces/¾ cup/100 g type "00" flour or all-purpose (plain) flour
2 ounces/½ cup/50 g unsweetened cocoa powder
2 ounces/scant ⅓ cup/50 g brown sugar

FOR THE FROSTING (ICING)
5 ounces/¾ cup/150 g mascarpone cheese
1½ ounces/⅓ cup/40 g confectioners' (icing) sugar
3½ ounces/⅔ cup/100 g fresh blueberries

EQUIPMENT NEEDED
Baking sheet
Parchment paper
Chef's knife
Chopping board
Bain-marie or double boiler
Mixing bowls
Electric whisk
Silicone spatula
Strainer (sieve)
Plastic wrap (cling film)
Wooden spoon
Cooling rack
Pastry (piping) bag
½ inch/1-cm plain piping tip (nozzle)

Preheat the oven to 350°F/180°C/160°C Fan/Gas 4 and line the baking sheet with parchment paper.

Finely chop the chocolate and melt in a bain-marie or double boiler. Place the butter in a mixing bowl, add the golden superfine (caster) sugar, and beat together with an electric whisk until creamy. Add a pinch of salt, the egg yolk, and the melted chocolate and mix with a silicone spatula to combine. Add the sifted flour and cocoa powder, knead to incorporate and form a dough. Shape the dough into a ball, cover in plastic wrap (cling film), and rest in the refrigerator for 1 hour.

Place the brown sugar in a small shallow dish. Take a small piece of dough and roll into a ball with a diameter of about 1¼ inches/ 3 cm. Roll each dough ball in the brown sugar and place on the lined baking sheet, spacing them about 1¼ inches/3 cm apart to allow for them to spread during baking. Press into the center of each dough ball with your index finger to make a dimple and bake the cookies (biscuits) in the preheated oven for 10 minutes. Remove the baking sheet from the oven and check if the cookies are ready. If the dimple in the cookies has risen, press lightly with the handle of a wooden spoon to create an indent, and bake for a further 5 minutes. Transfer the cookies to a cooling rack to cool completely.

To make the frosting (icing), place the mascarpone in a mixing bowl with the confectioners' sugar and whisk together until light and fluffy. Fit a pastry (piping) bag with a plain piping tip (nozzle), and fill with the mascarpone frosting. Fill the dimples on the cookies with piped frosting. Wash and dry the blueberries and arrange on the mascarpone frosting. Serve immediately.

COFFEE, ORANGE, AND CHOCOLATE SPICED COOKIES

Biscottini pepati al caffè, arancia e cioccolato

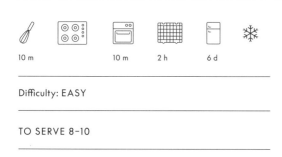

10 m   10 m   2 h   6 d

Difficulty: EASY

TO SERVE 8–10

FOR THE COOKIES
7 ounces/1¾ sticks/200 g unsalted butter,
    at room temperature
Pinch of salt
½ teaspoon ground allspice
4¾ ounces/generous 1 cup/140 g confectioners' (icing) sugar
Grated zest of 1 unwaxed orange
7 ounces/1⅔ cups/200 g type "00" flour or all-purpose
    (plain) flour
2 ounces/½ cup/50 g unsweetened cocoa powder
1½ teaspoons instant coffee

EQUIPMENT NEEDED
Baking sheet
Parchment paper
Mixing bowl
Zester
Electric whisk
Strainer (sieve)
Chef's knife
Embossed rolling pin

Preheat the oven to 350°F/180°C/160°C Fan/Gas 4 and line the baking sheet with parchment paper.

Place the butter in a mixing bowl, add a pinch of salt, the ground allspice, confectioners' (icing) sugar, and orange zest, and beat together using an electric whisk until creamy. Sift in the flour and cocoa powder, add the coffee, and mix to incorporate and form a dough.

Place the dough on a sheet of parchment paper and roll inside the parchment to form a cylinder with a diameter measuring 1¼ inches/3 cm. Wrap the dough in the same parchment sheet and chill in the refrigerator for at least 2 hours.

Remove the parchment, cut the roll into ¼-inch/5-mm-thick slices, and shape into balls. Flatten each ball of dough with the embossed rolling pin, and place the cookies (biscuits) on the lined baking sheet spacing them about 1¼ inches/3 cm apart to allow for them to spread during baking. Bake in the preheated oven for 10 minutes. Remove from the oven and rest on the baking sheet for 5 minutes, then transfer to a cooling rack to cool completely. Serve the cookies with coffee.

CHOCOLATE AND BROWNED BUTTER MINI FINANCIERS

Mini financier al cioccolato con burro nocciola

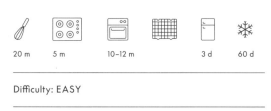

20 m   5 m   10–12 m   3 d   60 d

Difficulty: EASY

TO SERVE 8–10

FOR THE FINANCIERS

4 ounces/1 stick/120 g unsalted butter, plus extra for greasing
1½ ounces/½ cup/40 g sliced (flaked) almonds
1½ ounces/⅓ cup/40 g type "00" flour or all-purpose (plain) flour
1 ounce/¼ cup/30 g unsweetened cocoa powder
5 ounces/1¼ cups/150 g confectioners' (icing) sugar
Pinch of salt
4 ounces/1¼ cups/125 g almond meal (ground almonds)
4 ounces/125 g egg whites

EQUIPMENT NEEDED

Mini financier pan (tin) with 12 rectangular cavities
    measuring 1 × 3 inches/2.5 × 8 cm
Mixing bowls
Small saucepan
Strainer (sieve)
Silicone spatula
Paper towels
Cooling rack

Preheat the oven to 350°F/180°C/160°C Fan/Gas 4 and grease the financier pan (tin) with butter.

Place the sliced (flaked) almonds in a bowl of cold water to soak and set aside. Place the butter in a small saucepan and heat until it turns a nutty brown color. Remove from the heat and leave to cool to room temperature. Sift the flour, cocoa powder, and confectioners' (icing) sugar into a mixing bowl. Add a pinch of salt, the almond meal (ground almonds), and the egg whites and mix with a silicone spatula to incorporate. Pour in the browned butter and mix to a smooth batter.

Fill the financier pan with the batter, then drain the sliced almonds, pat dry with paper towels, and place a couple on each cake.

Bake in the preheated oven for 10–12 minutes, until cooked through. Remove from the oven and leave to cool in the pan for a few minutes, then transfer to a cooling rack to cool completely.

DOUBLE CHOCOLATE COOKIES

Cookies ai due cioccolati

20 m   10–12 m   3 d

Difficulty: EASY

TO SERVE 6

FOR THE COOKIES
13 ounces/2¾ cups/360 g type "00" flour or all-purpose
    (plain) flour
1 teaspoon baking soda (bicarbonate of soda)
½ teaspoon baking powder
1 vanilla bean (pod)
8 ounces/2 sticks/225 g unsalted butter, at room temperature
7 ounces/generous 1 cup/200 g brown sugar
Pinch of salt
2 large eggs
6¼ ounces/180 g 70% dark chocolate
5 ounces/150 g gianduja

EQUIPMENT NEEDED
Baking sheet
Parchment paper
Strainer (sieve)
Mixing bowls
Paring knife
Electric whisk
Silicone spatula
Chef's knife
Chopping board
Large ice cream scoop
Cooling rack

Preheat the oven to 350°F/180°C/160°C Fan/Gas 4 and line
the baking sheet with parchment paper.

Sift the flour, baking soda (bicarbonate of soda), and baking
powder into a mixing bowl. Split the vanilla bean (pod) lengthwise
using a sharp paring knife, and scrape out the seeds. Place the
butter, sugar, a pinch of salt, and the vanilla seeds in a separate
mixing bowl and beat using an electric whisk until fluffy. Add
the eggs, one at a time, alternating with a tablespoon of the dry
ingredients. Stir in the remaining dry ingredients with a silicone
spatula to make the cookie (biscuit) dough.

Coarsely chop the two types of chocolate and fold into the dough.
Use a large ice cream scoop to scoop a ball of cookie dough and
arrange on the lined baking sheet. Repeat until all the dough is
used up, spacing the balls 1¼–1½ inches/3–4 cm apart to allow
for them to spread during baking. Bake in the preheated oven for
10–12 minutes until they turn light golden. Remove from the oven
and leave the cookies to rest for a few minutes, then transfer to
a cooling rack to cool completely.

CHOCOLATE LADYFINGERS

Savoiardi al cioccolato

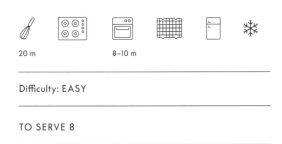

20 m   8–10 m

Difficulty: EASY

TO SERVE 8

FOR THE LADYFINGERS
3 eggs
Pinch of salt
3 ounces/⅓ cup/80 g superfine (caster) sugar
¾ ounce/scant ¼ cup/25 g type "00" flour or all-purpose (plain) flour
¾ ounce/2 heaping tablespoons/20 g unsweetened cocoa powder
1¾ ounces/45 g potato starch
Confectioners' (icing) sugar, for dusting

EQUIPMENT NEEDED
Baking sheet
Parchment paper
Mixing bowls
Electric whisk
Silicone spatula
Strainer (sieve)
Pastry (piping) bag
½-inch/1-cm plain piping tip (nozzle)

Preheat the oven to 400°F/200°C/180°C Fan/Gas 6 and line the baking sheet with parchment paper.

Separate the eggs and place the whites in a clean grease-free mixing bowl with a pinch of salt. Whisk the egg whites using an electric whisk, while gradually adding the sugar.

In a separate bowl, beat the egg yolks with a fork, then slowly pour into the whisked whites, and fold in using a silicone spatula. Add the sifted flour, cocoa powder and potato starch, and fold into the mixture.

Fit a pastry (piping) bag with a plain piping tip (nozzle), fill with the batter, and pipe uniform lines 4 inches/10 cm long, spaced 1¼–1½ inches/3–4 cm apart to allow for them to spread during baking, on the lined baking sheet.

Dust with a little confectioners' (icing) sugar and rest for 5 minutes, then dust again and bake in the preheated oven for 8–10 minutes. Remove from the oven and leave the ladyfingers to cool completely on the baking sheet before detaching from the parchment. Store in an airtight container for up to 8 days.

CHOCOLATE AND PINEAPPLE OATMEAL COOKIES

Biscotti di fiocchi d'avena con cioccolato e ananas

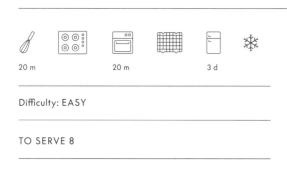

20 m   20 m   3 d

Difficulty: EASY

TO SERVE 8

FOR THE COOKIES
6¼ ounces/180 g 70% dark chocolate
3 ounces/80 g dried pineapple
4 ounces/1 stick/120 g unsalted butter, at room temperature
4¼ ounces/scant ¾ cup/130 g brown sugar
1 egg
Pinch of salt
4¾ ounces/generous 1 cup/140 g type "1" flour
½ teaspoon baking powder
3 ounces/⅔ cup/80 g steel-cut oats (coarse oatmeal)

EQUIPMENT NEEDED
Baking sheet
Parchment paper
Chef's knife
Chopping board
Mixing bowl
Wooden spoon or hand whisk
Strainer (sieve)
Ice cream scoop
Cooling rack

Preheat the oven to 350°F/180°C/160°C Fan/Gas 4 and line the baking sheet with parchment paper.

Roughly chop the chocolate and cut the dried pineapple into small pieces. Place the butter in a mixing bowl, add the sugar, and beat together with a wooden spoon or hand whisk until creamy. Beat in the egg and a pinch of salt.

Add the sifted flour and baking powder, the oats, chocolate, and dried pineapple, and mix to make the cookie (biscuit) dough.

Use the ice cream scoop to scoop a ball of cookie dough and arrange on the lined baking sheet. Repeat until all the dough is used up, spacing the balls 1¼–1½ inches/3–4cm apart to allow for them to spread during baking. Bake in the preheated oven for 20 minutes until they turn light golden. Remove from the oven and leave the cookies to rest for a few minutes, then transfer to a cooling rack to cool completely.

TIPS AND TRICKS
Because the dough spreads as it bakes, space the mounds of cookie dough at least 1¼–1½ inches/3–4 cm apart on the baking sheet.

DULCE DE LECHE BROWNIES

Brownie al dulce de leche

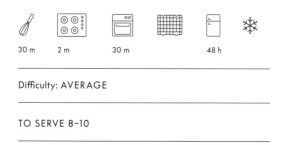

30 m   2 m   30 m   48 h

Difficulty: AVERAGE

TO SERVE 8–10

FOR THE BROWNIES
7 ounces/200 g 80% dark chocolate
7 ounces/1¾ sticks/200 g unsalted butter
14 ounces/1⅓ cups/400 g dulce de leche
Pinch of salt
4 ounces/½ cup/120 g superfine (caster) sugar
4 eggs
4¼ ounces/generous 1 cup/130 g type "00" flour or
    all-purpose (plain) flour
2 ounces/½ cup/50 g unsweetened cocoa powder

EQUIPMENT NEEDED
9-inch/23-cm square baking pan (tin)
Parchment paper
Chef's knife
Chopping board
Saucepan
Silicone spatula
Mixing bowls
Electric whisk
Strainer (sieve)
Palette knife
Disposable pastry (piping) bag or cone

Preheat the oven to 350°F/180°C/160°C Fan/Gas 4 and line the baking pan (tin) with parchment paper.

Coarsely chop the chocolate. Melt the butter in a saucepan over a very low heat, then remove from the heat, add the coarsely chopped chocolate, and stir with a silicone spatula until the chocolate has melted. In a separate bowl, mix 6¼ ounces/⅔ cup/180 g dulce de leche with a pinch of salt and set aside.

Pour the remaining dulce de leche into another bowl, add the sugar and eggs, and beat together using an electric whisk. Add the butter and chocolate mixture, and beat it to combine, then sift in the flour and cocoa powder, stirring to incorporate.

Pour half the batter into the baking pan (tin), then pour over the reserved salted dulce de leche, spreading it evenly over the batter with a palette knife. Cover with the remaining brownie batter, spreading it evenly, without mixing the layers. Fill a disposable pastry (piping) bag with the remaining dulce de leche, cut off the tip, and pipe over the top of the batter in a continuous zigzag pattern. Bake in the preheated oven for 30 minutes. Remove from the oven and leave to cool completely in the pan, then cut into cubes.

DARK AND RUBY CHOCOLATE KISSES

Baci al cioccolato fondente e ruby

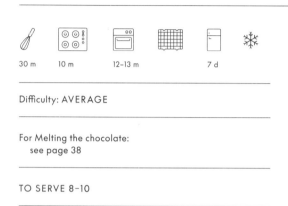

30 m   10 m   12–13 m   7 d

Difficulty: AVERAGE

For Melting the chocolate:
see page 38

TO SERVE 8–10

FOR THE KISSES
2 ounces/60 g 70% dark chocolate
6¾ ounces/1½ cups/190 g type "00" flour or all-purpose (plain) flour
2¼ ounces/generous ½ cup/60 g unsweetened cocoa powder
8 ounces/2 sticks/220 g unsalted butter, at room temperature
4 ounces/scant ⅔ cup/130 g superfine (caster) sugar
Pinch of salt
1 egg
7 ounces/200 g ruby chocolate

EQUIPMENT NEEDED
Baking sheet
Parchment paper
Chef's knife
Chopping board
Bain-marie or double boiler
Strainer (sieve)
Mixing bowls
Hand or electric whisk
Silicone spatula
Pastry (piping) bag
Large star piping tip (nozzle)
Cooling rack

Preheat the oven to 350°F/180°C/160°C Fan/Gas 4 and line the baking sheet with parchment paper.

Finely chop the dark chocolate and melt in a bain-marie or double boiler. Sift the flour and cocoa powder into a mixing bowl. Place the butter in a separate bowl, add the sugar and a pinch of salt, and beat together with a hand or electric whisk until fluffy, then beat in the egg until incorporated. Add the melted dark chocolate, stirring with a silicone spatula to combine, then add the sifted flour and cocoa, 1 tablespoon at a time, stirring after each addition.

Fit the pastry (piping) bag with a star piping tip (nozzle), fill with the cookie (biscuit) dough, and pipe the 'kisses' onto the lined baking sheet.

Bake in the preheated oven for 12–13 minutes. Remove from the oven and leave the cookies to rest for a few minutes before transferring to a cooling rack to cool completely.

Finely chop the ruby chocolate and melt in a bain-marie. Transfer to a bowl and leave to cool to room temperature.

Dip the flat side of half the cookies in the ruby chocolate and sandwich together with the remaining cookies. Drizzle any remaining melted chocolate over the kisses and set aside for the chocolate to harden before serving.

WHOOPIE PIES WITH WHITE CHOCOLATE BUTTERCREAM

Whoopie pie al cioccolato bianco

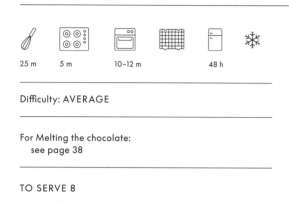

25 m   5 m   10–12 m   48 h

Difficulty: AVERAGE

For Melting the chocolate:
   see page 38

TO SERVE 8

FOR THE WHOOPIE PIES
9 ounces/2 cups/250 g type "00" flour or all-purpose
   (plain) flour
1 heaping teaspoon baking soda (bicarbonate of soda)
2½ ounces/⅔ cup/70 g unsweetened cocoa powder
1 vanilla bean (pod)
3¾ ounces/1 stick/110 g unsalted butter, at room
   temperature
5 ounces/⅔ cup/150 g superfine (caster) sugar
1 large egg
Pinch of salt
4¾ fl oz/scant ⅔ cup/140 ml whole (full-fat) milk
A few drops of lemon juice

FOR THE BUTTERCREAM
3 ounces/80 g white chocolate
3¾ ounces/1 stick/110 g unsalted butter
9 ounces/2 cups/250 g confectioners' (icing) sugar

EQUIPMENT NEEDED
Baking sheet
Parchment paper
Strainer (sieve)
Mixing bowls
Paring knife
Electric whisk
Ice cream scoop
Cooling rack
Chef's knife
Chopping board
Bain-marie or double boiler
Disposable pastry (piping) bag or cone

Preheat the oven to 350°F/180°C/160°C Fan/Gas 4 and line the baking sheet with parchment paper.

Sift the flour, baking soda (bicarbonate of soda), and cocoa powder into a mixing bowl. Split the vanilla bean (pod) lengthwise with a sharp paring knife and scrape out the seeds. Place the butter, sugar, and vanilla seeds in a separate bowl and beat together using an electric whisk until pale and fluffy. Add the egg, the sifted dry ingredients, and a pinch of salt and mix to incorporate. Sour the milk with 2–3 drops of lemon juice and stir into the dough mix.

Use the ice cream scoop to scoop a ball of dough and arrange on the lined baking sheet. Repeat until all the dough is used up, spacing the balls 1¼–1½ inches/3–4cm apart to allow for them to spread during baking. Bake in the preheated oven for 10–12 minutes, until cooked through. Remove from the oven and leave to rest on the baking sheet for a few minutes, then transfer to a cooling rack to cool completely.

To make the buttercream, finely chop the white chocolate, melt in a bain-marie or double boiler, and leave to cool a little. Place the butter in a mixing bowl and beat with an electric whisk, adding the confectioners' (icing) sugar 1 tablespoon at a time. Reduce the mixer speed to low, add the melted chocolate, and beat for 3–4 minutes. Fill a disposable pastry (piping) bag with the buttercream and cut off the tip. Pipe the buttercream over the flat bottom of half of the cookies (biscuits) and sandwich together with the remaining cookies.

CHOCOLATE CANDIES

ORANGE AND CHILI CHOCOLATE BONBONS

Cioccolatini all'arancia e peperoncino

30 m   10 m   4 h 10 m   7 d

Difficulty: ADVANCED

For Melting the chocolate:
   see page 38
For the Ganache for Bonbons and Truffles:
   see page 74
For Tempering the chocolate:
   see page 40
For the Chocolate Shells:
   see page 44

TO SERVE 10

FOR THE BONBONS
10½ ounces/300 g 75% dark chocolate
5 fl oz/scant ⅔ cup/150 ml heavy (whipping) cream
1½ ounces/40 g candied orange peel
Pinch of chili powder
14 ounces/400 g 60% dark chocolate

EQUIPMENT NEEDED
Chef's knife
Chopping board
Bain-marie or double boiler
Measuring cup or jug
Small saucepan
Silicone spatula
Kitchen thermometer
Marble board
Metal spatula or palette knife
Polycarbonate chocolate bonbon mold
Cooling rack
Metal tray
Ladle
Disposable pastry (piping) bag or cone

Finely chop the 75% dark chocolate and melt in a bain-marie or double boiler. Pour the cream into a small saucepan and bring to a simmer. Remove from the heat and drizzle the warm cream into the melted chocolate, stirring continuously with a silicone spatula until incorporated. Finely chop the candied orange peel and add to the bowl with a pinch of chili powder. Stir to combine, then refrigerate in the bowl for 4 hours until the mixture sets.

Temper the 60% dark chocolate following the basic technique and pour into the bonbon mold. Tilt the mold in all directions to cover the bottom and sides of the cavities following the basic technique to make the chocolate shells. Invert the mold to remove the excess chocolate and place the excess in a clean container to reuse. Set the shells aside to set.

When the chocolate shells have hardened, fill a disposable pastry (piping) bag with the chocolate and orange ganache and cut off the tip. Use the pastry bag to fill each shell two-thirds full with the ganache. Pour tempered chocolate over the chocolates to seal the filling inside following the basic technique. Chill the mold in the refrigerator for about 10 minutes for the bonbons to set, then tap the mold against the work surface to release the bonbons.

MISTAKES TO AVOID
When tempering the chocolate, do not stir it with a whisk. Only use a silicone spatula so that air is not incorporated into the melted chocolate, preventing the formation of bubbles.

CARAMEL-FILLED CHOCOLATE CUPS

Ciotoline di cioccolato al caramello

30 m   20 m   48 h   6 d

Difficulty: AVERAGE

For Melting the chocolate:
  see page 38
For Tempering the chocolate:
  see page 40
For the Chocolate Shells:
  see page 44

TO SERVE 6

FOR THE CHOCOLATE CUPS
7 ounces/200 g 85% dark chocolate
3½ ounces/½ cup/100 g brown sugar
1¾ fl oz/scant ¼ cup/50 ml heavy (whipping) cream
3 ounces/¾ stick/80 g unsalted butter

EQUIPMENT NEEDED
Bain-marie or double boiler
Kitchen thermometer
Marble board
Metal spatula or palette knife
Silicone spatula
Polycarbonate chocolate bonbon mold with
  2-inch/5-cm-diameter and ½-inch/1-cm-deep
  dome cavities
Cooling rack
Ladle
Saucepans
Measuring cup or jug
Disposable pastry (piping) bag or cone

Temper the chocolate following the basic technique and pour into the dome mold. Tilt the mold in all directions to cover the bottom and sides of the cavities following the basic technique to make the chocolate shells. Invert the mold to remove the excess chocolate and place the excess in a clean container to reuse. Set the shells aside to set.

When the chocolate has hardened, unmold the chocolate cups by inverting the mold and gently tapping it on the work surface.

Place the sugar in a saucepan with 2 tablespoons water and cook over a high heat until an amber caramel forms. Pour the cream into a separate saucepan and bring to a simmer, then drizzle into the caramel, stirring with a silicone spatula to combine. Take care not to scald yourself as the caramel will be very hot. Continue to cook for 2–3 minutes. Meanwhile, cut the butter into small cubes. Remove the caramel from the heat, stir in the butter, and leave to cool to room temperature.

Fill a disposable pastry (piping) bag with the caramel, cut off the tip, and fill half of the chocolate cups with the caramel. Use the remaining chocolate cups as lids, placing them over the caramel-filled cups.

TIPS AND TRICKS
When the chocolate shells have hardened and it is time to remove them from the molds, do not touch them with your bare hands. Wear a pair of disposable gloves to avoid heating the chocolate and leaving fingerprints on the smooth, shiny surface.

RUBY CHOCOLATE AND GANACHE LOLLIPOPS

"Lecca lecca" di cioccolato ruby con ganache

| 25 m | 10 m | | | 1 h 30 m | 3 d | |

Difficulty: AVERAGE

For Melting the chocolate:
   see page 38
For Tempering the chocolate:
   see page 40
For the Ganache for Bonbons and Truffles:
   see page 74

TO SERVE 10

FOR THE LOLLIPOPS
14 ounces/400 g ruby chocolate

FOR THE GANACHE
7½ ounces/215 g 70% dark chocolate
4 fl oz/½ cup/120 ml heavy (whipping) cream
2 ounces/½ stick/55 g unsalted butter, at room temperature
2–3 drops food-grade bergamot essential oil, for flavoring

EQUIPMENT NEEDED
Bain-marie or double boiler
Kitchen thermometer
Marble board
Metal spatula or palette knife
Silicone spatula
Disposable pastry (piping) bags or cones
2 large acetate sheets
Chef's knife
Chopping board
Mixing bowl
Measuring cup or jug
Saucepan
10 lollipop sticks

Temper the ruby chocolate following the basic technique. Fill a disposable pastry (piping) bag with the tempered chocolate, cut off the tip, and pipe 20 disks measuring 2-inch/5-cm in diameter onto two acetate sheets. Set aside to harden at room temperature, then carefully peel the disks off the acetate.

To make the ganache, finely chop the chocolate and place in a mixing bowl. Pour the cream into a small saucepan and heat to 185°F/85°C, then pour into the chocolate. Stir with a silicone spatula until the temperature of the ganache falls to 95°F/35°C. Cut the butter into small cubes and add to the ganache mixture with a few drops of bergamot oil. Mix to combine and chill in the refrigerator for 1 hour.

Fill a disposable pastry bag with the ganache, cut off the tip, and pipe ganache onto half of the ruby chocolate disks. Lay the lollipop sticks on the ganache and sandwich together with the remaining ruby chocolate disks. Press lightly to seal, then rest for 30 minutes in the refrigerator before serving.

TIPS AND TRICKS
To make disks of uniform size, draw circles on a sheet of parchment paper, lay the acetate sheet on top, and use the circles as a template.

Decorate one side of the lollipops with piped swirls of melted chocolate of your choice, if desired.

WHITE CHOCOLATE AND RASPBERRY BONBONS

Cioccolatini bianchi con ganache ai lamponi

30 m   10 m   4 h 10 m   7 d

Difficulty: ADVANCED

For the Ganache for Bonbons and Truffles:
  see page 74
For Melting the chocolate:
  see page 38
For Tempering the chocolate:
  see page 40
For the Chocolate Shells:
  see page 44

TO SERVE 10

FOR THE BONBONS
5 ounces/scant 1¼ cups/150 g fresh raspberries
1 pound 9 ounces/700 g white chocolate
6¼ fl oz/¾ cup/180 ml heavy (whipping) cream

EQUIPMENT NEEDED
Mixing bowls
Immersion (stick) blender
Strainer (sieve)
Chef's knife
Chopping board
Bain-marie or double boiler
Measuring cup or jug
Small saucepan
Silicone spatula
Kitchen thermometer
Marble board
Metal spatula or palette knife
Polycarbonate chocolate bonbon mold
Cooling rack
Metal tray
Ladle
Disposable pastry (piping) bag or cone

Puree the raspberries using an immersion (stick) blender then filter through a strainer (sieve) to remove the seeds, and set aside. Finely chop 10½ ounces/300 g of the chocolate and melt in a bain-marie or double boiler. Pour the cream into a small saucepan and bring to a simmer, then drizzle into the melted chocolate, stirring with a silicone spatula to combine. Stir in the raspberry pulp and leave the ganache to cool to room temperature, then refrigerate for 4 hours until set.

When the ganache has set, temper the remaining chocolate following the basic technique and pour into the bonbon mold. Tilt the mold in all directions to cover the bottom and sides of the cavities following the basic technique to make the chocolate shells. Invert the mold to remove the excess chocolate and place the excess in a clean container to reuse. Set the shells aside to set.

When the chocolate shells have hardened, fill a disposable pastry (piping) bag with the chocolate and raspberry ganache and cut off the tip. Use the pastry bag to fill each shell two-thirds full with the ganache. Pour tempered chocolate over the chocolates to seal the filling inside following the basic technique. Chill the mold in the refrigerator for about 10 minutes for the bonbons to set, then tap the mold against the work surface to release the bonbons.

MENDIANTS WITH NUTS AND CANDIED FRUIT

Mendiant alla frutta secca e candita

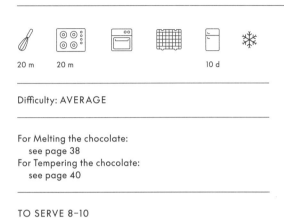

20 m   20 m   10 d

Difficulty: AVERAGE

For Melting the chocolate:
  see page 38
For Tempering the chocolate:
  see page 40

TO SERVE 8–10

FOR THE MENDIANTS
3½ ounces/100 g white chocolate
3½ ounces/100 g ruby chocolate
3½ ounces/100 g 60% dark chocolate
3½ ounces/100 g milk chocolate
1 ounce/scant ¼ cup/30 g roasted hazelnuts
½ ounce/10 g cocoa beans
1½ ounces/40 g candied orange peel
¾ ounce/scant ¼ cup/20 g goji berries

EQUIPMENT NEEDED
Bain-marie or double boiler
Kitchen thermometer
Marble board
Metal spatula or palette knife
Silicone spatula
4 × squeeze bottles or pastry (piping) bags
Acetate sheets
Chef's knife
Chopping board
Mortar and pestle

Temper the four types of chocolate following the basic technique. Fill a squeeze bottle with one of each type of chocolate and pipe out disks measuring 1½–2 inches/4–5 cm in diameter onto the acetate sheets.

Coarsely chop the hazelnuts, crush the cocoa beans using a mortar and pestle, and julienne the candied orange peel.

While the chocolate is still soft, arrange the goji berries on top of the ruby chocolate, the hazelnuts on the white chocolate, the crushed cocoa beans on the milk chocolate, and the candied orange peel on the dark chocolate. Set aside for the chocolate to harden fully, then carefully peel off the acetate sheets.

SESAME BRITTLE AND GANACHE CANDIES

Cioccolatini morbidi con croccantini al sesamo

30 m 10 m 10 m 2 h 7 d

Difficulty: AVERAGE

For Melting the chocolate:
   see page 38
For the Ganache for Bonbons and Truffles:
   see page 74

TO SERVE 10

FOR THE CANDIES
3 ounces/½ cup/80 g black sesame seeds,
   plus extra to garnish (optional)
¾ ounce/1 tablespoon/20 g acacia honey
3 ounces/⅓ cup/80 g superfine (caster) sugar
10½ ounces/300 g 85% dark chocolate
¾ ounce/1½ tablespoons/20 g unsalted butter
4 fl oz/½ cup/120 ml heavy (whipping) cream

EQUIPMENT NEEDED
Baking sheet
Saucepans
Silicone spatula
Parchment paper
Rolling pin
Chef's knife
Chopping board
Bain-marie or double boiler
Measuring cup or jug
Mixing bowl
Plastic wrap (cling film)
Electric whisk
Pastry (piping) bag
⅝-inch/1.5-cm plain piping tip (nozzle)

Preheat the oven to 325°F/160°C/140°C Fan/Gas 3.

Spread the sesame seeds on a baking sheet and toast in the oven for 10 minutes. Place the honey and sugar in a small saucepan and cook until you have a golden caramel. Add the sesame seeds and stir to combine. Lay a sheet of parchment paper over a work surface and pour the caramel onto the center of the paper. Cover with a second sheet of paper and use a rolling pin to roll out the caramel to a thickness of about ¹⁄₁₆ inch/2 mm. Take care not to burn yourself as the caramel will be very hot. Leave the caramel to cool and harden fully, then remove the parchment paper and cut the sesame brittle into squares about ¾ inch/2 cm wide.

While the brittle is cooling, make the ganache. Finely chop the chocolate and melt in a bain-marie or double boiler with the butter. Pour the cream into a saucepan and bring to a simmer, then drizzle into the melted chocolate, a third at a time, stirring with a silicone spatula to combine. Leave the ganache to cool to room temperature, then cover with plastic wrap (cling film) and refrigerate for 2 hours.

Whisk the ganache with an electric whisk for 1 minute until it becomes paler. Fill a pastry (piping) bag fitted with a plain piping tip (nozzle) and pipe a hazelnut-sized mound of ganache onto each sesame brittle square. Decorate, if desired, with black sesame seeds.

DARK CHOCOLATE AND GINGER BONBONS

Cioccolatini fondenti allo zenzero

30 m   15 m   4 h   7 d

Difficulty: ADVANCED

For Melting the chocolate:
   see page 38
For Tempering the chocolate:
   see page 40
For Enrobing:
   see page 42
For Decorating Bonbons:
   see page 64

TO SERVE 10

FOR THE GANACHE
2½ ounces/scant ⅓ cup/70 g superfine (caster) sugar
5½ fl oz/⅔ cup/160 ml heavy (whipping) cream
1 teaspoon acacia honey
8 ounces/225 g milk chocolate
¾ ounce/1½ tablespoons/20 g unsalted butter,
   at room temperature
½ teaspoon ground ginger

FOR THE BASE
5 ounces/150 g 70% dark chocolate

FOR ENROBING
14 ounces/400 g 70% dark chocolate

EQUIPMENT NEEDED
Saucepans
Measuring cup or jug
Chef's knife
Chopping board
Silicone spatula
Kitchen thermometer
8-inch/20-cm square baking pan (tin)
Plastic wrap (cling film)
Palette knife
Bain-marie or double boiler
Acetate sheet
Marble board
Chocolate dipping fork

To make the ganache, place the sugar in a saucepan, add 2 tablespoons water, and cook until an amber caramel forms. Meanwhile, pour the cream into a separate saucepan, add the honey, and bring to a simmer. Finely chop the milk chocolate and cut the butter into small cubes.

When the caramel is ready, remove from the heat and slowly drizzle in the cream, stirring with a silicone spatula to combine. Take care not to scald yourself as the caramel will be very hot. Add the chocolate and stir until the chocolate has melted. When the temperature of the mixture has cooled to 95°F/35°C, stir in the butter and ginger. Line the square baking pan (tin) with plastic wrap (cling film) and fill with the ganache. Level the surface using a palette knife and tap the pan against the work surface to remove any air bubbles. Freeze for 2 hours.

To make the base, finely chop the 5 ounces/150 g dark chocolate and melt in a bain-marie. Remove the ganache from the pan, turn upside down to remove the plastic wrap, and spread the melted dark chocolate over the top, using a palette knife to spread it evenly. Level the surface and return the ganache to the freezer for a further 2 hours.

Transfer the ganache to an acetate sheet with the chocolate base facing downward. Heat a knife under hot running water, wipe dry, and cut the ganache into rectangles measuring 1¼ × ¾ inches/3 × 2 cm.

Temper the 14 ounces/400 g dark chocolate for enrobing following the basic technique. Use the dipping fork to enrobe the chocolate rectangles in the tempered chocolate following the basic technique and use the same fork to decorate the bonbons with parallel lines following the basic technique.

CHOCOLATE, BEER, AND ACACIA HONEY TRUFFLES

Tartufi alla birra e miele d'acacia

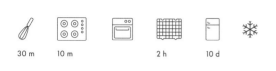

30 m   10 m   2 h   10 d

Difficulty: AVERAGE

For Melting the chocolate:
   see page 38
For Tempering the chocolate:
   see page 40
For Enrobing:
   see page 42
For Decorating Bonbons:
   see page 64

TO SERVE 8

FOR THE TRUFFLES
5 ounces/150 g 60% dark chocolate
¾ ounce/1 heaping tablespoon/25 g acacia honey
4 fl oz/½ cup/120 ml heavy (whipping) cream
½ ounce/1 tablespoon/15 g unsalted butter
2 tablespoons/30 ml beer

FOR ENROBING
9 ounces/250 g 60% dark chocolate

EQUIPMENT NEEDED
Chef's knife
Chopping board
Bain-marie or double boiler
Measuring cup or jug
Silicone spatula
Baking sheet
Parchment paper
Electric whisk
Kitchen thermometer
Marble board
Metal spatula or palette knife
Chocolate dipping forks
Acetate sheets

To make the ganache for the truffles, finely chop the chocolate and place in the bowl of a bain-marie or double boiler. Add the honey, cream, butter, and beer, and heat in the bain-marie, stirring gently with a silicone spatula until the chocolate has melted and all the ingredients are incorporated. Set aside to cool in the refrigerator for 2 hours.

Line the baking sheet with parchment paper. Whisk the ganache with an electric whisk until thick, then use two teaspoons to shape hazelnut-sized truffles; avoid touching the ganache with your hands as it will melt. Place each truffle, as it is made, on the lined baking sheet, then place in the refrigerator.

Temper the dark chocolate for enrobing following the basic technique. Enrobe the truffles following the basic technique, dipping one truffle at a time in the tempered chocolate, tapping off the excess, and arranging on an acetate sheet. Decorate with the dipping fork following the basic technique and continue until all the truffles are complete.

TIPS AND TRICKS

Immediately after enrobing each truffle in the tempered chocolate, decorate it as quickly as possible with the appropriate utensil before the chocolate hardens. Otherwise, the decoration will not be perfect.

MINT GANACHE-FILLED CHOCOLATE CUPS

Ciotoline di cioccolata con ganache alla menta

30 m   10 m   2 h 30 m   3 d

Difficulty: ADVANCED

For Melting the chocolate:
    see page 38
For Tempering the chocolate:
    see page 40
For the Chocolate Shells:
    see page 44
For the Ganache for Bonbons and Truffles:
    see page 74
For the Chocolate Shards:
    see page 54

TO SERVE 8–10

FOR THE CHOCOLATE CUPS
7 ounces/200 g 60% dark chocolate
1 bunch of mint
4 fl oz/½ cup/120 ml heavy (whipping) cream
7 ounces/200 g 75% dark chocolate
¾ ounce/scant ¼ stick/25 g unsalted butter
Chocolate Shards, for decoration

EQUIPMENT NEEDED
Bain-marie or double boiler
Kitchen thermometer
Marble board
Metal spatula or palette knife
Silicone spatula
Silicone mold with 1¼-inch/3-cm-diameter
    cylindrical cup cavities
Cooling rack
Metal tray
Ladle
Chef's knife
Chopping board
Saucepans
Measuring cup or jug
Fine-mesh strainer (sieve)
Electric whisk
Mixing bowl
Pastry (piping) bag
Star piping tip (nozzle)

Temper the 60% dark chocolate following the basic technique and pour into the mold. Tilt the mold in all directions to cover the bottom and sides of the cavities following the basic technique to make the chocolate shells. Invert the mold to remove the excess chocolate and place the excess in a clean container to reuse. Set the shells aside to set.

When the chocolate has hardened, unmold the chocolate cups by inverting the mold and gently tapping it on the work surface.

Roughly chop about 30 mint leaves and place in a saucepan with the cream. Bring the cream to a simmer, turn off the heat, and set aside to steep for 30 minutes.

Chop the 75% dark chocolate and melt in a bain-marie or double boiler with the butter. Strain the mint-infused cream through a fine-mesh strainer (sieve), then pour into the melted chocolate, and stir with a silicone spatula to combine. Leave the ganache to cool in the refrigerator for at least 2 hours.

Whisk the ganache with an electric whisk for 1 minute until it becomes paler and fluffy. Fill a pastry (piping) bag fitted with a star piping tip (nozzle) with the ganache and fill the chocolate cups with the mint ganache. Decorate, as desired, with chopped fresh mint leaves and the Chocolate Shards.

CHOCOLATE CUPS FILLED WITH CLEMENTINE MOUSSE

Bicchierini con mousse di clementine al cioccolato

30 m   15 m   24 h

Difficulty: ADVANCED

For Melting the chocolate:
    see page 38
For Tempering the chocolate:
    see page 40
For the Chocolate Shells:
    see page 44
For the Chocolate Shards:
    see page 54

TO SERVE 6

FOR THE CHOCOLATE CUPS
7 ounces/200 g 60% dark chocolate
3⅓ sheets (10 g) gelatin
1½ tablespoons/20 ml Grand Marnier
2 unwaxed clementines
4 egg yolks
4 ounces/scant ⅔ cup/125 g superfine (caster) sugar
8½ fl oz/1 cup/250 ml heavy (whipping) cream
¾ ounce/2 heaping tablespoons/20 g unsweetened
    cocoa powder
Chocolate Shards, for decoration

EQUIPMENT NEEDED
Bain-marie or double boiler
Kitchen thermometer
Marble board
Metal spatula or palette knife
Silicone spatula
Espresso-sized compostable coffee cups
Cooling rack
Metal tray
Ladle
Mixing bowls
Saucepan
Measuring cup or jug
Zester
Juicer
Electric whisk
Fine-mesh strainer (sieve)
Hand whisk

Temper the chocolate following the basic technique and pour into the coffee cups, using them as a mold. Tilt the cups in all directions to cover the bottom and sides following the basic technique to make the chocolate shells. Invert the cups to remove the excess chocolate and place the excess in a clean container to reuse. Set the shells aside to set.

Soak the gelatin sheets in a small bowl of cold water for 10 minutes until they are completely rehydrated and soft, making sure they are fully immersed in the water. Pour the Grand Marnier into a saucepan, add the grated zest and juice of one clementine, and cook for 5 minutes over a low heat.

Place the egg yolks and sugar in a mixing bowl and beat with an electric whisk until pale and fluffy. Strain the boiling clementine juice mixture and drizzle into the beaten eggs, stirring with a hand whisk. Transfer to a saucepan and cook the custard over a low heat, stirring often, until the temperature reaches 185°F/85°C.

Drain the sheets of gelatin and squeeze them with your hands to remove as much water as possible. Add the gelatin to the custard and stir until the gelatin has completely dissolved. Set aside to cool to room temperature. Pour the cream into a clean mixing bowl and whip to soft peaks with an electric whisk, then gently fold into the custard.

Unmold the chocolate cups, and roll in the cocoa powder to coat. Fill the cups with the mousse and top with the grated zest of the remaining clementine and the Chocolate Shards to decorate. Store in the refrigerator before serving.

PRALINE TRUFFLES

Tartufi pralinati

30 m	20 m		2 h	48 h	6 d

Difficulty: AVERAGE

For Melting the chocolate:
  see page 38
For the Ganache for Bonbons and Truffles:
  see page 74

TO SERVE 8–10

FOR THE TRUFFLES
10½ ounces/300 g milk chocolate
1 ounce/¼ stick/30 g unsalted butter
7 fl oz/scant 1 cup/200 ml heavy (whipping) cream
2 ounces/½ cup/50 g unsweetened cocoa powder

FOR THE CANDIED ALMONDS
5 ounces/1 cup/150 g blanched almonds
4 ounces/scant ⅔ cup/130 g superfine (caster) sugar

EQUIPMENT NEEDED
Skillet (frying pan)
Parchment paper
Chef's knife
Chopping board
Bain-marie or double boiler
Measuring cup or jug
Small saucepan
Silicone spatula
Electric whisk
Fine-mesh strainer (sieve)

To make the candied almonds, place the almonds, sugar, and 2 tablespoons water in a skillet (frying pan) and cook over a high heat, stirring often, until the sugar crystallizes and coats the almonds. Lower the heat and continue to cook until the sugar begins to caramelize. Transfer the candied almonds to a sheet of parchment paper, spaced apart, and set aside to cool completely.

Finely chop the milk chocolate and melt in a bain-marie or double boiler with the butter. Pour the cream into a small saucepan and bring to a simmer. Drizzle the hot cream into the melted chocolate, stirring with a silicone spatula to combine. Leave the ganache in the refrigerator to cool for 2 hours.

Whisk the ganache with an electric whisk for 1 minute until it becomes paler and fluffy. Finely chop two-thirds of the candied almonds and mix into the ganache, then take walnut-sized portions of the mixture, shape into uniform balls, and roll in the sifted cocoa powder. Decorate with the remaining almonds and serve.

CHOCOLATE CARAMELS WITH FLEUR DE SEL

Mou al cioccolato con fior di sale

30 m   20 m   12 h 5 m   10 d

Difficulty: AVERAGE

For Melting the chocolate:
   see page 38

TO SERVE 8–10

FOR THE CARAMELS
5 ounces/150 g 85% dark chocolate
¾ ounce/1½ tablespoons/20 g unsalted butter
Pinch of salt
7 ounces/scant 1 cup/200 g superfine (caster) sugar
7 fl oz/scant 1 cup/200 ml heavy (whipping) cream
Pinch of fleur de sel, plus extra for decoration

EQUIPMENT NEEDED
Chef's knife
Chopping board
Bain-marie or double boiler
Saucepans
Measuring cup or jug
Silicone spatula
Kitchen thermometer
7 × 8-inch/18 × 20-cm rectangular baking pan (tin)
Parchment paper

Finely chop the chocolate and melt in a bain-marie or double boiler with the butter and a pinch of salt. Place the sugar in a small saucepan with 2 tablespoons water and heat until you have an amber caramel.

Pour the cream into a small saucepan and bring to a simmer, then drizzle into the caramel, stirring with a silicone spatula to combine. Take care not to scald yourself as the caramel will be very hot. Continue to cook, stirring, until the mixture reaches a temperature of 239°F/115°C. Remove from the heat and leave to stand for 5 minutes, then pour the caramel into the chocolate and stir to incorporate.

Line the baking pan (tin) with parchment paper and pour the mixture into the pan. Sprinkle with a pinch of fleur de sel and refrigerate for 12 hours to harden. Cut the caramel into bite-sized squares, sprinkle with a little extra fleur de sel, and serve.

MISTAKES TO AVOID
Use caution when pouring the boiling cream into the caramel, it may splatter and scald you.

CHOCOLATE BARS WITH DRIED AND CANDIED FRUIT

Tavolette con frutta secca e candita

30 m   15 m   30 m   15 d

Difficulty: AVERAGE

For Melting the chocolate:
    see page 38
For Tempering the chocolate:
    see page 40
For the Chocolate Bars:
    see page 48

TO SERVE 6

FOR THE BARS
¾ ounce/⅛ cup/20 g pistachio nuts
7 ounces/200 g white chocolate
7 ounces/200 g milk chocolate
7 ounces/200 g 60% dark chocolate
3 dried apricots
½ ounce/10 g candied (crystallized) ginger

EQUIPMENT NEEDED
Saucepan
Dish towels (tea towels)
Chef's knife
Small skillet (frying pan)
Bain-marie or double boiler
Kitchen thermometer
Marble board
Metal spatula or palette knife
Silicone spatula
Disposable pastry (piping) bag or cone
Polycarbonate chocolate tablet molds
Cooling rack
Metal tray
Ladle
Chef's knife
Chopping board

Blanch the pistachios in a saucepan of boiling water for 30 seconds, then drain and peel by rubbing between two dish towels (tea towels) to remove the skins. Slice the pistachios lengthwise and toast in a dry skillet (frying pan) over a low heat for 1 minute.

Temper the three types of chocolate following the basic technique and fill the tablet molds following the basic technique to make the chocolate bars. Finely dice the apricots and crystallized ginger. Scatter the pistachios over the white chocolate, the dried apricots over the milk chocolate, and the candied (crystallized) ginger over the dark chocolate while it is still soft and warm.

Refrigerate the molds for 15 minutes, then rest at room temperature for a further 15 minutes to allow the chocolate to fully set. Turn the molds upside down and gently tap on the work surface, so the chocolate bars come out without breaking.

MISTAKES TO AVOID
When using polycarbonate or silicone molds for making bonbons or other confections, they must be perfectly clean and dry, with no marks on the inside that may make unmolding difficult.

DARK CHOCOLATE BONBONS WITH WHITE CHOCOLATE AND FENNEL GANACHE

Cioccolatini fondenti con ganache bianca al finocchio

30 m   15 m   1 h 20 m   7 d

Difficulty: ADVANCED

For Melting the chocolate:
   see page 38
For Tempering the chocolate:
   see page 40
For the Chocolate Shells:
   see page 44
For the Ganache for Bonbons and Truffles:
   see page 74

TO SERVE 10

FOR THE SHELLS
1 pound 2 ounces/500 g 80% dark chocolate

FOR THE GANACHE
½ small fennel bulb
4¼ fl oz/½ cup/125 ml heavy (whipping) cream
½ ounce/1 tablespoon/15 g unsalted butter,
   at room temperature
6¼ ounces/180 g white chocolate

EQUIPMENT NEEDED
Bain-marie or double boiler
Kitchen thermometer
Marble board
Metal spatula or palette knife
Silicone spatula
Polycarbonate chocolate bonbon mold
Cooling rack
Ladle
Chef's knife
Chopping board
Saucepans
Measuring cup or jug
Fine-mesh strainer (sieve)
Mixing bowl
Disposable pastry (piping) bag or cone

Temper the dark chocolate following the basic technique and pour into the bonbon mold. Tilt the mold in all directions to cover the bottom and sides of the mold cavities following the basic technique to make the chocolate shells. Invert the mold to remove the excess chocolate and place the excess in a clean container to reuse. Set the shells aside to set.

To make the ganache, clean, trim, and finely chop the fennel. Place the fennel in a saucepan with the cream and heat to a simmer. Turn off the heat, cover, and leave to steep for 40 minutes. Strain the cream through a fine-mesh strainer (sieve), pressing on the fennel with a spoon to recover as much cream as possible. There should be 2½ fl oz/⅜ cup/80 ml.

Cut the butter into small cubes and set aside. Finely chop the white chocolate and place in a mixing bowl. Bring the fennel cream to a boil, then drizzle into the chocolate and stir until the chocolate has melted. When the mixture cools to 95°F/35°C, add the butter and stir until melted and incorporated.

When the chocolate shells have hardened, fill a disposable pastry (piping) bag with the fennel ganache and cut off the tip. Use the pastry bag to fill each shell three-quarters full with the ganache. Set aside in the refrigerator for 30 minutes.

Pour tempered dark chocolate over the bonbons to seal the filling inside following the basic technique. Chill the mold in the refrigerator for about 10 minutes for the bonbons to set, then tap the mold against the work surface to release the bonbons.

CUSTARDS, MOUSSES, AND PUDDINGS

WHITE CHOCOLATE AND HAZELNUT MOUSSE

Mousse di cioccolato bianco alle nocciole

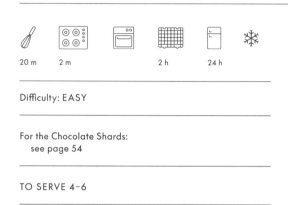

20 m   2 m   2 h   24 h

Difficulty: EASY

For the Chocolate Shards:
  see page 54

TO SERVE 4–6

FOR THE MOUSSE
7 ounces/200 g white chocolate
1½ ounces/scant ⅓ cup/40 g roasted hazelnuts
1 ounce/¼ stick/30 g unsalted butter
3½ fl oz/scant ½ cup/100 ml heavy (whipping) cream
2 egg whites
1½ ounces/⅓ cup/40 g confectioners' (icing) sugar

FOR THE DECORATION
1 ounce/scant ¼ cup/30 g roasted hazelnuts
Chocolate Shards made with 60% dark chocolate

EQUIPMENT NEEDED
Chef's knife
Chopping board
Food processor
Saucepan
Measuring cup or jug
Silicone spatula
Mixing bowl
Electric whisk
4–6 glasses

Finely chop the chocolate, then place the 1½ ounces/scant ⅓ cup/ 40 g hazelnuts in a food processor and blend until coarsely chopped. Place the butter in a saucepan and pour in the cream. Heat the pan until the butter has melted, then remove from the heat and add the chocolate. Stir with a silicone spatula until the chocolate has melted, then add the chopped hazelnuts. Stir to combine, then set aside to cool to room temperature.

Place the egg whites and confectioners' (icing) sugar in a clean, grease-free bowl and whisk to soft peaks with an electric whisk. Gently fold into the chocolate-hazelnut mixture, then divide the mousse equally between the glasses.

Finely chop the 1 ounce/scant ¼ cup/30 g hazelnuts. Stand a Chocolate Shard in each glass and sprinkle with the chopped hazelnuts. Rest in the refrigerator for 2 hours before serving.

TIPS AND TRICKS
If roasted hazelnuts are not available, roast raw nuts in a preheated oven at 350°F/180°C/160°C Fan/Gas 4 for about 10 minutes, or until they start to release their aroma. Wrap the roasted hazelnuts in a cloth, rub while still warm to remove their brown skins, then coarsely chop in a food processor.

BAKED GIANDUJA CUSTARD

Crema cotta al gianduia

20 m   5 m   35 m   6 h   48 h

Difficulty: AVERAGE

For the Chocolate Curls:
   see page 50

TO SERVE 6

FOR THE CUSTARD
7 ounces/200 g gianduja
1 vanilla bean (pod)
8½ fl oz/1 cup/250 ml whole (full-fat) milk
¾ ounce/4 teaspoons/20 g superfine (caster) sugar
8½ fl oz/1 cup/250 ml heavy (whipping) cream
6 egg yolks

FOR THE DECORATION
4 cocoa beans
Chocolate Curls made with gianduja

EQUIPMENT NEEDED
Chef's knife
Chopping board
Mixing bowls
Paring knife
Measuring cup or jug
Saucepan
Strainer (sieve)
Silicone spatula
Hand whisk
Fine-mesh strainer (sieve)
6 × 7-fl oz/scant 1 cup/200-ml capacity bowls
Deep baking pan (tin)
Mortar and pestle

Preheat the oven to 325°F/160°C/140°C Fan/Gas 3.

Finely chop the gianduja and place in a bowl. Use a sharp paring knife to split the vanilla bean (pod) lengthwise and scrape out the seeds. Pour the milk into a saucepan, add the sugar and vanilla seeds, and bring to a boil.

Strain the hot milk into the chocolate and stir with a silicone spatula until the chocolate has melted. Stir in the cream and set aside to cool to room temperature.

Place the egg yolks in a separate bowl and beat with a hand whisk. Slowly add the beaten yolks to the chocolate mixture, stirring continuously. Strain the custard through a fine-mesh strainer (sieve) and divide equally between the bowls.

Place the bowls inside a deep baking pan (tin) and fill the pan with enough boiling water to come two-thirds of the way up the sides of the bowls. Carefully place the baking pan in the preheated oven and bake for about 35 minutes. Remove the bowls from the baking pan and set aside to allow the custard to cool to room temperature, then refrigerate for 6 hours.

When ready to serve, coarsely crush the cocoa beans by pounding with the mortar and pestle, then sprinkle over the custard and finish decorating with gianduja Chocolate Curls.

TIPS AND TRICKS
If you prefer to use dark chocolate instead of gianduja, use double the amount of sugar.

DARK CHOCOLATE CUSTARD MOUSSE

Crema spumosa al cioccolato fondente

20 m   15 m   5–7 h   48 h

Difficulty: AVERAGE

TO SERVE 6

FOR THE MOUSSE
9 ounces/250 g 72% dark chocolate
1½ ounces/¼ cup/40 g dried apricots
2 ounces/¼ cup/50 g superfine (caster) sugar
1 clove
7 fl oz/scant 1 cup/200 ml whole (full-fat) milk
4 egg yolks
8½ fl oz/1 cup/250 ml heavy (whipping) cream

EQUIPMENT NEEDED
Chef's knife
Chopping board
Saucepans
Measuring cup or jug
Bain-marie or double boiler
Electric whisk
Silicone spatula
Kitchen thermometer
6 glasses
Mixing bowl
Pastry (piping) bag
Star piping tip (nozzle)

Finely chop the chocolate. Cut the apricots into chunks and place in a saucepan. Add 1 tablespoon of the sugar, the clove, and 3½ fl oz/scant ½ cup/100 ml water. Cook over a low heat for 5–6 minutes until all the liquid has evaporated. Set aside to cool to room temperature, then remove the clove.

Pour the milk into a saucepan and bring to a simmer. Place the egg yolks in the bowl of a bain-marie or double boiler, add the remaining sugar, and beat with an electric whisk until pale and fluffy. Drizzle the warm milk into the bowl and cook the custard in the bain-marie, stirring with a silicone spatula, for 7–8 minutes, until thick enough to coat the back of a spoon or until the temperature reaches 185°F/85°C. Add the chocolate and stir until the chocolate has melted. Set aside to cool to room temperature, then refrigerate for 3–4 hours.

Pour 7 fl oz/scant 1 cup/200 ml of the cream into a mixing bowl and whip to soft peaks with an electric whisk, then fold into the cold custard. Divide the mousse equally between the glasses and chill in the refrigerator for a further 2–3 hours.

When ready to serve, whip the remaining cream and fill a pastry (piping) bag fitted with a star piping tip (nozzle). Pipe a swirl of whipped cream on top of the mousse and decorate with a dried apricot piece.

TIPS AND TRICKS
Custard can also be cooked directly on the stove (hob). It should be watched carefully and stirred from time to time, and as soon as it begins to swell and bubbles form on the sides of the saucepan, it should immediately be transferred to a bowl.

CREAMY CHOCOLATE PUDDING WITH BAKLAVA ROSES

Budino cremoso al cioccolato con roselline di baklava

35 m   15 m   10 m   2 h   48 h

Difficulty: AVERAGE

TO SERVE 4

FOR THE PUDDING
1 ounce/scant ¼ cup/30 g roasted almonds
1 ounce/scant ¼ cup/30 g pistachio nuts, shelled and peeled
17 fl oz/2 cups/500 ml whole (full-fat) milk
3½ ounces/scant ½ cup/100 g superfine (caster) sugar
¾ ounce/2 tablespoons/20 g cornstarch (cornflour)
¾ ounce/scant ¼ cup/25 g unsweetened cocoa powder
Pinch of salt
1 egg
2 egg yolks
3 ½ ounces/100 g 60% dark chocolate
1 ounce/¼ stick/30 g unsalted butter

FOR THE BAKLAVA
¾ ounce/1½ tablespoons/20 g unsalted butter
¾ ounce/2 heaping tablespoons/20 g roasted almonds
¾ ounce/2 heaping tablespoons/20 g pistachio nuts, shelled and peeled
2 sheets (total 1½ ounces/40 g) phyllo (filo) pastry
4 ounces/½ cup/120 g superfine (caster) sugar
2 green cardamom pods
¾ ounce/1 tablespoon/20 g acacia honey
1 teaspoon lemon juice

FOR THE DECORATION
Chopped pistachio nuts, for sprinkling

EQUIPMENT NEEDED
Chef's knife
Chopping board
4 glasses
Measuring cup or jug
Saucepans
Strainer (sieve)
Mixing bowls
Hand whisk
Silicone spatula
Baking sheet
Parchment paper
Bain-marie or double boiler
Pastry brush
Mortar and pestle

Coarsely chop the almonds and pistachios, and divide equally between the glasses. Pour 13 fl oz/generous 1½ cups/400 ml of the milk into a saucepan, add the sugar, and place over a low heat, stirring until the sugar has dissolved. Sift the cornstarch (cornflour) and the cocoa powder into a mixing bowl, add a pinch of salt, and drizzle in the remaining milk, stirring with a hand whisk to combine.

Pour the cornstarch and cocoa mixture into the simmering milk, stirring with a whisk to prevent lumps from forming, and cook over a low heat for 3–4 minutes until thickened. Place the egg and extra egg yolks in a separate bowl, add a ladle of the boiling mixture, and stir with a whisk, then add the egg mixture to the saucepan and cook the pudding mixture over a very low heat for 2 minutes, stirring continuously.

Finely chop the chocolate and cut the butter into small pieces. Transfer the pudding mixture to a bowl, add the chocolate and butter, and stir with a silicone spatula until the chocolate and butter have melted. Divide the pudding equally between the glasses, pouring it over the chopped nuts. Leave to cool to room temperature, then refrigerate for 2 hours.

To make the baklava, preheat the oven to 350°F/180°C/160°C Fan/Gas 4 and line the baking sheet with parchment paper.

Melt the butter in a bain-marie or double boiler. Finely chop the nuts. Brush the phyllo (filo) sheets with the melted butter, and cut in half. Lay one sheet over another, sprinkle with the nuts and 2 tablespoons/20 g of the sugar, then cover with the other two buttered sheets. Cut the baklava into ¾-inch/2-cm-wide strips and shape into small roses by folding and rolling up the strips. Place the roses on the lined baking sheet and bake in the preheated oven for 10 minutes.

Meanwhile, crush the cardamom pods in a mortar and pestle. Pour 5 fl oz/scant ⅔ cup/150 ml water into a saucepan, add the honey, lemon juice, crushed cardamom pods, and the remaining sugar, and bring to a boil. Remove the baklava roses from the oven, pour the syrup over, and leave to cool completely. Remove the individual pudding glasses from the refrigerator, sprinkle with chopped pistachios, and decorate with the roses.

TRUFFLE CAKE WITH WASABI

Truffle cake con cuore al wasabi

30 m   5 m   6 h   48 h   30 d

Difficulty: AVERAGE

For Melting the chocolate:
   see page 38
For the Chocolate Strand:
   see page 56

TO SERVE 8

FOR THE CAKE
3½ ounces/scant 1 stick/100 g unsalted butter,
   at room temperature
4 ounces/1 cup/120 g confectioners' (icing) sugar
1 ounce/¼ cup/30 g unsweetened cocoa powder
4 egg yolks
9 ounces/250 g 70% dark chocolate
5 fl oz/scant ⅔ cup/150 ml heavy (whipping) cream
1 hazelnut-sized portion of wasabi

FOR THE DECORATION
Unsweetened cocoa powder, for dusting
1 Chocolate Strand

EQUIPMENT NEEDED
Mixing bowls
Electric whisk
Strainer (sieve)
Chef's knife
Chopping board
Bain-marie or double boiler
Silicone spatula
Measuring cup or jug
6¼-inch/16-cm round springform pan (tin)
Parchment paper
Acetate strip
Pastry (piping) bag
¾-inch/2-cm ribbon piping tip (nozzle)
Fine-mesh strainer (sieve)

Place the butter in a mixing bowl, add 2 ounces/scant ½ cup/ 50 g of the confectioners' (icing) sugar, and beat with an electric whisk until smooth and fluffy. Sift in the cocoa powder and beat to combine. Place the egg yolks in a separate bowl with the remaining sugar and beat with the whisk until the mixture turns pale and fluffy, and doubles in volume.

Finely chop the chocolate and melt in a bain-marie or double boiler. Leave to cool to room temperature, then add to the butter and sugar mixture, stirring with a silicone spatula to combine. Add the beaten egg yolks and stir until incorporated. Pour half the cream into a clean mixing bowl and whip to soft peaks with an electric whisk, then gently fold into the mixture. Place a heaped tablespoon of the mixture in a bowl, add the wasabi, mix, and set aside.

Line the base of the springform pan (tin) with parchment paper and the sides with the acetate strip. Pour in half of the chocolate mixture, spread the wasabi mixture over the top, and finish with the remaining chocolate mixture. Leave the truffle cake to set in the refrigerator for at least 6 hours.

When ready to serve, pour the remaining half of the cream into a mixing bowl and whip until firm. Fill a pastry (piping) bag fitted with a ribbon piping tip (nozzle) with the cream. Unmold the truffle cake onto a serving plate, dust with cocoa powder, pipe over the whipped cream, and decorate with a Chocolate Strand.

MISTAKES TO AVOID
When creaming the butter with the sugar, stop beating when the mixture is smooth and fluffy. Continuing to beat will overheat the butter and cause the liquid to separate from the solids, rendering it unusable and impossible to rectify. Add the chocolate to the butter and sugar mixture only when it has cooled to room temperature. If the chocolate is still too hot, it tends to melt the butter, compromising the final texture of the cake.

HAZELNUT "BONÈT"—CHOCOLATE AMARETTI PUDDING

"Bonèt" con le nocciole

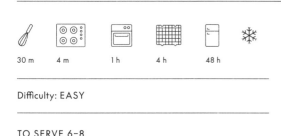

30 m	4 m	1 h	4 h	48 h	

Difficulty: EASY

TO SERVE 6–8

FOR THE PUDDING
1½ ounces/3 heaping tablespoons/40 g superfine
    (caster) sugar
7 ounces/1½ cups/200 g roasted hazelnuts
2 ounces/50 g amaretti cookies (biscuits)
5 eggs
3 ½ ounces/scant 1 cup/100 g confectioners' (icing) sugar
17 fl oz/2 cups/500 ml whole (full-fat) milk
3½ ounces/1 cup/100 g unsweetened cocoa powder
1¾ fl oz/3 tablespoons/50 ml brandy

FOR THE DECORATION
2 amaretti cookies (biscuits)
Chopped roasted hazelnuts, for sprinkling

EQUIPMENT NEEDED
Small saucepan
Dish towel (tea towel)
34-fl oz/1-liter capacity fluted savarin pan (tin) or
    mini Bundt pan
Food processor
Mixing bowls
Hand or electric whisk
Measuring cup or jug
Strainer (sieve)
Silicone spatula
Deep baking pan

Preheat the oven to 325°F/160°C/140°C Fan/Gas 3.

Place the superfine (caster) sugar in a small saucepan, add 4 tablespoons water, and cook until it is a golden caramel. Hold the savarin pan (tin) with a dish towel (tea towel) and carefully pour the caramel into the pan, tilting it in all directions to coat the bottom and sides.

Place the hazelnuts and cookies (biscuits) in a food processor and blend. Place the eggs in a mixing bowl with the confectioners' (icing) sugar, and beat with a hand or electric whisk until smooth. Drizzle the milk over, stirring continuously with a silicone spatula until incorporated, then stir in the chopped hazelnuts and cookies (biscuits). Add the sifted cocoa powder and brandy, and mix with a whisk to combine.

Pour the mixture into the prepared savarin pan. Place the savarin pan inside a deep baking pan and fill the deep baking pan with enough boiling water to come two-thirds of the way up the sides of the savarin pan. Carefully place the baking pan in the preheated oven and bake for about 1 hour. Remove the savarin pan from the baking pan and set aside to cool to room temperature, then refrigerate for at least 4 hours.

When ready to serve, turn out the pudding by inverting onto a serving plate and decorate, as desired, with crumbled amaretti cookies and the chopped hazelnuts.

CHOCOLATE BAVAROIS WITH MODICA CHOCOLATE

Bavarese al cioccolato al latte e cioccolato di Modica

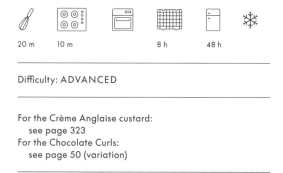

20 m   10 m   8 h   48 h

Difficulty: ADVANCED

For the Crème Anglaise custard:
   see page 323
For the Chocolate Curls:
   see page 50 (variation)

TO SERVE 6–8

FOR THE BAVAROIS
3⅓ sheets (10 g) gelatin
17 fl oz/2 cups/500 ml whole (full-fat) milk
3 egg yolks
2 ounces/¼ cup/50 g superfine (caster) sugar
7 ounces/200 g milk chocolate
13 fl oz/generous 1½ cups/400 ml heavy (whipping) cream

FOR THE DECORATION
3½ ounces/100 g fresh strawberries
½ ounce/10 g Modica chocolate
1 ounce/30 g milk chocolate

EQUIPMENT NEEDED
Small bowl
Measuring cup or jug
Saucepan
Bain-marie or double boiler
Hand whisk
Silicone spatula
Kitchen thermometer
Chef's knife
Chopping board
Mixing bowl
Electric whisk
10½ x 7-in/26 x 18-cm oval savarin pan (tin)
Chocolate grater
Vegetable peeler

Soak the gelatin sheets in a small bowl of cold water for 10 minutes until they are completely rehydrated and soft, making sure they are fully immersed in the water. Pour the milk into a small saucepan, set the pan over a low heat, and bring the milk almost to boiling point, then turn off the heat and set aside to cool to room temperature. Place the egg yolks and sugar in the bowl of a bain-marie or double boiler. Using a hand whisk, beat the egg yolks with the sugar until pale and fluffy. Slowly pour the warm milk into the bowl with the egg yolk mix, whisking continuously as you add the milk to make a smooth Crème Anglaise custard.

Heat the Crème Anglaise in the bain-marie, stirring continuously with a silicone spatula, until it starts to thicken, about 10 minutes. Constantly monitor the temperature with a kitchen thermometer and continue to cook the custard until it lightly coats the back of a spoon, or until the temperature reaches 185°F/85°C.

Finely chop the chocolate. Drain the sheets of gelatin and squeeze them with your hands to remove as much water as possible. Add the gelatin and chocolate to the Crème Anglaise, and stir until the gelatin has completely dissolved and the chocolate has melted. Set aside to cool to room temperature.

Pour the cream into a mixing bowl and whip to soft peaks with an electric whisk, then fold the cream into the chocolate custard and pour into the savarin pan (tin). Refrigerate for at least 8 hours.

When ready to serve, turn out the bavarois by dipping the base of the savarin pan in hot water for a few seconds, then inverting the pan onto a serving dish. Decorate with sliced strawberries, shredded (grated) Modica chocolate, and milk Chocolate Curls shaved with a vegetable peeler.

TIPS AND TRICKS
To cool the bavarois more quickly, after incorporating the gelatin and chocolate, place the mixing bowl in a cold bain-marie and continue to stir until the mixture begins to thicken.

RUBY CHOCOLATE CRÈME BRÛLÉE WITH PINK PEPPERCORNS

Crème brûlée al cioccolato ruby e pepe rosa

20 m   10 m   35 m   12 h 30 m   24 h

Difficulty: AVERAGE

For Melting the chocolate:
  see page 38

TO SERVE 6

FOR THE CRÈME BRÛLÉE
1 teaspoon pink peppercorns
10 fl oz/1¼ cups/300 ml whole (full-fat) milk
7 ounces/300 g ruby chocolate
10 fl oz/1¼ cups/300 ml heavy (whipping) cream
4 egg yolks
2 ounces/scant ½ cup/50 g confectioners' (icing) sugar
3 tablespoons turbinado (Demerara) sugar

EQUIPMENT NEEDED
Mortar and pestle
Measuring cup or jug
Saucepans
Chef's knife
Chopping board
Bain-marie or double boiler
Fine-mesh strainer (sieve)
Silicone spatula
Mixing bowl
Hand or electric whisk
6 shallow crème brûlée ramekins
Deep baking pan (tin)
Cook's blowtorch

Crush the pink peppercorns with a mortar and pestle. Pour the milk into a saucepan, add the crushed peppercorns, and bring to a boil. Turn off the heat, cover with a lid, and leave to steep for 30 minutes.

Preheat the oven to 350°F/180°C/160°C Fan/Gas 4.

Finely chop the chocolate and melt in a bain-marie or double boiler. Reheat the milk and pour it through a fine-mesh strainer (sieve) directly into the melted chocolate. Stir with a silicone spatula and set aside to cool to room temperature. Add the cream, stirring to combine. In a mixing bowl, lightly beat the egg yolks with the confectioners' (icing) sugar, using a hand or electric whisk, and add to the mixture.

Divide the crème brûlée mixture equally between the ramekins and place the ramekins inside a deep baking pan (tin). Fill the baking pan with enough boiling water to come two-thirds of the way up the sides of the ramekins. Carefully place the baking pan in the preheated oven and bake until just set, about 30 minutes. Remove the ramekins from the baking pan and set aside to cool to room temperature, then refrigerate for 12 hours.

When ready to serve, sprinkle the ramekins with the turbinado (demerara) sugar and caramelize with a cook's blowtorch. Leave the caramel to cool slightly then add a few pink peppercorns in the center of each crème brûlée, if desired.

TIPS AND TRICKS
Ruby chocolate tends to lose its bright color when mixed with light ingredients, such as milk or cream. If you would like to keep the color unchanged, you can add a few drops of pink food coloring gel to the mixture.

GIANDUJA PUDDING

Budino al gianduia

| 30 m | 5 m | 50 m | 4 h | 48 h | |

Difficulty: EASY

For the Chocolate Tuiles:
see page 52

TO SERVE 8

FOR THE PUDDING
1 ounce/¼ stick/30 g unsalted butter
3½ ounces/scant ½ cup/100 g superfine (caster) sugar
7 ounces/200 g gianduja
7 fl oz/scant 1 cup/200 ml whole (full-fat) milk
10 fl oz/1¼ cups/300 ml heavy (whipping) cream
6 eggs

FOR THE DECORATION
Unsweetened cocoa powder, for dusting
Chocolate Tuiles made from dark chocolate

EQUIPMENT NEEDED
8 × 4-fl oz/120-ml capacity pudding pans (tins)
Chef's knife
Chopping board
Measuring cup or jug
Saucepan
Silicone spatula
Mixing bowl
Hand or electric whisk
Deep baking pan (tin)
Fine-mesh strainer (sieve)

Preheat the oven to 325°F/160°C/140°C Fan/Gas 3.

Grease the pudding pans (tins) with the butter and sprinkle the bottom and sides with half the sugar. Finely chop the gianduja. Pour the milk and cream into a saucepan and bring to a simmer over a moderate heat. Remove from the heat, add the gianduja, and stir with a silicone spatula until melted. Break the eggs into a mixing bowl and beat with the remaining sugar, using a hand or electric whisk, then add to the chocolate mixture and mix to combine.

Divide the mixture equally between the prepared pudding pans and place the pans inside a deep baking pan (tin). Fill the baking pan with enough boiling water to come two-thirds of the way up the sides of the pudding pans. Carefully place the baking pan in the preheated oven and bake for 50 minutes. Remove the pudding pans from the baking pan and set aside to cool to room temperature. Refrigerate for at least 4 hours.

When ready to serve, unmold the puddings onto serving plates. Dust with cocoa powder and decorate with the Chocolate Tuiles.

RUBY CHOCOLATE PANNA COTTA WITH BERRIES

Panna cotta al cioccolato ruby con frutti di bosco

30 m   15 m   6–8 h   48 h

Difficulty: EASY

For the Chocolate Shavings:
  see page 50

TO SERVE 6

FOR THE PANNA COTTA
4 ounces/120 g ruby chocolate
3⅓ sheets (10 g) gelatin
1 vanilla bean (pod)
17 fl oz/2 cups/500 ml heavy (whipping) cream
1½ ounces/3 heaping tablespoons/40 g superfine
  (caster) sugar

FOR THE DECORATION
2 ounces/50 g ruby chocolate
3½ ounces/100 g mixed berries

EQUIPMENT NEEDED
Chef's knife
Chopping board
Mixing bowls
Paring knife
Measuring cup or jug
Saucepans
Fine-mesh strainer (sieve)
Silicone spatula
6 × 5-fl oz/150-ml capacity pudding pans (tins)
Medium grater
Bain-marie or double boiler
Pastry brush
Marble board
Metal spatula or palette knife

Finely chop the 4 ounces/120 g chocolate and place in a mixing bowl. Soak the gelatin sheets in a small bowl of cold water for 10 minutes until they are completely rehydrated and soft, making sure they are full immersed in the water. Split the vanilla bean (pod) lengthwise using a sharp paring knife. Pour the cream into a saucepan, add the vanilla bean and the sugar, and heat until the sugar has dissolved.

Drain the sheets of gelatin and squeeze them with your hands to remove as much water as possible. Add the gelatin to the hot vanilla cream and stir until the gelatin has completely dissolved. Slowly pour the vanilla cream mixture through a fine-mesh strainer (sieve) into the chocolate, stirring continuously with a silicone spatula until the chocolate has melted.

Divide the panna cotta mixture equally between the pudding pans (tins) and refrigerate for 6–8 hours to set.

When ready to serve, shred (grate) a little of the chocolate with a medium grater and set aside, then melt the remainder in a bain-marie and brush onto the plates. Unmold each panna cotta over the chocolate smear and top with the mixed berries and Chocolate Shavings.

TIPS AND TRICKS
To unmold the panna cotta onto plates, dip one pudding pan at a time in hot water for a few seconds and run a small knife around the edge of the pan. Then invert the pan onto the plate with a hard tap.

WHITE CHOCOLATE AND BLACKBERRY RICOTTA MOUSSE

Mousse di ricotta con cioccolato bianco e more

20 m 15 m 6 h 48 h

Difficulty: EASY

For Melting the chocolate:
    see page 38

TO SERVE 6

FOR THE MOUSSE
9 ounces/1⅔ cups/250 g fresh blackberries
½ lemon
2 ounces/¼ cup/50 g superfine (caster) sugar
10½ ounces/1¼ cups/300 g ricotta piemontese cheese
5 ounces/150 g white chocolate
5 fl oz/scant ⅔ cup/150 ml heavy (whipping) cream
2 ounces/50 g whole grain cookies (biscuits)

EQUIPMENT NEEDED
Paper towels
Saucepan
Juicer
Mixing bowls
Electric whisk
Chef's knife
Chopping board
Bain-marie or double boiler
Silicone spatula
Measuring cup or jug
6 glasses

Wash the blackberries and dry on paper towels. Place in a saucepan with the juice of ½ lemon and 1 ounce/2 tablespoons/30 g of the sugar, and cook over a high heat until they begin to release their juice. Transfer to a bowl and set aside to cool to room temperature.

Place the ricotta in a mixing bowl, add the remaining sugar, and beat with an electric whisk until fluffy. Finely chop the chocolate and melt in a bain-marie or double boiler. Leave to cool to room temperature, then stir into the cheese with a silicone spatula.

Pour the cream into a separate, clean bowl and whip to soft peaks with an electric whisk. Gently fold the whipped cream into the ricotta mixture. Divide half the ricotta mousse equally between the glasses, cover with two-thirds of the blackberries and their juice, and top with the remaining mousse.

Crumble the cookies (biscuits) over the mousses and refrigerate for at least 6 hours. Arrange the remaining blackberries on top, to serve.

ALMOND MOUSSE CAKE WITH MILK CHOCOLATE MOUSSE CENTER

Mousse di mandorle con cuore al latte

35 m   10 m   12 h   24 h

Difficulty: ADVANCED

For the Eggless Chocolate Mousse:
  see page 86
For the Chocolate Lace Collar:
  see page 58

TO SERVE 6–8

FOR THE MILK CHOCOLATE MOUSSE
6¼ ounces/180 g milk chocolate
⅓ sheet (1 g) gelatin
3½ fl oz/scant ½ cup/100 ml whole (full-fat) milk
7 fl oz/scant 1 cup/200 ml heavy (whipping) cream

FOR THE ALMOND MOUSSE
1½ sheets (4 g) gelatin
10 ounces/280 g almond paste (marzipan)
11½ fl oz/1⅓ cups/340 ml whole (full-fat) milk
11½ fl oz/1⅓ cups/340 ml heavy (whipping) cream

FOR THE DECORATION
4¾ ounces/140 g milk chocolate

EQUIPMENT NEEDED
Mixing bowls
Measuring cup or jug
Saucepans
Silicone spatula
Strainer (sieve)
Kitchen thermometer
Electric whisk
3-inch/8-cm silicone sphere mold
Immersion (stick) blender
6¼-inch/16-cm round deep springform pan (tin)
Parchment paper
2 × 5-inch/12-cm-wide acetate strips to fit the circumference
  of the springform pan
Disposable pastry (piping) bag or cone

Make the milk chocolate mousse following the basic technique for Eggless Chocolate Mousse, but using the ingredients and measures listed here. Fill the sphere mold with the mousse and freeze for 4 hours.

To make the almond mousse, soak the gelatin sheets in a small bowl of cold water for 10 minutes until they are completely rehydrated and soft, making sure they are fully immersed in the water. Break the almond paste (marzipan) into small pieces. Pour the milk into a saucepan and bring to a boil, add the almond paste, and stir with a silicone spatula until the paste has dissolved.

Drain the sheets of gelatin and squeeze them with your hands to remove as much water as possible. Add the gelatin to the milk, remove from the heat, and stir until the gelatin has completely dissolved. Blend until smooth with an immersion (stick) blender and set aside to cool to room temperature.

Pour the cream into a separate, clean bowl and whip to soft peaks with an electric whisk. Gently fold the whipped cream into the mixture.

Line the base of the springform pan (tin) with parchment paper and the sides with one of the acetate strips. Remove the frozen milk chocolate mousse sphere from the mold. Pour in a third of the mousse and arrange the frozen milk chocolate mousse sphere, in the center. Cover with the remaining mousse and freeze for 4 hours.

Unmold the mousse, remove the acetate strip, and transfer to a serving plate. Use 3½ ounces/100 g milk chocolate to make the Chocolate Lace Collar following the basic technique and using the second acetate strip. Wrap the collar around the mousse and peel off the acetate strip when the chocolate has hardened. Refrigerate the cake for 4 hours. Melt the remaining milk chocolate in a bain-marie, fill a disposable pastry (piping) bag with the melted chocolate, and cut off the tip. Decorate the top of the cake with milk chocolate piping.

CHOCOLATE SOUFFLÉ

Soufflé al cioccolato

20 m   5 m   20 m

Difficulty: ADVANCED

For Melting the Chocolate:
  see page 38

TO SERVE 6

FOR THE SOUFFLÉ
3 ounces/⅓ cup/80 g superfine (caster) sugar
1 ounce/¼ stick/30 g unsalted butter
5 ounces/150 g 60% dark chocolate
1¾ fl oz/3 tablespoons/50 ml whole (full-fat) milk
3 eggs
1 egg white
Confectioners' (icing) sugar, for dusting

EQUIPMENT NEEDED
Pastry brush
6 × 7-fl oz/200-ml capacity soufflé ramekins
Chef's knife
Chopping board
Bain-marie or double boiler
Measuring cup or jug
Mixing bowl
Silicone spatula
Electric whisk
Fine-mesh strainer (sieve)

Preheat the oven to 400°F/200°C/180°C Fan/Gas 6. Set aside 2 ounces/scant ¼ cup/50 g of the superfine (caster) sugar. Use a pastry brush to grease the ramekins with the butter and sprinkle with the remaining sugar, removing the excess.

Finely chop the chocolate and melt in a bain-marie or double boiler with the milk. Set aside to cool to room temperature. Separate the eggs and place the whites in a clean grease-free mixing bowl with the extra egg white. Add the yolks to the melted chocolate mixture with ¾ ounce/20 g of the sugar, and gently mix with a silicone spatula.

Use an electric whisk to whisk the egg whites with the remaining sugar to stiff, glossy peaks, then fold into the chocolate soufflé mixture.

Divide the mixture equally between the prepared ramekins, filling to ½ inch/1 cm below the rim, and bake in the preheated oven for 20 minutes. Serve the soufflés immediately, dusted with confectioners' (icing) sugar.

MISTAKES TO AVOID
Before baking, place the ramekins on a baking sheet so they can all be removed from the oven at the same time. Never open the oven door while baking to prevent the soufflés from collapsing.

WHITE CHOCOLATE AND PASSION FRUIT MOUSSE CAKE

Mousse al cioccolato bianco e frutti della passione

---

30 m   15 m   6 h   48 h   30 d

Difficulty: AVERAGE

For the Chocolate Curls:
    see page 50 (variation)

TO SERVE 6–8

FOR THE WHITE CHOCOLATE MOUSSE
2 large egg yolks
2 ounces/¼ cup/50 g superfine (caster) sugar
6¼ fl oz/¾ cup/180 ml whole (full-fat) milk
4¾ ounces/140 g white chocolate
6¼ fl oz/¾ cup/180 ml heavy (whipping) cream

FOR THE PASSION FRUIT MOUSSE
3⅓ sheets (10 g) gelatin
3 large egg yolks
2 ounces/generous ¼ cup/60 g superfine (caster) sugar
6¼ fl oz/¾ cup/180 ml passion fruit juice
2 tablespoons/30 ml whole (full-fat) milk
1 tablespoon/10 ml heavy (whipping) cream

FOR THE DECORATION
3 passion fruits
7 ounces/200 g papaya flesh
1½ ounces/40 g white chocolate

EQUIPMENT NEEDED
Mixing bowls
Electric whisk
Measuring cup or jug
Saucepans
Silicone spatula
Kitchen thermometer
Coarse grater
3-inch/8-cm hexagonal pastry ring
Plastic wrap (cling film)
Vegetable peeler

To make the white chocolate mousse, place the egg yolks in a mixing bowl, add the sugar, and beat using an electric whisk until pale and fluffy. Pour the milk into a small saucepan and bring to a simmer, then drizzle into the beaten egg yolks, stirring continuously with a silicone spatula.

Transfer the mixture to a heavy-bottomed saucepan and cook over a low heat until it reaches a temperature of 185°F/85°C and is thick enough to coat the back of a spoon. Leave the custard to cool to 122°F/50°C.

Shred (grate) the white chocolate with a coarse grater, add to the mousse mixture, and stir until the chocolate has melted. Set aside to cool to room temperature.

Pour the cream into a separate, clean mixing bowl and whip to soft peaks with an electric whisk, then gently fold the whipped cream into the mousse. Line the sides of the pastry ring with plastic wrap (cling film) and set it on a plate. Pour the mousse evenly into the pastry ring and refrigerate for 2 hours.

To make the passion fruit mousse, soak the gelatin sheets in a small bowl of cold water for 10 minutes until they are completely rehydrated and soft, making sure they are fully immersed in the water. Place the egg yolks in a mixing bowl with the sugar and beat using an electric whisk, then incorporate the passion fruit juice.

Pour the milk into a small saucepan and bring to a boil. Drain the sheets of gelatin and squeeze them with your hands to remove as much water as possible. Add the gelatin to the milk, remove from the heat, and stir until the gelatin has completely dissolved, then stir into the beaten egg mixture and set aside to cool to room temperature.

Pour the cream into a separate, clean bowl and whip with an electric whisk. Gently fold the whipped cream into the passion fruit mixture. Remove the hexagonal pastry ring from the refrigerator and evenly spread the passion fruit mousse on top of the white chocolate mousse. Refrigerate for a further 4 hours, or until the mousse has set.

When you are ready to serve, unmold the mousse cake onto a serving plate and remove the plastic wrap. Cut the passion fruit in half, scoop out the pulp with a teaspoon, and arrange on top. Finely dice the papaya and place in a mound at the center of the cake and finish with white Chocolate Curls made using a vegetable peeler.

MINT CHOCOLATE PUDDING WITH NECTARINE

Pudding cremoso al cioccolato e menta con pesche

35 m   7 m   15 m   48 h

Difficulty: EASY

For Melting the Chocolate:
   see page 38

TO SERVE 6

FOR THE PUDDING
6 ounces/1½ sticks/170 g unsalted butter, plus extra
   for greasing, at room temperature
2½ ounces/generous ½ cup/70 g type "00" flour or
   all-purpose (plain) flour, plus extra for dusting
6¼ ounces/180 g mint chocolate
3 large eggs
3 large egg yolks
4 ounces/scant ⅔ cup/130 g superfine (caster) sugar
Pinch of salt
1 nectarine

EQUIPMENT NEEDED
6 × 2½-inch/6-cm cast-iron ramekins
Chef's knife
Chopping board
Bain-marie or double boiler
Mixing bowl
Hand or electric whisk
Strainer (sieve)
Silicone spatula
Skillet (frying pan)

Preheat the oven to 350°F/180°C/160°C Fan/Gas 4 and grease the ramekins with butter and a dusting of flour.

Finely chop the chocolate and melt in a bain-marie or double boiler. Set aside to cool to room temperature.

Place the eggs, the extra yolks, and 3½ ounces/scant ½ cup/100 g of the sugar in a mixing bowl, and whisk, using a hand or electric whisk, until pale and fluffy. Cut the butter into small pieces and gradually add to the bowl, whisking continuously. Add the melted chocolate, a pinch of salt, and the sifted flour, and mix with a silicone spatula to incorporate.

Pour the batter into the ramekins and bake in the preheated oven for 15 minutes.

Pit and cut the nectarine into wedges. Halve each wedge crosswise and sauté in a skillet (frying pan) with the remaining sugar for about 2 minutes until lightly caramelized. Serve the puddings warm with a few nectarine pieces arranged on top.

CHOCOLATE, CUSTARD, AND RASPBERRY "TIRAMISU"

"Tiramisù" di cioccolato, crema cotta e lamponi

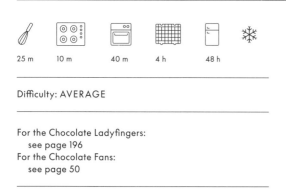

25 m   10 m   40 m   4 h   48 h

Difficulty: AVERAGE

For the Chocolate Ladyfingers:
    see page 196
For the Chocolate Fans:
    see page 50

TO SERVE 4

FOR THE VANILLA CUSTARD
1 vanilla bean (pod)
2 fl oz/¼ cup/60 ml whole (full-fat) milk
7 fl oz/scant 1 cup/200 ml heavy (whipping) cream
4 egg yolks
2 ounces/¼ cup/50 g superfine (caster) sugar
3½ ounces/generous ¾ cup/100 g fresh raspberries

FOR THE CHOCOLATE CREAM
3 ounces/80 g 70% dark chocolate
4¼ fl oz/½ cup/130 ml whole (full-fat) milk
¾ ounce/4 teaspoons/20 g superfine (caster) sugar
½ teaspoon/1 g agar agar

FOR THE ASSEMBLY AND DECORATION
3½ ounces/100 g Chocolate Ladyfingers
2 ounces/scant ½ cup/50 g fresh raspberries
8 Chocolate Fans

EQUIPMENT NEEDED
Paring knife
Chopping board
Measuring cup or jug
Saucepans
Mixing bowl
Hand or electric whisk
4 × sturdy glass ramekins
Deep baking pan (tin)
Chef's knife
Silicone spatula

To make the vanilla custard, preheat the oven to 300°F/150°C/130°C Fan/Gas 1.

Split the vanilla bean (pod) lengthwise using a sharp paring knife. Pour the milk and cream into a saucepan, add the vanilla bean, and bring to a boil, then set aside to cool to room temperature. Place the egg yolks in a mixing bowl with the sugar and beat with a hand or electric whisk. Once cooled, remove the vanilla bean from the milk and cream mixture, add the yolk mixture, and incorporate with a hand or electric whisk. Divide the custard equally between the ramekins.

Place the ramekins inside a deep baking pan (tin) and fill the baking pan with enough boiling water to come two-thirds of the way up the sides of the ramekins. Carefully place the baking pan in the preheated oven and bake until just set, about 40 minutes. Remove the ramekins from the baking pan and set aside to cool to room temperature.

Break up the Chocolate Ladyfingers into small pieces and coarsely crush the 3½ ounces/generous ¾ cup/100 g of the raspberries with a fork. Cover the baked custard with the Chocolate Ladyfingers and raspberries, and refrigerate.

To make the chocolate cream, finely chop the chocolate and place in a bowl. Pour the milk, sugar, and agar-agar into a saucepan and bring to a boil over a low heat. Pour the hot milk, a third at a time, over the chocolate and stir, with a silicone spatula, until the chocolate has melted. Leave the chocolate cream to cool to room temperature, then pour over the baked custard in the ramekins and refrigerate for 4 hours. Serve decorated with fresh raspberries and the Chocolate Fans.

SEMIFREDDI AND FROZEN DESSERTS

CHOCOLATE GELATO

Gelato al cioccolato

20 m   15 m   60 d

Difficulty: EASY

For the Chocolate Cigarette Curls:
see page 50

TO SERVE 4

FOR THE GELATO
3½ ounces/100 g 60% dark chocolate
1 vanilla bean (pod)
10 fl oz/1¼ cups/300 ml whole (full-fat) milk
6 egg yolks
Pinch of salt
4 ounces/½ cup/120 g superfine (caster) sugar
10 fl oz/1¼ cups/300 ml heavy (whipping) cream

FOR THE DECORATION
Chocolate Cigarette Curls (optional)

EQUIPMENT NEEDED
Chef's knife
Chopping board
Paring knife
Measuring cup or jug
Small saucepan
Mixing bowls
Electric whisk
Silicone spatula
Bain-marie or double boiler
Kitchen thermometer
Ice cream maker

Finely chop the chocolate. Use a sharp paring knife to split the vanilla bean (pod) lengthwise and scrape out the seeds. Pour the milk into a small saucepan, add the vanilla bean and seeds, and place over a low heat. Place the egg yolks in a bowl, add a pinch of salt and the sugar, and beat together using an electric whisk until very light and fluffy. Drizzle the warm milk into the egg yolk mixture, stirring continuously with a silicone spatula, then mix in the cream.

Cook the custard in a bain-marie or double boiler, stirring often, until thick enough to coat the back of a spoon, or until the temperature reaches 185°F/85°C. Remove the vanilla bean, add the chocolate, and stir until the chocolate has melted. Transfer the custard to a bowl and set aside to cool to room temperature.

When the custard has completely cooled, pour into the ice cream maker and churn, according to the manufacturer's instructions. Serve cold, decorated with Chocolate Cigarette Curls, if desired.

TIPS AND TRICKS
You can cook the custard directly on the stove (hob). Use a heavy-bottomed saucepan and cook over a low heat while stirring continuously. When the custard starts to thicken, without allowing it to come to a boil, immediately remove the pan from the heat and cool in a cold bain-marie.

CHOCOLATE SORBET

Sorbetto al cioccolato

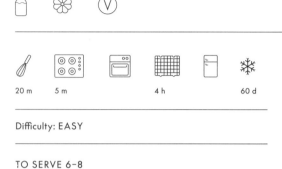

20 m   5 m   4 h   60 d

Difficulty: EASY

TO SERVE 6–8

FOR THE SORBET
7 ounces/200 g 70% dark chocolate
1 vanilla bean (pod)
4 ounces/generous 1 cup/120g unsweetened cocoa powder
40 fl oz/4¾ cups/1.2 liters just boiled water
9 ounces/1¼ cups/250 g superfine (caster) sugar
Pinch of salt
2 cocoa beans

EQUIPMENT NEEDED
Chef's knife
Chopping board
Paring knife
Strainer (sieve)
Saucepan
Measuring cup or jug
Hand whisk
Immersion (stick) blender
Baking pan (tin)
Food processor

Finely chop the chocolate. Use a sharp paring knife to split the vanilla bean (pod) lengthwise and scrape out the seeds. Sift the cocoa powder into a saucepan and add the hot water, mixing with a hand whisk.

Add the sugar and bring to a boil. Cook the syrup for 2–3 minutes, stirring, until the sugar has dissolved. Remove from the heat, add a pinch of salt and the vanilla seeds.

Add the chocolate to the syrup and stir until the chocolate has melted. Blend the mixture for a few seconds with an immersion (stick) blender, then pour the mixture into a baking pan (tin). Freeze the sorbet for 1 hour, remove from the freezer and blend in a food processor, then return to the freezer for a further hour. Repeat a further three times until the sorbet has been in the freezer for a total of 4 hours.

When ready to serve, finely chop the cocoa beans and sprinkle over the sorbet.

MILK CHOCOLATE CHAI SEMIFREDDO

Semifreddo chai di cioccolato al latte

30 m   15 m   8 h 35 m   60 d

Difficulty: AVERAGE

For Melting the chocolate:
    see page 38
For the Chocolate Pâte à Bombe:
    see page 92
For the Chocolate Batons:
    see page 60

TO SERVE 8

FOR THE SEMIFREDDO
1 heaped tablespoon masala chai blend (loose leaf tea)
1 quantity Chocolate Pâte à Bombe made with 4 ounces/
    120 g milk chocolate and masala chai
7 fl oz/scant 1 cup/200 ml heavy (whipping) cream

FOR THE DECORATION
Milk Chocolate Batons made with 7 ounces/200 g
    milk chocolate

EQUIPMENT NEEDED
7-inch/18-cm round springform pan (tin)
Plastic wrap (cling film)
Measuring cup or jug
Small saucepan
Chef's knife
Chopping board
Bain-marie or double boiler
Fine-mesh strainer (sieve)
Mixing bowl
Electric whisk
Silicone spatula
Ladle
Large acetate sheet
Metal spatula
Chocolate grater

Line the springform pan (tin) with plastic wrap (cling film).

Pour 4 fl oz/½ cup/120 ml water into a small saucepan and bring to a simmer. Turn off the heat, add the tea, and set aside to steep for 5 minutes.

Meanwhile, finely chop 4 ounces/120 g of chocolate and melt half in a bain-marie or double boiler. Strain the tea and stir into the melted chocolate, then leave to cool to room temperature. Melt the remaining chocolate and set aside.

Make the Pâte à Bombe as described in the basic technique, substituting the melted milk chocolate and tea mixture for the dark chocolate, and set aside to cool to room temperature.

Pour the cream into a mixing bowl and whip with an electric whisk. Fold the whipped cream into the Pâte à Bombe, using a silicone spatula, and incorporate the melted chocolate. Fill the springform pan with the mixture and place in the freezer for 8 hours.

Meanwhile, make the Chocolate Batons as described in the basic technique.

Remove the semifreddo from the freezer 30 minutes before you wish to serve it and unmold by inverting directly onto a serving plate. Peel off the plastic wrap and refrigerate for 30 minutes. Arrange the Chocolate Batons around the edge of the semifreddo, and shred (grate) the remaining milk chocolate over the top.

CHOCOLATE, RUM AND RAISIN MERINGATA

Meringata al cioccolato con uvetta al rum

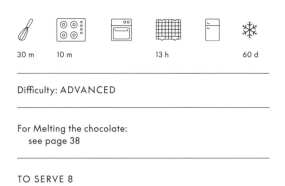

30 m   10 m   13 h   60 d

Difficulty: ADVANCED

For Melting the chocolate:
   see page 38

TO SERVE 8

FOR THE SEMIFREDDO
3 ounces/⅔ cup/80 g raisins
1¾ fl oz/3 tablespoons/50 ml rum
2 ounces/60 g hard meringues
6¼ ounces/180 g 60% dark chocolate
2 large eggs
2 large egg yolks
3½ ounces/scant ½ cup/100 g superfine (caster) sugar
8½ fl oz/1 cup/250 ml heavy (whipping) cream

FOR THE SOFT MERINGUE TOPPING
6 ounces/¾ cup/170 g superfine (caster) sugar
3 large egg whites

EQUIPMENT NEEDED
8-inch/20-cm square pan (tin)
Plastic wrap (cling film)
Mixing bowls
Chef's knife
Chopping board
Bain-marie or double boiler
Electric whisk
Measuring cup or jug
Silicone spatula
Saucepan
Kitchen thermometer
Cook's blowtorch

Line the square pan (tin) with plastic wrap (cling film).

Soak the raisins in the rum for 1 hour and break the hard meringues into coarse crumbs. Finely chop the chocolate and melt in a bain-marie or double boiler. Transfer to a bowl and leave to cool to room temperature. Place the eggs, the extra yolks, and the sugar in a separate bowl and beat with an electric whisk until pale and fluffy.

Add the melted chocolate and stir with a silicone spatula to combine. Add the raisins with the rum and meringue crumbs. Pour the cream into a mixing bowl and whip with an electric whisk. Gently fold the whipped cream into the mixture, pour into the pan, cover with plastic wrap and freeze for 12 hours.

When you are ready to serve the semifreddo, make the soft meringue topping. Pour 2 fl oz/¼ cup/60 ml water into a saucepan, add the sugar, and bring to a boil. Cook the syrup until it reaches 225°F/107°C. Place the egg whites in a clean, grease-free bowl and whisk to soft peaks with an electric whisk. Slowly drizzle the boiling syrup into the whisked egg whites, whisking continuously to combine. Continue to whisk the mixture until the meringue cools completely.

Remove the semifreddo from the freezer and unmold by inverting directly onto a serving plate. Peel off the plastic wrap, spread the meringue over the top, and use a cook's blowtorch to evenly brown the surface of the meringue.

VARIATION
If you love more intense chocolate notes, you can substitute 80% dark chocolate for the 60% dark chocolate. The bitterness of the chocolate will also balance the sweetness of the meringue.

CHOCOLATE AND BANANA MILKSHAKE

Milkshake di banane e cioccolato

15 m   10 m

Difficulty: EASY

For the Chocolate Gelato:
see page 272

TO SERVE 4

FOR THE MILKSHAKE
3 ounces/80 g 75% dark chocolate
1 ounce/2½ tablespoons/30 g superfine (caster) sugar
7 fl oz/scant 1 cup/200 ml heavy (whipping) cream
3 bananas
1 pound 2 ounces/500 g Chocolate Gelato
7 fl oz/scant 1 cup/200 ml whole (full-fat) milk
2 cocoa beans

EQUIPMENT NEEDED
Chef's knife
Chopping board
Measuring cup or jug
Small saucepan
Silicone spatula
Mixing bowl
Electric whisk
Food processor
Mortar and pestle
4 tall glasses
Pastry (piping) bag
Large star piping tip (nozzle)

Finely chop the chocolate. Pour 5 fl oz/scant ⅔ cup/150 ml water into a small saucepan, add the sugar, and bring to a boil, stirring with a silicone spatula, until the sugar has dissolved. Cook the syrup for 5 minutes then turn off the heat. Add the chocolate and stir until the chocolate has melted.

Pour the cream into a mixing bowl and whip with an electric whisk, then set aside in the refrigerator. Peel two of the bananas and place in a food processor, add the Chocolate Gelato and milk, and blend to a smooth consistency. Slice the remaining banana widthwise, and crush the cocoa beans by pounding in a mortar and pestle.

Divide the milkshake equally between four tall glasses. Fit a pastry (piping) bag with a large star piping tip (nozzle) and fill with the whipped cream. Pipe the cream on top of the milkshake, and top with a few banana slices, the chocolate syrup, and crushed cocoa beans.

TIPS AND TRICKS
When it comes to pounding cocoa beans with a mortar and pestle, first peel off the light outer shell and crush the inner part into small crumbs, known as nibs. If you cannot find cocoa beans or nibs, use unsweetened cocoa powder instead.

CHOCOLATE AND ORANGE RICOTTA SEMIFREDDO CAKE

Torta semifreddo alla ricotta con arancia e cioccolato

40 m · 35 m · 9 h 5 m · 60 d

Difficulty: ADVANCED

For the Classic Whisked Sponge:
see page 317
For the Chocolate Shards:
see page 54

TO SERVE 8

FOR THE CHOCOLATE SPONGE
3 eggs
2¼ ounces/¼ cup/60 g superfine (caster) sugar
Pinch of salt
2½ ounces/generous ½ cup/70 g type "00" flour or
all-purpose (plain) flour
1¼ ounces/scant ⅓ cup/35 g unsweetened cocoa powder

FOR THE SEMIFREDDO
3½ ounces/100 g 80% dark chocolate
2½ ounces/70 g candied orange peel
8½ fl oz/1 cup/250 ml heavy (whipping) cream
10½ ounces/1¼ cups/300 g sheep ricotta cheese
2 ounces/scant ½ cup/50 g confectioners' (icing) sugar

FOR THE DECORATION
Chocolate Shards made with 3½ ounces/100 g
60% dark chocolate

EQUIPMENT NEEDED

6¼-inch/16-cm round springform pan (tin)
Stand mixer fitted with whisk attachment or
electric whisk and bowl
Strainer (sieve)
Silicone spatula
Parchment paper
Cooling rack
Serrated knife
Chef's knife
Chopping board
Food processor
Measuring cup or jug
Mixing bowls
Immersion (stick) blender
7-inch/18-cm round springform pan
Plastic wrap (cling film)
Acetate sheets
Metal spatula or palette knife

To make the sponge cake, preheat the oven to 350°F/180°C/160°C Fan/Gas 4 and line the base of the 6¼-inch/16-cm springform pan (tin) with parchment paper.

Break the eggs into the bowl of a stand mixer fitted with a whisk attachment or use a mixing bowl and electric whisk, add the sugar and a pinch of salt, and beat together until the mixture is pale and very fluffy, about 10 minutes. Add the flour sifted with the cocoa powder and, using a silicone spatula, gently fold to combine, taking care not to knock any air out of the mixture.

Pour the batter into the prepared springform pan (tin) and bake in the preheated oven for 35 minutes. Turn off the oven and leave the cake to rest in the oven for 5 minutes, leaving the door slightly ajar. Remove from the oven and set aside to cool slightly, then remove from the pan and place on a cooling rack. When the sponge has cooled completely, use a serrated knife to cut the sponge horizontally into three even layers.

To make the semifreddo, finely chop the chocolate. Blend the candied orange peel to a paste in a food processor. Pour the cream into a mixing bowl and whip with an electric whisk. In a separate bowl, blend the ricotta cheese with the confectioners' (icing) sugar using an immersion (stick) blender until creamy, then fold in the orange peel paste, finely chopped chocolate, and whipped cream.

Line the 7-inch/18-cm springform pan with plastic wrap (cling film) and place a sponge layer on the bottom of the pan. Spread one-third of the ricotta mixture over the top and sides. Repeat the process until all the sponge layers and the ricotta cream have been used, finishing with a layer of the ricotta cream.

Freeze for 8 hours, then remove the semifreddo from the pan. Peel off the plastic wrap and transfer to a serving plate. Decorate with the Chocolate Shards and leave to stand at room temperature for 1 hour before serving.

DARK AND WHITE CHOCOLATE GELATO POPS

Stecco al cioccolato bianco e nero

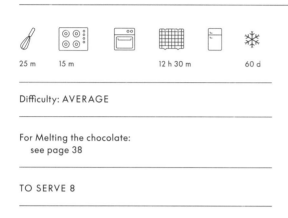

25 m   15 m   12 h 30 m   60 d

Difficulty: AVERAGE

For Melting the chocolate:
   see page 38

TO SERVE 8

FOR THE GELATO POPS
5 ounces/150 g white chocolate
10 fl oz/1¼ cups/300 ml heavy (whipping) cream
20 fl oz/2½ cups/600 ml whole (full-fat) milk
3 egg yolks
1½ ounces/3 heaping tablespoons/40 g superfine
   (caster) sugar
10½ ounces/300 g 70% dark chocolate

EQUIPMENT NEEDED
Chef's knife
Chopping board
Measuring cup or jug
Saucepans
Bain-marie or double boiler
Electric whisk
Silicone spatula
Kitchen thermometer
Cold bain-marie
Ice cream maker
Ice pop molds
Ice pop sticks

Finely chop the white chocolate. Pour the cream and milk into a saucepan and bring to a boil. Place the egg yolks in the bowl of a bain-marie or double boiler, add the sugar, and beat with an electric whisk until pale and fluffy. Pour the hot milk and cream into the bowl and cook the custard in the bain-marie, stirring with a silicone spatula, until thick enough to coat the back of a spoon, or until the temperature reaches 185°F/85°C.

Remove from the heat, add the white chocolate, and stir until the chocolate has melted. Transfer the bowl from the bain-marie to a cold bain-marie and quickly cool the custard.

Make the gelato by churning the custard in the ice cream maker according to the manufacturer's instructions. Fill the ice pop molds with gelato and freeze for 30 minutes, then insert the ice pop sticks and freeze for a further 12 hours.

When the ice pops are fully frozen, finely chop and melt the dark chocolate in a bain-marie. Remove the gelato pops from the molds, quickly dip each one into the melted chocolate, and serve.

MISTAKES TO AVOID
To prevent the gelato from melting, rest the melted dark chocolate for 5 minutes, to cool slightly, before dipping the gelato pops.

WHITE CHOCOLATE GELATO WITH WALNUTS AND FENNEL SEED BRITTLE

Gelato al cioccolato bianco, noci e finocchio caramellato

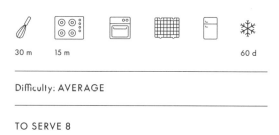

30 m   15 m   60 d

Difficulty: AVERAGE

TO SERVE 8

FOR THE GELATO
6¼ ounces/180 g white chocolate
4 egg yolks
4 ounces/½ cup/120 g superfine (caster) sugar
25 fl oz/3 cups/750 ml heavy (whipping) cream
2 ounces/⅓ cup/60 g brown sugar
2 teaspoons fennel seeds
3 ounces/¾ cup/80 g red walnut kernels

EQUIPMENT NEEDED
Chef's knife
Chopping board
Mixing bowls
Bain-marie or double boiler
Electric whisk
Measuring cup or jug
Small saucepans
Silicone spatula
Kitchen thermometer
Cold bain-marie
Ice cream maker
Baking sheet
Parchment paper
8 glasses

Finely chop the chocolate and place in a mixing bowl. Place the egg yolks in the bowl of a bain-marie or double boiler, add the superfine (caster) sugar, and beat with an electric whisk until pale and fluffy. Pour the cream into a small saucepan and bring to a simmer. Pour the hot cream into the chocolate, stirring continuously, until the chocolate has melted.

Pour the white chocolate cream into the beaten egg yolks and cook the custard in a bain-marie, stirring with a silicone spatula, until thick enough to coat the back of a spoon, or until the temperature reaches 185°F/85°C.

Transfer the bowl from the bain-marie to a cold bain-marie and quickly cool the custard.

Make the gelato by churning the custard in the ice cream maker according to the manufacturer's instructions. Place the brown sugar in a small saucepan, add 1 tablespoon of water, and cook to a golden caramel, swirling the pan from time to time until the sugar has completely dissolved. Stir in the fennel seeds, then pour the caramel onto a baking sheet lined with parchment paper. Spread in a thin layer and set aside to cool and harden, forming a brittle.

Coarsely crush the fennel seed brittle, and add two-thirds to the gelato during the last few minutes of churning. Coarsely chop the walnuts, divide them equally between the glasses, and top with a scoop of gelato. Serve sprinkled with the remaining crushed fennel seed brittle.

RUBY CHOCOLATE AND ROASTED PLUM SEMIFREDDI

Semifreddo di cioccolato ruby con prugne arrosto

30 m	5 m	40 m	9 h 10 m		60 d

Difficulty: AVERAGE

For the Chocolate Pâte à Bombe:
   see page 92
For the Chocolate Curls:
   see page 50 (variation)

TO SERVE 8

FOR THE SEMIFREDDI
1 pound 2 ounces/500 g red plums
1 vanilla bean (pod)
1 ounce/1½ tablespoons/30 g acacia honey
1 quantity Chocolate Pâte à Bombe made with
   8¾ ounces/240 g ruby chocolate
7 fl oz/scant 1 cup/200 ml heavy (whipping) cream

FOR THE DECORATION
Chocolate Curls made from 1 × 3½-ounce/100-g bar
   ruby chocolate

EQUIPMENT NEEDED
Baking sheet
Parchment paper
Paring knife
Chopping board
Mixing bowls
Food processor
Kitchen thermometer
Measuring cup or jug
Electric whisk
Silicone spatula
8 × 2½-inch/6-cm round, smooth, deep pudding pans (tins)
Plastic wrap (cling film)
Marble board
Small round pastry cutter

Preheat the oven to 350°F/180°C/160°C Fan/Gas 4 and line the baking sheet with parchment paper.

Wash and dry the plums. Halve, pit, and cut each half into two wedges. Split the vanilla bean (pod) lengthwise, using a sharp paring knife, and remove the seeds. Place the plums in a bowl with the honey and vanilla seeds, and mix to combine. Transfer to the lined baking sheet and roast in the preheated oven for 10 minutes.

Remove from the oven and set aside 8 plum wedges, then return to the oven and roast the remaining plums for a further 30 minutes. Set aside to cool then transfer to a food processor and briefly pulse to coarsely chop the plums.

Make the Pâte à Bombe as shown in the basic technique, substituting melted ruby chocolate at a temperature of 108°F/42°C for the dark chocolate.

Pour the cream into a mixing bowl and whip with an electric whisk. Fold the whipped cream into the Pâte à Bombe, using a silicone spatula, then add the chopped plums and stir gently to combine.

Line the pudding pans (tins) with plastic wrap (cling film), then divide the mixture equally between the pans, and freeze for 8 hours.

One hour before you are ready to serve the semifreddi, unmold them by inverting directly onto small plates, remove the plastic wrap, and refrigerate for 1 hour.

Decorate with the reserved plum wedges and the ruby Chocolate Curls. Leave to stand at room temperature for 10 minutes before serving.

TIPS AND TRICKS
To make large chocolate curls, the chocolate bar should be neither too cold nor too warm. If the bar is too cold you can warm it slightly between the palms of your hands, and if it is too warm, place it in the refrigerator for a few minutes.

ZABAIONE AND CHOCOLATE SEMIFREDDO

Semifreddo zabaione e cioccolato

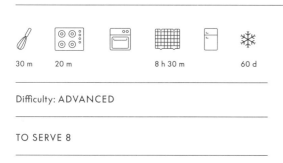

30 m	20 m			8 h 30 m	60 d

Difficulty: ADVANCED

TO SERVE 8

FOR THE SEMIFREDDO
3 egg yolks
Pinch of salt
3½ ounces/scant ½ cup/100 g superfine (caster) sugar
1¾ fl oz/3 tablespoons/50 ml Vin Santo dessert wine
3½ fl oz/scant ½ cup/100 ml heavy (whipping) cream
3½ ounces/100 g 80% dark chocolate
1 egg white

FOR THE CHOCOLATE SAUCE
3½ ounces/100 g 70% dark chocolate
3½ fl oz/scant ½ cup/100 ml heavy (whipping) cream
3½ fl oz/scant ½ cup/100 ml whole (full-fat) milk

EQUIPMENT NEEDED
Bain-marie or double boiler
Electric whisk
Measuring cup or jug
Mixing bowls
Chef's knife
Chopping board
Kitchen thermometer
Silicone spatula
9 × 3-inch/23 × 8-cm loaf pan (tin)
Plastic wrap (cling film)
Small saucepan

Place the egg yolks, a pinch of salt, and 2 ounces/¼ cup/50 g of the sugar in the bowl of a bain-marie or double boiler, and beat with an electric whisk until pale and fluffy. Add the wine and 1 tablespoon plus 2 teaspoons/25 ml water and stir to combine. Cook the zabaione in the bain-marie, whisking continuously, until thick and fluffy. Transfer to a bowl and set aside to cool to room temperature. Pour the cream into a mixing bowl and whip with an electric whisk, then set aside in the refrigerator.

Finely chop the 80% dark chocolate and melt in the bain-marie. Add the remaining sugar with 1 tablespoon water and cook until the temperature reaches 230°F/110°C.

Place the egg white in a clean, grease-free bowl and whisk to soft peaks with an electric whisk. Slowly drizzle the boiling chocolate syrup into the whisked egg white, whisking continuously to combine. Continue to whisk the mixture until the meringue cools completely.

Using a silicone spatula, fold the meringue into the zabaione, followed by the whipped cream. Line the loaf pan (tin) with plastic wrap (cling film) and pour the mixture into the pan. Freeze for 8 hours.

Just before you are ready to serve the semifreddo, make the sauce. Finely chop the chocolate and melt in the bain-marie. Pour the cream and milk into a small saucepan and bring to a simmer. Add to the melted chocolate, a third at a time, stirring to combine. Unmold the semifreddo onto a serving plate and peel off the plastic wrap. Rest at room temperature for 30 minutes, and serve with the hot chocolate sauce.

MILK CHOCOLATE AND MACADAMIA SEMIFREDDO

Semifreddo di cioccolato al latte con noci macadamia

20 m   15 m   6–8 h   60 d

Difficulty: AVERAGE

For Melting the chocolate:
  see page 38
For the Chocolate and Cream Glaze:
  see page 70

TO SERVE 8

FOR THE SEMIFREDDO
10½ ounces/300 g milk chocolate
3 eggs
2 egg yolks
2¼ ounces/½ cup/60 g confectioners' (icing) sugar
3½ ounces/scant ⅔ cup/100 g blanched macadamia nuts
13 fl oz/generous 1½ cups/400 ml heavy (whipping) cream
½ quantity Chocolate and Cream Glaze

EQUIPMENT NEEDED
Chef's knife
Chopping board
Bain-marie or double boiler
Heat-resistant bowl
Electric whisk
Heavy-bottomed skillet (frying pan)
Food processor
Silicone spatula
Measuring cup or jug
Mixing bowl
7 x 3-inch/18 x 8-cm amor polenta sponge baking pan (tin)
Plastic wrap (cling film)

Finely chop the chocolate and melt in a bain-marie or double boiler, then set aside. Place the eggs and the extra egg yolks in a heat-resistant bowl, add the confectioners' (icing) sugar, place over the bain-marie, and beat with an electric whisk until pale and fluffy.

Remove the bowl from the bain-marie and continue to beat the eggs until the mixture cools completely. Toast the macadamia nuts in a dry, heavy-bottomed skillet (frying pan) over a low heat until they begin to turn golden. Set aside until cool enough to handle, then thinly slice 4 or 5 nuts and set aside. Blend the remaining nuts in a food processor until coarsely ground.

Fold the melted chocolate into the beaten egg mixture, using a silicone spatula. Pour the cream into a mixing bowl and whip with an electric whisk to soft peaks, then gently fold into the mixture together with the chopped nuts.

Pour the mixture into the baking pan (tin). Cover the pan with plastic wrap (cling film) and freeze for 6–8 hours. To unmold, dip the bottom of the pan in boiling water for a few seconds then invert directly onto a serving plate. Cover the semifreddo with the Chocolate and Cream Glaze, and decorate with the reserved sliced nuts.

BEVERAGES

HOT CHOCOLATE WITH COCONUT AND CINNAMON

Cioccolata al cocco e cannella

5 m   10 m   15 m

Difficulty: EASY

TO SERVE 4

FOR THE HOT CHOCOLATE
1 vanilla bean (pod)
7 fl oz/scant 1 cup/200 ml whole (full-fat) milk
2 ounces/½ cup/50 g unsweetened cocoa powder
2 ounces/50 g 60% dark chocolate
7 fl oz/scant 1 cup/200 ml coconut milk
4 long cinnamon sticks

EQUIPMENT NEEDED
Paring knife
Measuring cup or jug
Saucepan
Fine-mesh strainer (sieve)
Mixing bowls
Chef's knife
Chopping board
Hand whisk
Silicone spatula
4 cups

Split the vanilla bean (pod) lengthwise with a sharp paring knife. Pour the milk into a saucepan, add the vanilla bean, and bring to a boil. Turn off the heat and leave to steep for 15 minutes.

Sift the cocoa powder into a small bowl, then finely chop the chocolate and place in a separate bowl. Remove the vanilla bean and drizzle the milk over the cocoa, stirring continuously with a hand whisk. Return the milk to the pan and bring back to a boil, then pour over the chocolate and stir with a silicone spatula until all the chocolate has melted. Return to the pan and add the coconut milk, bring to a simmer, then serve in cups with a cinnamon stick in each one.

TIPS AND TRICKS
If your hot chocolate is not smooth, blend it for a few seconds with an immersion (stick) blender, then tap the container on the work surface to remove any air bubbles.

BICERIN

Bicerin

5 m   5 m

Difficulty: EASY

For Melting the chocolate:
   see page 38

TO SERVE 4

3½ ounces/100 g 60% dark chocolate
4 shots boiling hot espresso coffee, sweetened to taste
3½ fl oz/scant ½ cup/100 ml whole (full-fat) milk
3½ fl oz/scant ½ cup/100 ml heavy (whipping) cream

EQUIPMENT NEEDED
Chef's knife
Chopping board
Bain-marie or double boiler
Silicone spatula
Measuring cup or jug
Mixing bowl
Electric whisk
4 heat-resistant glasses

Finely chop the chocolate and melt in a bain-marie or double boiler. Add the boiling coffee and milk, and stir with a silicone spatula until hot.

Pour the cream into a bowl and lightly whip with an electric whisk until it begins to thicken. Pour the hot chocolate into glasses, add the whipped cream, and serve.

TIPS AND TRICKS
To make sure the cream does not sink as you add it to the chocolate, carefully let it slide over the back of a spoon placed in the center of the glass.

VIENNESE HOT CHOCOLATE

Cioccolata viennese

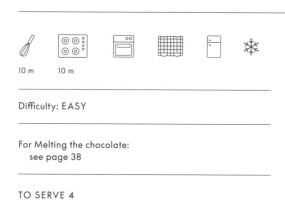

10 m   10 m

Difficulty: EASY

For Melting the chocolate:
  see page 38

TO SERVE 4

FOR THE HOT CHOCOLATE
5 ounces/150 g 70% dark chocolate
27 fl oz/3⅓ cups/800 ml whole (full-fat) milk
7 fl oz/scant 1 cup/200 ml boiling water
Sugar, to taste
5 fl oz/scant ⅔ cup/150 ml heavy (whipping) cream
¾ ounce/2 tablespoons/20 g confectioners' (icing) sugar
Unsweetened cocoa powder, for dusting

EQUIPMENT NEEDED
Chef's knife
Chopping board
Bain-marie or double boiler
Measuring cup or jug
Hand whisk
Mixing bowl
Strainer (sieve)
Electric whisk
Silicone spatula
Pastry (piping) bag
⅝-inch/1.5-cm star piping tip (nozzle)
4 heat-resistant glasses

Finely chop the chocolate and melt in a bain-marie or double boiler. Add the milk and boiling water and heat the chocolate mix for 5 minutes, stirring continuously with a hand whisk. Sweeten, to taste, and set aside to cool to room temperature.

Use an electric whisk to whip the cream with the confectioners' (icing) sugar. Add the sugar towards the end, once the cream is partially whipped. Fill a pastry (piping) bag fitted with a star piping tip (nozzle). Reheat the chocolate and serve in glasses. Pipe the whipped cream on top of the chocolate and dust with the cocoa powder.

VARIATION
If you do not like the intense flavor of dark chocolate, you can make this chocolate using milk, white, or ruby chocolate, omitting the sugar.

CHOCOLATE LIQUEUR

Liquore al cioccolato

10 m   5 m   45 d   6 mths

Difficulty: EASY

MAKES 50 FL OZ / 6½ CUPS / 1.5 LITERS

FOR THE LIQUEUR
1 pound/2¼ cups/450 g cane sugar
1 ounce/¼ cup/30 g unsweetened cocoa powder
9 ounces/250 g 70% dark chocolate
13 fl oz/generous 1½ cups/400 ml neutral spirit

EQUIPMENT NEEDED
Saucepan
Strainer (sieve)
Measuring cup or jug
Hand whisk
Chef's knife
Chopping board
3 × 17 fl oz/½-liter bottles with airtight stopper,
    clean and completely dry
Fine-mesh strainer (sieve)

Place the sugar into a saucepan, add the sifted cocoa powder, and slowly pour in 22 fl oz/2¾ cups/650 ml water, stirring continuously with a hand whisk. Cook over a moderate heat, stirring often, until the sugar has dissolved. Finely chop the chocolate. Remove the pan from the heat and add the chocolate to the cocoa mixture, stirring until the chocolate has melted. Set aside to cool to room temperature.

When cooled, add the spirit, and stir. Fill the bottles with the liqueur, replace the stopper, and seal closed. Rest the bottles in a dark place for 2 weeks, shaking them occasionally.

Strain the liqueur through a fine-mesh strainer (sieve), refill the bottles, and rest for a month in a cool, dark place before serving. This liqueur can be stored in the refrigerator or pantry for up to 6 months.

THICK PINK HOT CHOCOLATE

Cioccolata densa rosa

10 m   15 m

Difficulty: EASY

For Melting the chocolate:
see page 38

TO SERVE 4

FOR THE HOT CHOCOLATE
7 ounces/200 g ruby chocolate
½ ounce/10 g sugar
¾ ounce/18 g rice starch
17 fl oz/2 cups/500 ml whole (full-fat) milk
Ground black pepper, for sprinkling (optional)

EQUIPMENT NEEDED
Chef's knife
Chopping board
Bain-marie or double boiler
4 cups
Mixing bowl
Measuring cup or jug
Saucepan
Hand whisk

Finely chop the chocolate and melt in a bain-marie or double boiler. Dip the rim of the cups in the melted chocolate and shake to remove any excess. Dip the chocolate-coated rims in the sugar and leave to set.

Place the rice starch in a bowl and pour in 3½ fl oz/scant ½ cup/100 ml of the milk. Mix to combine then stir in the remaining milk with a hand whisk. Transfer to a saucepan and cook for 5 minutes.

Add the remaining melted ruby chocolate and cook, stirring continuously with a whisk until it reaches the desired consistency.

Pour the chocolate into the cups and sprinkle with ground black pepper, if desired.

COCOA BEAN AND SAGE INFUSION

Infuso di fave di cacao e salvia

2 m   5 m   10 m

Difficulty: EASY

TO SERVE 4

FOR THE INFUSION
5 sage leaves
3 teaspoons cane sugar
6 cocoa beans

EQUIPMENT NEEDED
Measuring cup or jug
Saucepan
Heat-resistant pitcher (jug)
4 heat-resistant glasses

Bring 17 fl oz/2 cups/500 ml water to a boil in a saucepan. Place the sage leaves in a pitcher (jug) and add the sugar and cocoa beans. Pour in the boiling water and leave to steep for 10 minutes.

Remove the sage, place a cocoa bean in each glass, and serve the infusion warm, or cold with ice.

MILK CHOCOLATE WITH PORT

Cioccolata al latte al Porto

5 m   5 m

Difficulty: EASY

For the Chocolate Shavings:
    see page 50

TO SERVE 4

FOR THE CHOCOLATE
3½ ounces/100 g milk chocolate
17 fl oz/2 cups/500 ml whole (full-fat) milk
2 fl oz/¼ cup/60 ml ruby port
Milk Chocolate Shavings, to decorate

EQUIPMENT NEEDED
Chef's knife
Chopping board
Mixing bowl
Measuring cup or jug
Saucepan
Hand whisk
Pitcher (jug)
4 heat-resistant glasses

Finely chop the chocolate and place in a bowl. Pour the milk into a saucepan and bring to a boil. Remove from the heat and drizzle the hot milk into the chocolate, stirring with a hand whisk until the chocolate has melted.

Transfer to a pitcher (jug), add the port, and leave to cool. When ready to serve, pour into glasses and decorate with the Chocolate Shavings.

MISTAKES TO AVOID
You can melt the chocolate in a bain-marie or double boiler before mixing it with the hot milk. However, you need to pay close attention to the temperature of the water in the water bath. The water should not be brought to a boil as both milk chocolate and white chocolate tend to burn very easily, making them unusable.

CHOCOLATE AND VANILLA CAFFÈ SHAKERATO—ITALIAN-STYLE ICED COFFEE

Caffè shakerato al cioccolato e vaniglia

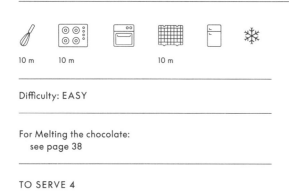

10 m   10 m   10 m

Difficulty: EASY

For Melting the chocolate:
   see page 38

TO SERVE 4

FOR THE ICED COFFEE
2 ounces/50 g white chocolate
1 vanilla bean (pod)
7 fl oz/scant 1 cup/200 ml whole (full-fat) milk
13 fl oz/generous 1½ cups/400 ml hot coffee
3½ ounces/100 g 60% dark chocolate
Ice cubes

EQUIPMENT NEEDED
Chef's knife
Chopping board
Bain-marie or double boiler
4 tall glasses
Paring knife
Measuring cup or jug
Saucepan
Chocolate grater
Silicone spatula
Cocktail shaker

Finely chop the white chocolate and melt in a bain-marie or double boiler. Use a teaspoon to smear a little of the melted chocolate down one side of each glass, for decoration. Place the glasses in the freezer for 10 minutes for the chocolate to harden.

Split the vanilla bean (pod) lengthwise with a sharp paring knife. Pour the milk into a saucepan, add the vanilla bean, and warm over a low heat. Add the coffee and shred (grate) in the dark chocolate.

Gently stir with a silicone spatula until the chocolate has melted, then pour into a cocktail shaker with 3–4 ice cubes and shake.

Fill the chilled glasses with the chocolate-flavored iced coffee and serve.

BASIC RECIPES

CLASSIC (SWEET) PIE DOUGH (SHORTCRUST PASTRY)

Pasta frolla classica

15 m   1 h   24 h   60 d

Difficulty: AVERAGE

FOR THE DOUGH
10½ ounces/2½ cups/300 g type "00" flour or all-purpose
 (plain) flour, plus extra for dusting
5 ounces/1⅓ sticks/150 g cold unsalted butter
3 ounces/⅓ cup/80 g superfine (caster) sugar
Grated zest of 1 unwaxed lemon
Pinch of salt
1 egg
2 egg yolks

EQUIPMENT NEEDED
Strainer (sieve)
Chef's knife
Zester
Plastic wrap (cling film)

AS USED IN
– Chocolate and Chili Tart (page 142)
– Dark Chocolate Baked Custard Torte (page 150)
– White Chocolate and Raspberry Tart (page 164)

Sift the flour into a mound on a clean work surface and make a well in the middle. Cut the cold butter into small cubes and place in the well with the sugar, lemon zest, and a pinch of salt.

Working quickly to ensure the ingredients do not become too warm, rub everything together using your fingertips. Starting from the center and working outwards, gradually incorporate all the flour into the butter until the mixture resembles coarse bread crumbs.

Rub the mixture between the palms of your hands to break it down into fine crumbs. When the mixture resembles sand, heap it back into a mound and make a well in the middle, then add the egg and two additional egg yolks to the well.

Using your fingertips, combine all the ingredients, then shape the dough (pastry) into a ball, work quickly and do not handle the dough more than necessary.

Gently flatten the ball of dough slightly, then wrap it in plastic wrap (cling film). Leave to rest in the refrigerator for at least 1 hour.

If you often use pie dough, you can multiply the ingredients to make more dough and divide it into individual portions. Wrap each portion individually, and place in a freezer bag for freezing.

When it is time to use the pie dough, roll it out to ⅛ inch/2–3 mm thick on a lightly floured work surface, then carefully lift the rolled-out dough and transfer it to a prepared pan (tin). Press down firmly on the base and sides and trim away any excess dough that is overhanging the sides with a small sharp knife. Bake as instructed in your recipe.

VARIATIONS
Classic (sweet) pie dough has many different variations, depending on the percentage of butter used, the type and amount of sugar, and whether part of the flour is replaced with a nut meal or flour. Pâte sucrée is mainly used for blind baking. It is made by mixing 9 ounces/2 cups/250 g flour with 3½ ounces/scant 1 stick/100 g butter, 3 ounces/scant ⅔ cup/80 g confectioners' (icing) sugar, 2 eggs, and a pinch of salt. Chocolate pie dough, on the other hand, is made with 9 ounces/2 cups/250 g flour, 4¾ ounces/ 1¼ sticks/140 g butter, ¾ ounce/2 heaping tablespoons/20 g sifted unsweetened cocoa powder, 3 ounces/⅓ cup/80 g superfine (caster) sugar, 1 egg, and 1 egg yolk. Sweet nut dough is made by mixing 9 ounces/2 cups/250 g flour with 3½ ounces/1 cup/100 g nut meal (almonds, hazelnuts, pistachios, or walnuts), 3½ ounces/ scant 1 cup/100 g confectioners' sugar, 4¾ ounces/1¼ sticks/140 g butter, 1 egg, and a pinch of salt.

ALL-BUTTER PIE DOUGH (PASTRY)

Pasta brisée

10 m · 1 h · 24 h · 60 d

Difficulty: AVERAGE

FOR THE DOUGH
7 ounces/1⅔ cups/200 g type "00" flour or all-purpose
    (plain) flour, plus extra for dusting
1 ounce/2½ tablespoons/30 g superfine (caster) sugar
Pinch of salt
3½ ounces/scant 1 stick/100 g cold unsalted butter

EQUIPMENT NEEDED
Strainer (sieve)
Chef's knife
Metal dough scraper
Measuring cup or jug
Plastic wrap (cling film)

Sift the flour into a mound on a clean work surface and make a well in the middle. Add the sugar and a pinch of salt. Cut the cold butter into small cubes and place in the well along with the sugar and salt.

Working quickly to ensure the ingredients do not become too warm, mix the ingredients together using a metal dough scraper. Starting from the center and working outwards, gradually incorporate all of the flour into the butter until the mixture resembles coarse bread crumbs.

Heap the crumbs back into a mound and make a well in the middle, then add 1¾ fl oz/3 tablespoons/50 ml cold water to the well.

Using your fingertips, combine all the ingredients then shape the dough (pastry) into a small block of even thickness. Again, work quickly and do not handle the dough more than necessary to prevent it becoming too warm.

Wrap the dough in plastic wrap (cling film) and leave to rest in the refrigerator for at least 1 hour.

When it is time to use the pie dough, roll it out to ⅛ inch/2–3 mm thick on a lightly floured work surface, then carefully lift the rolled-out dough and transfer it to a prepared pan (tin). Press down firmly on the base and sides, then prick the base of the dough with a fork. Trim away any excess dough that is overhanging the sides with a small sharp knife. Bake as instructed in your recipe. Alternatively, line the pastry case with parchment paper, then fill with baking beans and place in the lower part of the oven preheated to 350°F/180°C/160°C Fan/Gas 4 for 15–20 minutes to blind bake. After 15–20 minutes, remove the baking beans and parchment paper and return to the oven for a further 10–15 minutes, or until the pastry case has dried out.

VARIATION
One variation includes egg. To make the dough, mix 7 ounces/1⅔ cups/200 g flour with 3¼ ounces/¾ stick/90 g butter, 1 egg, 1 ounce/2½ tablespoons/30 g sugar, and a pinch of salt. Once you have lined the pan (tin) with the dough, it should rest for at least 10 minutes in the refrigerator before being baked at 350°F/180°C/160°C Fan/Gas 4.

CRUMBLE MIX

Impasto per crumble

10 m   24 h   60 d

Difficulty: EASY

FOR THE MIX
5½ ounces/scant 1½ sticks/160 g cold unsalted butter
9 ounces/2 cups/250 g type "00" flour or all-purpose
    (plain) flour
2 ounces/¼ cup/50 g turbinado (Demerara) sugar,
    plus extra for sprinkling (optional)
Pinch of salt
Grated zest of ½ unwaxed orange or lemon, or seeds of
    1 vanilla bean (pod)

EQUIPMENT NEEDED
Chef's knife
Mixing bowl

Cut the butter into small cubes and place in a mixing bowl. Add the flour to the bowl with the sugar, cold butter, and a pinch of salt.

Working quickly to ensure the ingredients do not become too warm, rub everything together using your fingertips. Gradually incorporate all the flour into the butter until the mixture resembles coarse bread crumbs.

Chop your chosen fruit into small chunks and sprinkle with sugar, if using. Add any flavorings, such as citrus zest or vanilla. Spoon the fruit into a single ovenproof dish or divide it equally between individual ovenproof dishes.

Spoon the crumble mix onto your fruit pieces, covering them completely. Bake in a preheated oven at 400°F/200°C/180°C Fan/Gas 6 for 30–35 minutes, or until the crumble topping is lightly golden and the fruit is soft and its juices are bubbling around the edges.

MISTAKES TO AVOID
As with other types of dough (pastry), it is very important to prevent the crumble mix from becoming too warm while it is being worked. Always use cold butter, cut into small cubes, and do not overwork the dough. If soft butter is used or the crumble mix is allowed to get too warm, you will end up with a smooth dough instead of the characteristic crumb-like texture. If this happens, wrap the dough in plastic wrap (cling film) and leave to cool in the refrigerator for 1–2 hours, or until firm, then shred (grate) it directly onto the fruit, using a grater with large holes.

CLASSIC WHISKED SPONGE

Pan di Spagna

 20 m   40 m 20 m

Difficulty: EASY

FOR THE SPONGE
6 eggs
4 ounces/scant ⅔ cup/130 g superfine (caster) sugar
Flavoring to taste (seeds of 1 vanilla bean (pod) or the
    grated zest of ½ unwaxed lemon)
Pinch of salt
5 ounces/scant 1¼ cups/150 g type "00" flour or
    all-purpose (plain) flour
1 ounce/30 g potato starch

EQUIPMENT NEEDED
8-inch/20-cm round springform cake pan (tin)
Parchment paper
Stand mixer fitted with whisk attachment or
    electric whisk and bowl
Mixing bowl
Strainer (sieve)
Silicone spatula
Cooling rack
Plastic wrap (cling film)

AS USED IN
– Chocolate and Orange Ricotta Semifreddo Cake
    (page 282)

Preheat the oven to 350°F/180°C/160°C Fan/Gas 4 and line the cake pan (tin) with parchment paper. Do not butter or flour the pan, simply line it with parchment paper.

Break the eggs into the bowl of the stand mixer fitted with a whisk attachment, or use an electric whisk and a mixing bowl. Add the sugar, any flavoring, and a pinch of salt. Start the mixer on a slow speed and start to beat the ingredients together. Gradually increase the speed, and continue to beat for 10 minutes, until the mixture falls from the whisk in wide ribbons and leaves a visible trace on the mixture below.

Combine the flour and potato starch in a bowl then sift one-third directly onto the whisked egg mixture. Using a silicone spatula, gently fold the flour into the mixture with an upwards motion, taking care not to knock any air out of the mixture.

Sift in the remaining flour, one-third at a time, and gently fold in to combine. Pour the sponge mixture into the lined pan.

Bake the sponge in the preheated oven for 40 minutes, or until golden, risen, and firm on top—the sponge should be starting to shrink away from the pan and a skewer inserted into the center comes out clean. Do not open the oven door until the end of the cooking time to prevent the cake from sinking in the center. Leave the sponge to cool for 20 minutes before removing it from the pan. If necessary, run a silicone spatula in between the pan and cake to loosen the sponge. Place the sponge on a cooling rack to cool completely.

The sponge can be stored for 72 hours when wrapped in plastic wrap (cling film) and kept at room temperature. As there is no fat in the mixture, it is susceptible to drying out.

The sponge can be sliced and layered with any filling. In which case, it is best to bake the sponge the day before as it is easier to cut the day after baking. It should never be cut while still warm, as it will be too soft and crumbly.

MISTAKES TO AVOID
To whisk the eggs perfectly, they must be at room temperature and not cold from the refrigerator. It is possible to mix the eggs and sugar, then start to whisk in a bain-marie or double boiler with gently simmering water, without letting the temperature exceed 104°F/40°C, then transfer to the stand mixer and continue to beat until pale and mousse-like and falling in ribbons. It is also advisable to use this bain-marie method if using only a hand mixer.

SAVOY SPONGE
Pasta biscuit

15 m   7–10 m

Difficulty: EASY

FOR THE SPONGE
4 eggs
4 ounces/½ cup/120 g superfine (caster) sugar,
   plus extra for sprinkling
Pinch of salt
4 ounces/1 cup/125 g type "00" flour or all-purpose
   (plain) flour

EQUIPMENT NEEDED
15 × 10-inch/38 × 25-cm jelly roll pan (Swiss roll tin) or
   baking tray (pan)
Parchment paper
Mixing bowls
Electric whisk
Silicone spatula
Strainer (sieve)
Palette knife

AS USED IN
– Chocolate Charlotte with Rum, Banana, and Coconut
   (page 140)
– Chocolate and Pistachio Vertical Cake (page 166)

Preheat the oven to 425°F/220°C/200°C Fan/Gas 7 and line the jelly roll pan (Swiss roll tin) with parchment paper.

Separate the egg yolks from the whites and place the whites in a grease-free bowl. Add half the sugar and a pinch of salt to the egg whites and whisk with an electric whisk until the mixture reaches soft peaks, and the sugar has completely dissolved.

Add the remaining sugar and 1 tablespoon of water to the egg yolks in a separate bowl. Beat with an electric whisk until the mixture is pale and fluffy. Add a quarter of the whisked egg whites to the beaten yolk mixture and gently fold it in using a silicone spatula.

Sift all the flour directly onto the beaten yolk mixture and gently fold it into the mix using the spatula. Add the remaining whisked egg whites and gently fold in until fully combined.

Pour the sponge mixture into the lined baking pan (tin), spreading it evenly with a palette knife. Place in the preheated oven and bake for 7–10 minutes, or until lightly golden, risen, and just firm to the touch, and a skewer inserted into the center comes out clean. Leave the sponge to cool slightly in the pan, then turn out onto a sheet of parchment paper dusted with superfine (caster) sugar.

TIPS AND TRICKS
As well as the preparation of roulades with different fillings, this type of sponge can also be used for the base and layers of a cake. It can also be used in a charlotte. In this case, you can make the sponge more decorative by piping the mixture onto a lined baking sheet using a pastry (piping) bag fitted with a ½-inch/1-cm plain piping tip (nozzle), creating oblique lines close to each other. Bake for 8–10 minutes at 350°F/180°C/160°C Fan/Gas 4. Cut the sponge to fit the bottom and sides of the pan for the charlotte.

CHOUX PASTRY

Pasta choux per bignè

30 m   10 m   35 m   30 m   48 h

Difficulty: AVERAGE

FOR THE CHOUX PASTRY
3¾ ounces/1 stick/115 g unsalted butter
Pinch of salt
1 teaspoon superfine (caster) sugar
4¾ ounces/generous 1 cup/140 g type "00" flour or
   all-purpose (plain) flour
5 eggs

EQUIPMENT NEEDED
2 baking sheets
Parchment paper
Measuring cup or jug
Saucepan
Silicone spatula
Mixing bowl
Pastry (piping) bag
½-inch/1-cm smooth piping tip (nozzle)

AS USED IN
– Choux Wreaths (page 134)

Preheat the oven to 400°F/200°C/180°C Fan/Gas 6 and line two baking sheets with parchment paper.

Pour 8½ fl oz/1 cup/240 ml water into a saucepan, add the butter, a pinch of salt, and the sugar, and bring to a boil over a low heat. Remove from the heat, add all the flour, and stir until smooth. Place the saucepan over a very low heat and cook for 5 minutes, stirring continuously with a silicone spatula.

Transfer the mixture to a bowl and leave to cool slightly. Add one egg at a time, mixing with the spatula until incorporated. Leave to cool completely, then fill a pastry (piping) bag fitted with a plain piping tip (nozzle) and pipe apricot-sized mounds of choux pastry in a large ring on each of the lined baking sheets. Leave a space of about ½ inch/1 cm between each mound.

Dip your finger in cold water and smooth the surface of the choux paste. Bake the wreaths in the preheated oven for 35 minutes. Then turn off the oven, leave the door slightly ajar, and rest for a further 30 minutes.

TIPS AND TRICKS
To fill the wreaths, cut in half through the center with a serrated knife, use a teaspoon to add the filling, then replace the top. This is the best method for very thick fillings, ice cream, or chopped fruit. If filling with a cream, however, it is easier to use a pastry bag. Use a thin piping tip to make a small hole in the bottom of each choux puff in the wreath and pipe the cavity full of the cream.

ITALIAN MERINGUE

Meringa italiana

20 m   10 m

Difficulty: ADVANCED

FOR THE MERINGUE
9 ounces/1¼ cups/240 g superfine (caster) sugar
3 egg whites

EQUIPMENT NEEDED
Small saucepan
Measuring cup or jug
Hand whisk
Kitchen thermometer
Stand mixer fitted with whisk attachment or
   electric whisk and bowl

Place 7 ounces/1 cup/200 g of the sugar in a small saucepan and pour in 1¾ fl oz/3 tablespoons/50 ml water. Set the pan over a low heat and let the sugar dissolve, gently stirring with a hand whisk. Once the sugar has dissolved completely, increase the heat to medium and bring the syrup to a boil. Using a kitchen thermometer (digital is best), continuously monitor the temperature.

When the syrup reaches 230°F/110°C, start to whisk the egg whites. Place the egg whites in the bowl of the stand mixer with the remaining sugar. It is important that the bowl is grease-free and that the egg whites are at room temperature and do not contain any trace of the egg yolks. Whisk the egg whites on a medium speed to soft peaks.

As soon as the syrup reaches 250°F/121°C, remove from the heat and very slowly drizzle the hot syrup into the whisked egg whites, whisking continuously to combine. Continue to whisk the mixture until the meringue has cooled down. Do not pour the syrup onto the whisks as it will set into sugar strands; instead, pour the syrup down the side of the bowl.

Increase the speed of the mixer to incorporate more air into the meringue and whisk for about 10 minutes, until it is cold and forms stiff, glossy peaks.

HOW TO USE
This type of meringue can be used for meringues that are to be browned with a cook's blowtorch, in the preparation of creams that require no further cooking, or as a base for buttercream. It adds the correct amount of sweetness and airiness in the preparation of semifreddi or fruit mousses.

FRENCH MERINGUE

Meringa francese

15 m

Difficulty: EASY

FOR THE MERINGUE
4 ounces/scant ⅔ cup/125 g superfine (caster) sugar
4 ounces/1 cup/125 g confectioners' (icing) sugar
5 egg whites

EQUIPMENT NEEDED
Mixing bowl
Stand mixer fitted with whisk attachment or
    electric whisk and bowl

AS USED IN
– Chocolate Pavlova (page 138)

Mix the superfine (caster) sugar with the confectioners' (icing) sugar in a bowl. Place the egg whites in the bowl of the stand mixer fitted with a whisk attachment. It is important that the bowl is grease-free and that the egg whites are at room temperature and do not contain any trace of the egg yolks.

Add half the sugar mix to the egg whites and start to whisk them on a medium speed, until the whisk starts to form a trace on the surface.

Add the remaining sugar, 1 tablespoon at a time, whisking continuously to incorporate. Continue to whisk for about 10 minutes at maximum speed, until you obtain a very firm and glossy meringue.

HOW TO USE
This recipe for French meringue is used to make classic meringues and pavlova meringues. To make a pavlova meringue, whisk in 1 teaspoon of lemon juice and ¾ ounce/2 heaping tablespoons/ 25 g cornstarch (cornflour) once the meringue is at the firm and glossy stage to make the meringue even firmer and more compact.

PASTRY CREAM

Crema pasticciera

10 m   7 m   48 h

Difficulty: EASY

FOR THE CREAM
17 fl oz/2 cups/500 ml whole (full-fat) milk
Pared zest of 1 unwaxed lemon or 1 vanilla bean (pod)
6 egg yolks
3½ ounces/scant ½ cup/100 g superfine (caster) sugar
3 ounces/⅔ cup/80 g type "00" flour or all-purpose
    (plain) flour

EQUIPMENT NEEDED
Measuring cup or jug
Saucepans
Paring knife
Mixing bowls
Hand or electric whisk
Strainer (sieve)
Silicone spatula
Cold bain-marie
Plastic wrap (cling film)

Pour the milk into a saucepan and add the pared lemon zest or the vanilla bean (pod), split lengthwise. Set the pan over a low heat and bring the milk almost to boiling point, then turn off the heat and set aside to cool slightly.

Place the egg yolks and sugar in a bowl. Using a hand or electric whisk, beat the egg yolks with the sugar until they are pale and fluffy. Add the flour and stir into the yolk mixture to combine.

Strain the warm milk through a strainer (sieve) into a clean saucepan. Slowly pour the milk into the bowl with the egg yolk mixture. Whisk continuously as you add the milk to avoid any lumps forming.

Strain the pastry cream mixture through a strainer into a clean saucepan and bring to a simmer, then continue cooking over a low heat for a further 5 minutes. Stir the pastry cream continuously with a silicone spatula until it becomes quite thick.

Pour the pastry cream into a bowl and set it in a cold bain-marie to cool completely. Cover it with plastic wrap (cling film), ensuring the wrap touches the surface of the cream, and use immediately, or set aside in the refrigerator.

Pastry cream can be used to fill cakes, brioches, and pastries. It can be stored in the refrigerator for up to 3 days; stir before use if chilled.

TIPS AND TRICKS
Pastry cream is one of the most used base creams of pastry making. As well as flour, it can be made with potato starch or cornstarch (cornflour), which imparts a more delicate flavor. Rice flour or rice starch can be used for those who are gluten intolerant. Depending on the type of recipe, the pastry cream can be flavored with spices, citrus fruits, coffee, or shredded (grated) chocolate.

CRÈME ANGLAISE

Crema inglese

15 m   10 m   48 h

Difficulty: AVERAGE

FOR THE CUSTARD
17 fl oz/2 cups/500 ml whole (full-fat) milk
1 vanilla bean (pod)
6 egg yolks
5 ounces/⅔ cup/150 g superfine (caster) sugar

EQUIPMENT NEEDED
Measuring cup or jug
Saucepans
Paring knife
Bain-marie or double boiler
Hand or electric whisk
Fine-mesh strainer (sieve)
Silicone spatula
Kitchen thermometer
Strainer (sieve)
Mixing bowl
Cold bain-marie
Plastic wrap (cling film)

AS USED IN
– Chocolate Bavarois with Modica Chocolate
   (page 250)

Pour the milk into a saucepan and add the vanilla bean (pod), split lengthwise. Set the pan over a low heat and bring the milk almost to boiling point, then turn off the heat and set aside to cool slightly.

Place the egg yolks and sugar in a bain-marie or double boiler. Using a hand or electric whisk, beat the egg yolks with the sugar until pale and fluffy.

Strain the warm milk through a fine-mesh strainer (sieve) into a clean saucepan. Slowly pour the milk into the bowl with the egg yolk mix. Whisk continuously as you add the milk to make a smooth custard.

Heat the custard in the bain-marie. Stir the custard continuously with a silicone spatula until it starts to thicken. Constantly monitoring the temperature with a kitchen thermometer, continue to cook the custard until it lightly coats the back of a spoon and do not allow the temperature to exceed 180–185°F/82–85°C.

Strain the custard into a mixing bowl and set it in a cold bain-marie to quickly cool. Cover the crème anglaise with plastic wrap (cling film), ensuring the wrap touches the surface of the custard, and use immediately, or set aside in the refrigerator.

Crème anglaise can be flavored to taste with spices, citrus peel, coffee, or finely chopped chocolate, which should be added at the end of cooking, when it is still warm.

Crème anglaise is the classic custard served with many desserts and can be used as a base in the preparation of gelato, or mixed with whipped cream and gelatin to make Bavarian cream (bavarois).

MISTAKES TO AVOID
Crème anglaise is a very delicate custard that needs extreme care during cooking. In fact, its temperature must never exceed 185°F/85°C, because at higher temperatures the egg yolks solidify and the cream curdles, forming small lumps. If you are experienced, you can cook it directly on the stove (hob), using a kitchen thermometer (digital is best) to monitor the temperature.

GLOSSARY

ACETATE SHEET
A flexible, clear plastic sheet with a glossy coating used in chocolate making. The flexibility of the sheet can help with molding and shaping chocolate, and the smooth surface allows the chocolate to release easily after working.

AGAR AGAR
A tasteless, vegetable-based thickener derived from a red seaweed. It is available in powder form, in flowers, or in bars. Thanks to its high gelling-thickening power, it is used in confectionery for the preparation of desserts, ice creams, puddings, creams, etc. A teaspoon of this seaweed is equivalent to about 8 sheets of gelatin and, on average, the proportion to use is 1 teaspoon to 17 fl oz/2 cups/500 ml of liquid. It is used by dissolving it in water or other liquids brought to a boil.

BAIN-MARIE COOKING
A cooking method that involves immersing a container holding the preparation to be cooked in another larger container, which is full of hot water that is kept constantly at just boiling. In particular, it is used for delicate sauces or, more frequently, to heat a preparation without altering its taste and texture. It is especially good for melting and tempering chocolate.

BAVAROIS
With a frothy and light appearance, this spoon dessert is very similar to a pudding, characterized by a base of custard and whipped cream set with gelatin and flavored with fruit, preserves (jam), chocolate, coffee, or vanilla.

BICERIN
A traditional triple-layered hot drink from Turin, consisting of chocolate, coffee, and cream. The word *"bicerin"* means "small, round glass" in Piedmontese.

BLIND BAKING
When the empty "shell" of a pie dough (pastry) case is baked in the oven with no filling, it is said to be blind-baked. Later on, this blind-baked pastry case becomes a filled tart or quiche. A tart pan (tin) is lined with dough, the base is covered with parchment paper, then the pastry case is filled with ceramic pie weights or baking beans—this prevents the pastry swelling excessively during cooking, thereby losing its shape. In the absence of these ceramic beans, dried pulses or coarse salt can be used. After the initial baking, remove the pan from the oven, remove the paper and baking beans, then return the pan to the oven, so that the dough dries out in the center and takes on a light golden color.

BONBONS
Small, molded chocolate confections, often coated (enrobed) in another layer of chocolate.

"BONET"
A traditional Piedmontese dessert of chocolate, rum, and amaretti biscuits that takes the form of a soft, rich Italian-style chocolate-caramel custard pudding.

BUNDT CAKE
Bundt cakes are baked in bundt pans (tins), which are ring-shaped and indented to create a decorative appearance when the cake is turned out. The resulting cake is quite dense and moist. The name comes from the German *"bund,"* meaning "to have a gathering."

CAFFÈ SHAKERATO
Espresso coffee is shaken with ice to create this Italian-style iced coffee, perfect for enjoying on hot summer days.

CANDIED
The process of making candied fruits involves dipping the fruit several times in a sugar solution, until the sugar is absorbed. Depending on the type of fruit, this process may be preceded by a cooking phase. During the process, the water content of the fruit is progressively replaced by sugar, which gives the candied fruit its texture, aroma, and shelf life. The candying of citrus peel is very common.

CARAMEL
The process consists of melting sugar with a little water, then boiling the syrup until it reaches an amber color and using it to make decorative shapes, spun sugar, or for coating nuts and sometimes fruits. It can also be used as the base for a caramel sauce. It requires a lot of attention, to prevent the sugar from burning or crystallizing.

CHARLOTTE
A spoon dessert of French origin, it has many variations. It is made with a special round and flared mold, lined with sponge biscuits or sponge cake soaked in liqueur, then filled with mousses, creams, and fruit compotes.

CHEESECAKE
Cheesecakes are usually made with cream cheese (fresh, spreadable white cheese) that can be flavored with fruit, chocolate, and vanilla. They have a base made from cookie (biscuit) crumbs or sponge cake.

COOK'S BLOWTORCH

An instrument with an adjustable flame used for heating different types of surfaces. In confectionery, a blowtorch is used to caramelize shaped surfaces, for example, meringue, custard cream, and crème brûlée. There are professional blowtorches for use in commercial kitchens, with high power and an adjustable flame, however there are also smaller domestic blowtorches suitable for home use, with non-adjustable flame intensity.

CORNSTARCH (CORNFLOUR)

A fine white flour obtained from the processing of maize. Its function in pâtisserie is mainly that of a thickener, along with potato starch.

CREAM OF TARTAR

A natural acidic leavening agent obtained usually from grapes and tamarind. It is a white potassium salt which has the characteristic of being odorless and tasteless. It is usually mixed with baking soda (bicarbonate of soda) to make baking powder, used for leavening cakes, muffins, and cookies (biscuits). It is widely used in natural and vegan cuisine due to the certainty of its non-animal origin and the total absence of stabilizers that could contain fatty acids of animal origin. It can also sometimes replace brewer's yeast for people with intolerances.

CRÈME ANGLAISE

Crème anglaise ("English cream") is a light custard made from sugar, egg yolk, hot milk, and vanilla. It can be used as a base ingredient in desserts, or served alongside or over desserts as a pouring custard.

CUPCAKE

Also known as a fairy cake in the UK and a patty cake in Australia, a cupcake is a small sweet sponge baked in a baking pan (tin) with cups that is similar to a muffin mold. The classic cupcake recipe calls for a topping—royal icing, glacé icing, sugar paste, or buttercream—and some decoration, which can be candied (glacé) cherries, nuts, fruits, or more elaborate sugar-paste figures.

ENROBING

A technique designed to coat a bonbon or piece of solid chocolate in a thin layer of tempered chocolate. The bonbon is dipped carefully into the tempered chocolate, and any excess allowed to drip away, before being left to set. You could also enrobe dried or candied fruit and nuts, for example.

FLEUR DE SEL

Fleur de sel ("flower of salt") is a pure form of sea salt flake that adds flavor, texture, and decoration to both savory and sweet dishes. Harvested from the surface of seawater as it evaporates, fleur de sel is noted for its superior flavor.

FRENCH MERINGUE

The easiest style of meringue to make, but the least stable until baked. Sugar is whisked gradually into beaten egg whites, then the mixture is formed into shapes and baked. It can also be folded into batters for cake mixes.

GANACHE

A wonderfully rich, smooth filling or frosting (icing) for cakes and bonbons, made by combining chocolate and cream over a low heat. Cooled ganache can also be whipped to create a lighter, fluffier texture.

GELATIN

This is the most common gelatin substance of animal origin, once obtained from the processing of fish but now more commonly derived from animal sources. Easily available, it generally comes in the form of thin and transparent sheets weighing a few grams. To use, it is softened for a few minutes in cold water, then drained and squeezed, then combined with the mixture to be thickened.

GIANDUJA

A soft, sweet blend of chocolate and hazelnuts, gianduja can be found in the form of bonbons, bars, or spreads. Gianduja is chocolate with at least 32% cocoa mixed with hazelnut meal, which originated in Turin in the early 1800s. Chopped almonds and walnuts can also be added to the mixture, provided their weight in combination with the hazelnut meal does not exceed 60% of the total.

GLAZE

From the French glacer, "to freeze," glazing involves covering the surface of cakes, cookies (biscuits), or other sweets with a shiny and sugary layer. Glazes can be flavored with chocolate, cocoa, caramel, syrups, liqueurs, and other flavorings, or enriched with other ingredients, such as egg whites, and colored with food dye.

INCORPORATING

The term "incorporating" is used when a solid ingredient is mixed into a liquid or semi-liquid. It is best to carry out this process in several stages to obtain a homogeneous mixture: small quantities of each ingredient are combined, with more of each being added only when the previous additions are fully mixed together.

ITALIAN MERINGUE
More stable than French meringue, Italian meringue is made by whisking a hot sugar syrup into beaten egg whites. It doesn't require any baking, and is often used as a piped frosting (icing) as it holds its shape well.

MELTING
Melt ingredients such as butter or chocolate in a bain-marie or double boiler, microwave oven, or over a low heat. A low temperature is important so that the ingredients just melt and do not boil, as boiling could affect the flavor and texture.

MODICA CHOCOLATE
Traditional to Sicily, Modica chocolate is designated a P.G.I. (protected geographical indication) product. Traditionally, the chocolate is cold-processed, with no added fats, and the cocoa beans ground manually, giving a granular texture and retaining all the beneficial properties of cocoa.

MUFFINS
Muffins are individual sponge cakes that differ from cupcakes in that they usually contain a higher proportion of liquid and are chemically leavened with baking powder and/or baking soda (bicarbonate of soda).

PATE A BOMBE
A light yet rich base for many creams, mousses, and semifreddi, made by whisking egg yolks with hot sugar syrup, or combining them over a low heat in a bain-marie or double boiler.

PIE
A pie is a pie dough (pastry) case baked in the oven that contains either a savory or sweet filling. Traditionally, a pie uses particular types of pie dough (pastry), which can be a classic pie dough (shortcrust pastry), sweet shortcrust pastry, or puff pastry. Sweet pies can have a variety of fillings, such as fruit, custards, ganache, or frangipane.

PIE WEIGHTS/BAKING BEANS
Small ceramic or metal heatproof balls used to weigh down an empty pie shell while blind-baking, to avoid the shell shrinking or bubbling as it cooks without its filling. The pie shell should be lined with parchment paper and the weights sit inside the paper.

POTATO STARCH
The starch extracted from potatoes creates a very light, flavorless, and odorless fine white flour. It is used, like wheat flour and cornstarch (cornflour), to thicken creams or sauces, and also in the preparation of cakes and other baked desserts, making them soft and light.

RUBBING IN
The action of mixing fat and flour for pastry. This can be done in a food processor or by hand, with a pastry cutter or with the fingertips, and gives a mixture that looks like bread crumbs. It should be done as quickly as possible, so that the butter doesn't become too warm and start to melt.

SEMIFREDDO
Semifreddo means "half cold/frozen," and is a traditional partially frozen Italian dessert made from base ingredients of egg yolks, sugar, and cream. Ingredients such as chocolate, fruit, and nuts can also be incorporated, and the semifreddo is often made in a loaf pan (tin).

SIFTING
Dry ingredients, such as flour and cocoa, can be passed through a fine-mesh strainer (sieve) to remove lumps and to aerate the ingredients. It is also possible to sift ingredients with a special hand-held sifter.

SOFTENED BUTTER
Butter brought to room temperature, around 68°F/20°C. It can then be beaten until pale and soft, to use in cakes or to add to doughs, such as brioche.

TEMPERING
A technique that puts melted chocolate through three different temperature points. The process of tempering aligns the cocoa and fat molecules in chocolate, giving the chocolate shine and a certain brittleness (called "snap"). Chocolate is tempered to be used for chocolates and chocolate decorations.

TORTA CAPRESE
A traditional flourless Italian cake from the island of Capri, made with chocolate and nuts—traditionally almond, but you can also use hazelnuts, pistachios, or other nuts of your choice. The resulting cake is rich, moist in the center, with a slightly firmer crust. A perfect gluten-free option.

WHIPPING OR WHISKING
Incorporating air using a fork, hand whisk, or electric stand mixer. It will make the ingredients, such as cream and egg whites, more frothy and increase the volume. When whisking egg whites, start on low speed and gradually increase the speed to help the whites reach maximum volume and create a stable foam.

INDEX

RECIPE NOTES

Flour is type "00" or all-purpose (plain) flour, unless specified otherwise.

Sugar is white superfine (caster) sugar, unless specified otherwise.

Butter is unsalted butter, unless specified otherwise.

Milk is whole (full-fat) milk, unless specified otherwise.

Cream is fresh heavy (whipping) cream, unless specified otherwise.

Eggs are assumed to be US size large (UK size medium) and preferably organic and/or free-range, unless specified otherwise.

Gelatin is platinum gelatin sheets, unless specified otherwise.

Chocolate is bittersweet (dark) chocolate and with a minimum of 70% cocoa solids, unless specified otherwise.

Bread crumbs are fresh unless specified otherwise.

Individual fruits, such as apples and pears, are assumed to be of medium size, unless specified otherwise, and should be peeled and/or washed, unless specified otherwise.

When the zest of a citrus fruit is used, always use unwaxed organic fruit.

Cooking and preparation times given are for guidance only, as individual ovens vary.

If using a convection (fan) oven, follow the manufacturer's instructions concerning oven temperatures.

Exercise a high level of caution when following recipes involving any potentially hazardous activity. This includes the use of high temperatures and open flames, such as using a cook's blowtorch. In particular, when deep-frying, slowly and carefully lower the food into the hot oil to avoid splashes, wear long sleeves to protect your arms, and never leave the pan unattended.

When no quantity is specified for an ingredient—for example, strips of citrus zest, chocolate shavings, or edible flowers for decorating finished dishes—then quantities are discretionary and flexible.

Imperial and metric measurements, as well as volumetric cup measurements, are given for each recipe. Follow only one set of measurements throughout a recipe, and not a mixture, as they are not interchangeable.

All volumetric cup measurements given are level. Flour cup measures are spooned and leveled. Brown sugar cup measures are packed, while other dry ingredient measures are loosely packed.

All tablespoon and teaspoon measurements given are level, and not heaping, unless otherwise stated.
1 teaspoon – 5 ml
1 tablespoon = 15 ml
Australian standard tablespoons are 20 ml, so any Australian readers are advised to use 3 teaspoons in place of 1 tablespoon when measuring small quantities.

Some recipes include uncooked or very lightly cooked eggs. These should be avoided by the elderly, infants, pregnant women, convalescents, and anyone with an impaired immune system.

Phaidon Press Limited
2 Cooperage Yard
London E15 2QR

Phaidon Press Inc.
65 Bleecker Street
New York, NY 10012

phaidon.com

The recipes in this book were first published in 2021 as
Il Cucchiaio d'Argento: Cioccolato
© Editoriale Domus

This English edition first published in 2023
© 2023 Phaidon Press Limited

Translated from the original Italian by Cillero & de Motta.

ISBN 978 1 83866 709 2

A CIP catalogue record for this book is available from
the British Library and the Library of Congress.

Commissioning Editor: Emilia Terragni
Project Editor: Rachel Malig
Production Controllers: Zuzana Cimalova and Adela Cory
Typesetting: Cantina

Cover designed by Julia Hasting
Designed by Hans Stofregen

Photography on pages 117, 199, 227, 243, 257 by Haarala
Hamilton. All other photography by Luca Colombo at
Studio XL.

Printed in China

The publisher would like to thank Vanessa Bird, James
Brown, Liz Hamilton, Max Hamilton, Jo Ireson, João Mota,
Pene Parker, Rosie Reynolds, Ellie Smith, Tracey Smith, Kathy
Steer, and Emilia Terragni for their contribution to this book.